THE MAZE
OF
MORMONISM

WALTER MARTIN

VISION HOUSE PUBLISHERS
Santa Ana, California 92705

Except where otherwise indicated, all Scripture quotations are taken from the King James Version of the Bible. Scripture quotations taken from the *New American Standard Bible* are designated NASB. Those taken from the *New International Version* of the Bible are designated NIV.

The Maze of Mormonism

Copyright ©1962, 1978 by Walter Martin
(Revised and enlarged 1978)

Library of Congress Catalog Card Number 78-66067
ISBN 0-88449-017-3

Printed in the United States of America.

TO THE MEMORY
OF MY MOTHER,
MAUD AINSWORTH MARTIN,

descendant of Brigham Young, but disciple of Jesus Christ—a constant source of encouragement to my father and to his youngest son in the pursuit of a difficult calling.

Acknowledgments

The author wishes to acknowledge a great debt of gratitude to Jerry and Marian Bodine, who spent literally hundreds of hours in research and verification of documentary evidence; to the Reverend Mr. R. Odell Brown; to Mr. Arthur Budvarson; to the Reverend H.M.S. Richards, Sr., whose personal collection on Mormonism is unsurpassed; to Gary Metz for his primary research; and to Jerald and Sandra Tanner, whose primary research into the roots of Mormon history and doctrine has been of inestimable value. The Reverend Wesley P. Walters, H. Michael Marquardt, and the Reverend Marvin Cowan cannot be overlooked for their tireless efforts to uncover the whole truth of what can only be called "the Mormon masquerade."

My thanks also are given to the late Pierson Curtis, former senior master of the Stony Brook School for Boys in Stony Brook, New York, who corrected the proofs and contributed many helpful suggestions; and to Shiela Kenney for typing and Mrs. Gretchen Passantino for editing and updating the last two printings of this book.

I extend my gratitude to my former research assistant, the Reverend Anthony Collarile, particularly for his Old Testament research.

Whatever shortcomings may exist in the work, however, are solely the responsibility of the author, with whom the final decision for the manner of organization and the mode of presentation for the data has rested.

CONTENTS

Appendices:

PREFACE

One of the truly great problems which the Christian church faces today is that of effectively evangelizing and combating false and divisive teachers and their teachings, both those which bore from within the church and those which attack from without. The Apostle Paul anticipated just such happenings nineteen centuries ago, and urgently warned the church against them (Acts 20:28-31).

In this work we have tried both to recognize and to deal effectively with one group of such teachings and their promulgators. This work is designed primarily to be a concise handbook on Mormon history and theology for Christian workers, and one which by necessity includes a systematic apologetic in defense of the historic Christian faith.

In two other books *(The Rise of the Cults* and *The Kingdom of the Cults)* we have dealt with the larger problem of cults in general and have attempted to provide an introduction to the problem of contemporary American cults. Then we have attempted to sketch some ground rules with which interested readers could answer the cultists from the Scriptures.

We also described some of the methods and approaches of dealing with cultists which the author has found successful throughout thirty years of research and of personal relationships with many such persons.

This book, however, is designed to deal in survey form with a particular problem—the Mormon Church, its gospel, and its zealous advocates. To be sure, there is no magic panacea for the problem of the rapidly growing cults of our time (of which Mormonism is the largest), but an answer must be sought. Those who propose that we either dismiss such growth by ignoring its presence, or else attack the cults without first understanding the basis for their beliefs as well as the Biblical basis for answering them, postulate grave folly, and we would be foolish to follow their counsel.

The Christian church must realize, however, that the situation, while serious, is by no means hopeless, for throughout the preceding ages the church has always had to face the doctrinal ancestors of the very people with whom we must deal today. Perversions of the truth of the gospel have existed in every age, the first century not excepted; so the problem of false doctrine is nothing new. It is merely the same old denial couched in twentieth-century phraseology and dressed with the air of respectability in an age when religion for religion's sake is popular, and criticism of the religious convictions of others is highly unpopular. It is no secret that the defense of the cross always incurs a mounting displeasure or offense on the part of some people who, possessing no real convictions themselves, are disturbed to see such convictions manifested in the activities of others.

In addition to this, there are many poorly informed Christians who, in apparent ignorance of the Biblical command to "earnestly contend for the faith" (Jude 3) against the avowed enemies of the gospel, hinder the cause of cult evangelism and apologetics by a misguided sense of "Christian love." They forget that love for one's enemies in the Biblical context does *not* mean abandonment of the responsibility of vigorously opposing their errors, which we are called upon to do time and again in Scripture (Ephesians 6:10, 11).

Christian workers everywhere are daily meeting the challenge of the cults, at home and on the mission fields, and the great scarcity of thoroughly documented material upon which to base an effective defense of the historic Christian position continues to be a real problem in many areas of the world.

In this book we have dealt as much as possible with primary sources and have documented our conclusions accordingly. In our study of the Mormon religion, the author openly acknowledges that we have approached Mormonism with the theological tenets of historic Christianity foremost in our thinking, and we have weighed the faith of the Mormon "saints" theologically in this light. We feel that this position is perfectly valid, since Mormonism claims that it is *the* Christian faith and therefore stands or falls on the historic teachings of the Christian church as found in the Bible and the Bible alone.

We have, however, consulted numerous sources, including the famous Berrian collection of the New York Public Library (reputedly one of the world's finest sources of information on the history of Mormonism), as well as the extensive documentation on file in the library of the Union Theological Seminary in New York City, the Huntington Library in California, and the archives of the Utah and the Reorganized Mormon Churches and Brigham Young University.

The results of our years of research as found in this book will doubtless be criticized by the Mormon Church and its friends, who will claim that much of the quoted material is from allegedly "hostile" sources, and that as a result the Mormons have not had a "fair" showing. In answer to this, we can only say that any material quoted has been documented wherever possible from primary source material, including many personal testimonies, affidavits, and exhaustively documented writings, contemporary in many cases with the founders and early advocates of the Mormon religion. Such facts cannot be easily discounted by anyone who considers himself an impartial scholar or investigator. The fact is that the Mormon Church has *not* produced contemporary evidence of the same caliber which in any way tends to disprove our basic findings.

We sincerely welcome any attempt in this direction that the Mormons may make, in the firm conviction that the facts support our conclusions. I would have been only too happy to quote Mormon sources of the same era (and have in many cases), but the majority of data I relied upon was better documented and verified. If the Mormon Church can produce such evidence, evidence which has been requested time and time again by many investigators, I shall be most willing to consider it and revise my conclusions accordingly.

The original edition of this book is the first attempt of its kind in over 38 years to present a complete, thoroughly documented, historical, theological, and apologetic survey of the Mormon religion. The author sends forth this book with the knowledge that the Mormon situation is of the utmost urgency. I also feel quite deeply that the facts contained in this book must be sound and reliable if my conclusions are to be considered valid and useful to the interested Christian. I have made every effort to accomplish this goal of accuracy.

This work is not to be construed as a personal attack upon Mormons in general or upon those persons who make up the Church hierarchy. Rather, let me say that this is a defense against the attacks of a rapidly multiplying and determined cultic system of religion which in one breath believes Joseph Smith, Brigham Young, and *The Book of Mormon* in preference to the Scriptures, and in the next breath pledges allegiance to those same Scriptures—a contradiction not to be taken lightly!

Against the pseudohistory and theological mazes carefully manufactured by overzealous Mormons and aided by their vast wealth and political prestige, I offer only the Word of God and the verdict of history, believing that the interested reader will see the great gulf that exists between Christianity and the religion of Joseph Smith and Brigham Young.

It is my abiding hope and prayer that many people will see these truths and will turn from Mormonism to the freedom that can be found only in the true Jesus of Biblical revelation (2 Corinthians 11:3, 4), the Son of God.

I therefore offer this volume as a step in the direction of proper Christian orientation toward the Mormon cult. It is my sincere hope that as the truths of the gospel are contrasted to the major teachings of Mormonism, the reader may see the challenge which lies before all true Christians and may be led to a deeper personal commitment to the task of both effectively witnessing to adherents of the cults and, when possible, refuting their un-Christian doctrines in obedience to the counsel of Scripture.

WALTER MARTIN

ONE

MORMON HISTORY AND JOSEPH SMITH, JR.
—
False Prophet or Martyred Saint?

Mormonism, the popular name for the Church of Jesus Christ of Latter-day Saints (LDS), owes its existence to Joseph Smith, Jr., born in Sharon, Windsor County, Vermont, December 23, 1805. Joseph was the fourth child and third son of Joseph and Lucy Mack Smith, the parents of ten children—poorly educated, generally given to superstitious beliefs, and destined to have their dream of historical immortality realized in the person of Joseph, Jr.

The story of how young Joseph began his career, his first vision, his encounters with angels, his discovery of miraculous records on plates of gold, and his subsequent bouts with doubt, the law, members of the church he was to found, and his self-proclaimed office as "prophet, seer, and revelator" of God have fascinated religious historians for 150 years.

All of these areas we shall explore in the following chapters. What Joseph Smith began in Fayette, New York, in 1830 by organizing the Church of Jesus Christ of Latter-day

Saints[1] goes on today on an international scale undreamed of by those around the budding young prophet.

The Mormon Church

The Mormon Church has grown from 30 members in 1830 to more than 4,800,000 as of February 1981, and its growth rate is a religious phenomenon. In 1900 the Church numbered 268,331; in 1910, 393,437; in 1920, 526,032; in 1930, 672,488; in 1940, 862,664; in 1950, 1,111,314; in 1960, 1,693,180; in 1962, 1,965,786; in 1964, over 2,000,000 members; and in 1976 their projection for the year 2000 was for more than 8,000,000 members!

The Mormons have more than 29,000 full-time missionaries active throughout the world today and have developed a business empire which *Time* magazine estimates, on an annual income basis, to be in excess of one billion dollars. A study by the United Press (1975) gave a partial breakdown of some Mormon holdings, and *New West* magazine expanded on this.

WHAT THE MORMON CHURCH OWNS

MEDIA

Bonneville International Corporation
A wholly owned church company with a total of seven FM radio stations (the maximum allowed by the Federal Communications Commission), four AM stations, two television stations. Stations on the West Coast are: KIRO-AM, KIRO-FM, KIRO-TV in Seattle, Washington; KOIT-FM, San Francisco; KBIG-FM, KBRT-AM in Los Angeles.

Assets: Refuse to disclose. (KSL, Inc., a Salt Lake City subsidiary, reported a 1976 sales range of $5 to $10 million.)

KBYU-TV, Provo
Owned and operated by the church's Brigham Young University.
Assets: Refuse to disclose.

Bonneville Productions
A subsidiary of Bonneville International. Produces com-

---

[1]First named "The Church of Christ," then later "The Church of the Latter-day Saints," and finally (in 1838) the present name, "The Church of Jesus Christ of Latter-day Saints."

mercials and public service announcements.
Assets: Refuse to disclose.

Deseret News Publishing Company
100 percent church-owned. Publishes the *Deseret News* (the Salt Lake City afternoon paper).
The company takes care of much of the church's printing

needs but also engages in commercial printing.
1976 sales: $9 million.

Deseret Book Company
Sells official church and church-approved literature at eight bookstores (including ones in Orange and Northridge).
1976 sales: $8 million.

FINANCE

Beneficial Life Insurance Company
Wholly owned by the church. California accounts for 14 percent of its business.
Assets: $284 million.

Utah Home Fire Insurance Company
Wholly owned by the church. California accounts for 18 percent of its business.

Assets: $30 million.

Continental Western Life Insurance Company of Iowa
Wholly owned by the church.
Assets: $31 million.

Deseret Mutual Benefit Association
Another insurance company owned by the church.
Assets: $63 million.

MAJOR REAL ESTATE HOLDINGS

Deseret Farms of California
Two commercial farms in Yolo County in Northern California sitting on a total of 5,500 acres. The nonunion farms produce almonds, walnuts, corn, safflower, wheat.
Assets: Refuse to disclose. (The real estate alone is valued at $6.53 million).

Deseret Ranches of Florida
300,000 acres near Disney World.
Assets: Refuse to disclose.

Elberta Farm Corporation
14,000 acres in southern Utah.
Assets: Refuse to disclose.

Deseret Farms of Texas
Assets: Refuse to disclose.

Deseret Trust Company
Administers gifts to the church, primarily to Brigham Young University.
Assets: $50 million (including $10 to $11 million of real property in California).

Zions Securities Corporation
Manages and owns the church's commercial real estate, particularly in Salt Lake City. Also owns a 7,000-acre Hawaiian village—Laie on the island of Oahu.
Assets: "In the eight figures"

(over $10 million), according to a spokesman.

Beneficial Development Company
The development arm of Zions Securities, also in the mortgage-loan business. Finances shopping centers, industrial parks, office buildings.
Assets: Refuse to disclose.

OTHER SIGNIFICANT CHURCH PROPERTY

36-story apartment complex and office building in New York.
$3.4 million worth of holdings in Nauvoo, Illinois, once the seat of church power.
Sixteen temples around the

INVESTMENTS

53.7 percent of the stock in U and I Incorporated (formerly Utah-Idaho Sugar Company), a company with assets exceeding $168 million.
Second largest stockholder in Utah Power and Light Company, the largest utility company in the state, with assets of over $1.1 billion.

OTHER ENTERPRISES

Management Systems Corporation
Church-owned data processing firm.
Assets: Refuse to disclose.
Deseret Industries
Similar to Salvation Army. Em-

EDUCATION

Elementary, secondary, postsecondary schools in Mexico,

Utah Motel Company
Owns and operates two hotels and a motel in Salt Lake City.
Assets: Refuse to disclose.

Polynesian Cultural Center
Major Hawaiian tourist attraction.
Assets: $7 million. (Income from 1971-1974; $31.35 million).

world, each worth several million dollars.
2,600 acres of land in Nevada recently purchased from Summa Corporation.
An estimated 65 acres of downtown Salt Lake City real estate.

Controlling stock (37 percent) in Zion's Co-operative Mercantile Institution department-store chain, with $44 million in assets.
$28 million worth of stock in Times Mirror Corporation, publishers of the Los Angeles Times.

ploys the handicapped; sells used goods.
Sales: Approximately $4 million.
Mormon Tabernacle Choir
Beehive Clothing Mills
Manufactures sacred church garments.

Central and South America, Pacific Islands.

Brigham Young University,
Utah
(enrollment 25,600).
Assets: $283.4 million.
Brigham Young University,
Hawaii
(enrollment 1,180).

Ricks College, Idaho
(enrollment 5,800).
LDS Business College, Utah
(enrollment 860).

Used by permission of *New West* Magazine

The Mormon Mutual Improvement Association has sponsored more than 26,000 dances, 1280 dance festivals, and 12,000 dramatic presentations. The Mormons have popularized what is known as "family home evening," emphasizing the unity of the family and the necessity for people to be together at least one night a week in a society whose family life is rapidly disintegrating.

The Mormon Church has extensive real estate holdings and boasts that a new Mormon Church building is begun each day across the earth.

The Mormon Church also leans heavily on building temples, and today has 17 temples and 5 more planned or under construction throughout the world, as well as a large Church school system which has more than 74,000 students, with Brigham Young University in Utah and Hawaii accounting for 26,780 of that number.

The followers of Joseph Smith's religion are usually missionary-minded, sincere, dedicated, and zealous, and they practice many principles of the Old and New Testaments, including tithing and care for the aged and infirm, if members of the LDS Church. The Mormons also have an employment agency and welfare department for their Church, and they encourage what are known as "fast offerings," or the giving up of two meals on the first Sunday of each month, the money from which sacrifice is contributed to the care of the poor of the Church. The Mormon Tabernacle Choir, famous for its recordings and public concerts, has been operative for almost 50 years on radio, and more recently on television.

There are more Mormons listed in *Who's Who in*

America than are members of any other religion. Politically-minded as a result of alleged early persecutions, Mormons have risen to responsible positions, penetrating into many areas of government, particularly the Department of Agriculture, the Federal Bureau of Investigation, and the Internal Revenue Service. Ezra Taft Benson, who is expected to become the next president of the Mormon Church, served as Secretary of Agriculture under Dwight Eisenhower, the late Ivy Baker Priest was Treasurer of California and of the United States, and the late Marriner S. Eccles was a former president of the U.S. Chamber of Commerce and chairman of the Federal Reserve Board. The former governor of Michigan, George Romney, is also a Mormon, as is Morris K. Udall, Representative of the Second Congressional District in Arizona.

The Mormons have made extensive inroads in the Hawaiian Islands, and their Polynesian Cultural Center operates at a generous profit and is an excellent front for Mormon propaganda throughout the Islands, as well as for contacts later made by Mormon missionaries when the tourists return home. The Mormon Church controls 78 percent of the sugar beet industry of the United States, controls U.S. Industries (a large conglomerate), and owns large blocks of stock in the Central Pacific Railroad.

The Mormon Church is extremely reluctant to reveal any information about its financial holdings. The wide diversity of investments reaches all over the world and is kept very private. It has been said, "The Mormon Church, this American Zion, wields more economic power effectively than the State of Israel or the Pope in Rome."[2]

The Mormons own an agricultural empire which in turn supplies products for Mormon canneries, which produce orange juice in Los Angeles, tuna in San Diego, and chili and fruit in Sacramento and Redwood City (California). They also own factories in various cities which turn out de-

---

[2]*New West magazine, May, 1978*

tergent boxes, shoe polish, furniture, and toothpaste. The sixteen hundred acres of Mormon orange orchards in Riverside, California, sells the fruit through Sunkist Growers, Inc. The amount of land owned by the Mormon Church is staggering; in only nine counties in California the value of that property amounts to over 183 million dollars!

J. Willard Marriott and the Osmond family are the largest contributors to the Mormon Church, resulting from their multimillion-dollar dynasty. Marriott owns 31 hotels and 1200 restaurants, including Big Boy restaurants, Roy Rogers Family Restaurant, and Farrell's Ice Cream Parlours. Zody's-Hartfield Department Stores are also Mormon-owned, and wages are paid directly to the Church.

The source from which the financial assets of the multi-billion-dollar Mormon empire are accumulated is the Church members themselves through their tithing program. Although the Church claims that tithing is not compulsory and no pressure is applied to force members to comply with this "law," we find that one cannot get a "Temple Recommend" unless a "full tithe has been paid for one year." This is 10 percent of the members' gross income, which goes directly to Church headquarters in Salt Lake City. If one is not a full-tithe payer, one cannot enter the Temple. If one is not married and/or sealed in the Temple (and thus performs his or her "work" here on earth), he or she can never hope to enter the Celestial Heaven, where the Mormon god and his sons dwell. Therefore, a devout Mormon quite literally pays his way into heaven. Most Mormons do not realize that they are not giving to the Lord, but to the furtherance of untold material wealth for the "Mormon Kingdom."

Local church-building programs, assistance for the welfare program of the Church, and support of Mormon missionaries all come from additional "offerings" and savings (mentioned earlier), but not from the "tithe money."

Those who would dismiss the threat of Mormons to orthodox Christianity (because in their vocabulary and practices they resemble the Christian church) must look to Mormon theology as well as to the history and teachings of its prophets before jumping to any hasty conclusions, as we shall see later on.

LDS Church Organization

The "General Authorities of the Church of Jesus Christ of Latter-day Saints" consists of: The First Presidency, which includes the President (Prophet, Seer, and Revelator to the Church) and his three Counselors; the Council of the Twelve; Patriarch to the Church; The Presidency of the First Quorum of the Seventy; the First Quorum of the Seventy; and the Presiding Bishopric.

Kimball, on a radio broadcast interview, affirmed that all authority resides in the Priesthood of the Mormon Church, and that he as President is in charge of its operation. There are two priesthoods in the Mormon Church: the Aaronic, which is lesser in spiritual authority, and the Melchizedek, which is greater. It is expected that every male Mormon in good standing with the Church must belong to one of these priesthoods. The administration of the Mormon Church is divided into "wards" and "stakes," the former consisting of from 500 to 1000 people. Every ward is composed of districts, known as "blocks," presided over by a bishop with two counselors as assistants. The wards are consolidated into stakes and are supervised by a president and two counselors, aided in turn by twelve men known as the Stake High Council. Today there are approximately 6000 wards, 1600 stakes, 1700 branches, and 200 missions functioning throughout the Mormon Church. These auxiliary groups form a powerful coalition for mutual assistance among Mormons; for example, during the Great Depression of 1929, Mormon Storehouse offerings assured that no Mormon was without the necessities of life. Note, however, that for the LDS Church charity begins and ends largely at home. Very little is given to non-Mormons, or "Gentiles," as they are called. For example, missions for alcoholics in

Salt Lake City, Ogden, and Provo (Utah) are supported by evangelical Christians rather than by the Mormon Church. The reason for this seems obvious: alcoholic derelicts cannot tithe!

In common with other cultic groups, Mormonism has endured persecution, slander, and the murder of its "prophet." Unlike many of the other cultic structures, who prefer to allow these things to slip into the past, the Mormon Church has attempted to place the blame for these problems on the established Christian church. The Mormons continue to defend their prophets, a practice which has led them into more than one precarious historical dilemma.

The Mormon missionary program is propelled by great zeal on the part of the missionaries, who are well-trained from their Mormon missionary handbook and can quote certain verses of the Bible quite profusely, though out of context and in total ignorance of historic Christian theology.

The average Mormon has many sound moral and ethical traits. Generally he is amiable and hospitable and is extremely devoted to his family, to the teachings of the Church, and to the proselyting of his neighbors. Unfortunately, the great majority of Mormons are ignorant of the grave historical and theological problems involved in the sources of their religion, and are frequently shocked when the carefully manufactured and doctored history[3] of the Church and its "revelations" through Joseph Smith, Brigham Young (Smith's successor), etc., is exposed and the truth is revealed.

The picture that Mormonism presents to the world is generally that of a form of Christian fundamentalism, with unique truths and claims. However, in the interests of truth

---

[3]See Jerald and Sandra Tanner, *Falsification of Joseph Smith's History* (Salt Lake City: Modern Microfilm, 1971) for extensive documentation and photocopies.

it is necessary that we review the facts behind the public image in the full light of Biblical theology. The real Mormon Church is a far cry from the pleasant image of its Tabernacle Choir and the King and Osmond families. Any good that is in Mormonism is derived from the Bible and Biblical principles. The evil in Mormonism has come from the revelations of its prophets and general authorities.

Historical Backgrounds

As we have observed, Joseph Smith, Jr., came from a large family, and his father, Joseph Smith, Sr., was known as a superstitious mystic and an individual who spent a great deal of his time digging for treasure and pursuing other such fruitless quests. Judge Daniel Woodward, of the County Court of Windsor, Vermont, a former neighbor of the Smith family, went on record as to the elder Smith's treasure-hunting escapades and declared that "he also became implicated with one Jack Downing counterfeiting money but turned state's evidence in escape of penalty" (*Historical Magazine*, 1850).

Lucy Mack Smith, Joseph's mother, held some extreme religious views as well as superstitious theories, and later embarrassed Brigham Young and the whole Mormon Church by the publication of her book *Biographical Sketches of Joseph Smith and His Progenitors for Many Generations.* "Mother Smith's History," as it came to be known, was published by the Mormons in Liverpool, England,[4] but Brigham Young, upon learning of it and the many "mistakes," suppressed it on the grounds that "should it ever be deemed best to publish these sketches, it will not be done until they are carefully corrected" (*Millennial Star* 17:298, personal letter dated January 31, 1858). Since Joseph Smith, Jr., did not go beyond the fourth grade, and his mother was even less educated than he, her history was in reality written by a Sister Corley and is available to-

---

[4]Available from Modern Microfilm Company, Salt Lake City, Utah, P.O. Box 1884.

day in photocopy. Its contents are a continuing source of embarrassment to Mormon historians.

The Smiths were not well-received by their neighbors after their move to Palmyra, New York, since more than sixty of these neighbors signed affidavits describing the Smiths in something less than complimentary terms:

> We, the undersigned, have been acquainted with the Smith family, for a number of years, while they resided near this place, and we have no hesitation in saying, that we consider them destitute of that moral character, which ought to entitle them to the confidence of any community. They were particularly famous for visionary projects, spent much of their time in digging for money which they pretended was hid in the earth; and to this day, large excavations may be seen in the earth, not far from their residence, where they used to spend their time in digging for hidden treasures. Joseph Smith, Senior, and his son Joseph, were in particular, considered entirely destitute of *moral character, and addicted to vicious habits.*
>
> E. D. Howe, *Mormonism Unveiled*
> (Painesville, Ohio, 1834), page 261.[5]

Other neighbors further stated of Joseph that he was known for

> ... his habits of exaggeration and untruthfulness ... and by reason of the extravagances of his statement, his word was received with the least confidence by those who knew him best. He could utter the most palpable exaggeration or marvelous absurdity with the utmost apparent gravity.
>
> Pomeroy Tucker, *The Origin, Rise and Progress of Mormonism* (New York, 1847), page 16.

In Appendix D we have quoted affidavits concerning the character of Joseph Smith, Jr., which support these alle-

---

[5]Mr. Howe was the editor of a newspaper in Painesville and a contemporary of Joseph Smith. His work was published in 1834 and updated in 1840. Both editions are rare, but the copies I possess contain devastating documentation, *prima facie* evidence of the highest veracity.

gations. The reader can judge for himself what Mormon historians have failed to effectively refute from contemporary sources.

The Palmyra Revival and Joseph Smith's First Vision

Two of the things which Mormon missionaries are extremely careful to avoid when visiting prospective converts is any truthful recitation of Joseph Smith, Jr.'s, so-called "First Vision" in its entirety, or the embarrassing details of the Palmyra, New York, "revival" which allegedly precipitated it.

According to Mormon history as recorded by Joseph Smith in *The Pearl of Great Price*, Joseph Smith 2:5, in the spring of 1820 "an unusual excitement on the subject of religion" generated great interest among the Methodists and

> . . . soon became general among all the sects in that region of country. Indeed, the whole district of country seemed affected by it, and great multitudes united themselves to the different religious parties, which created no small stir and division amongst the people, some crying, "Lo, here!" and others, "Lo, there!" Some were contending for the Methodist faith, some for the Presbyterian, and some for the Baptist.

Young Joseph, upset by all of this tumult of opinions, allegedly sought the will of God in response to the promise in the Bible:

> If any of you lack wisdom, let him ask of God, who giveth to all men liberally, and upbraideth not, and it shall be given him.
>
> James 1:5

There was to this alleged supplication an immediate, albeit confused, response on the part of the supernatural, and some of the response had ominous undertones. According to young Joseph:

> . . . immediately I was seized upon by some power which entirely overcame me, and had such an astonishing influence over me as to bind my tongue so that I could not

speak. Thick darkness gathered around me, and it seemed to me for a time as if I were doomed to sudden destruction.

But, exerting all my powers to call upon God to deliver me out of the power of this enemy which had seized upon me, and at the very moment when I was ready to sink into despair and abandon myself to destruction—not to an imaginary ruin, but to the power of some actual being from the unseen world, who had such marvelous power as I had never before felt in any being—just at this moment of great alarm, I saw a pillar of light exactly over my head, above the brightness of the sun, which descended gradually until it fell upon me.

It no sooner appeared than I found myself delivered from the enemy which held me bound.

Pearl of Great Price,
Joseph Smith 2:15b-17a

Smith was immediately told by the Personages that all of the sects were wrong, that "all of their creeds were an abomination in his sight," and that all those who were members were corrupt (*Pearl of Great Price*, Joseph Smith 2:19).

When young Joseph tried to recount his fabulous encounter, he claimed that "all the sects—all united to persecute me" (*ibid.*, 2:22).

In his carefully researched publication, *New Light On Mormon Origins From the Palmyra, New York Revival*, the Reverend Wesley P. Walters painstakingly demolishes in a scholarly and dispassionate manner Joseph's reliability as a historian and the attempts of Mormon mythmakers to repair the pieces of the Palmyra Humpty Dumpty. Walters demonstrates that no revival such as Joseph Smith, Jr., described took place in 1820, according to the records of the churches in that area. However, what does emerge is fascinating. The records of the Presbyterian Church in Palmyra reveal that there was indeed a revival in 1824, but that *no revival took place in 1820*. Far from being insignificant, the dating of the Palmyra revival is tremendously important to the whole fabric of Joseph Smith's story. According to Joseph, his "First Vision" occurred *after* the revival. However, since history tells us that the revival took place in 1824, Smith's *second* vision (which he says took place on September 21, 1823) would have had to precede the revival Joseph mentions. In the "Second Vision," the angel Moroni communicated the miraculous message concerning the "golden plates" of what was to become *The Book of Mormon*. But since the true date of the revival was 1824-25, the veracity of the "Second Vision" collapses. The dating of the Palmyra revival, then, is most important. Since it did not occur in 1820, Joseph could not have been asking God in 1820 which church was right and which to join, and the entire "First Vision" becomes a fraudulent story.

Further complicating the problems of zealous Mormon historians is the interesting fact that the initial account of the crucial "First Vision" informs us that *an angel* visited Joseph Smith (*Journal of Discourses* 13:77-78), but the revised edition of the story says that it was *God the Father and Jesus Christ* who appeared. The earliest account of the "First Vision" was published in *Times and Seasons* in 1842—twenty-two years after the vision was allegedly experienced by Joseph! In the *Journal of Discourses*, we are further told:[6]

> The Lord did not come with the armies of heaven, in power and great glory, nor send His messengers panoplied with aught else than the truth of heaven, to communicate to the meek, the lowly, the youth of humble origin, the sincere enquirer after the knowledge of God. But He did send His angel to this same obscure person, Joseph Smith jun., who afterwards became a Prophet, Seer, and Revelator, and informed him that he should not join any of the religious sects of the day, for they were all wrong; that they were following the precepts of men instead of the Lord Jesus, . . .
> *Journal of Discourses* 2:171

---

[6]For a more detailed picture of the conflicts in the story, see *Journal of Discourses* 2:196-97; 6:29, 335; 10:127; 12:333-34; 13:65-66, 294, 324; 18:239; 20:167; 14:261-62.

In 1833 Joseph Smith gave an account of his "First Vision" in which he omitted any mention of having seen God the Father, as well as the condemnation of all Christian churches and people. Further confusing and complicating the entire issue beyond any possible rational solution is the problem that apparently Joseph couldn't even remember the name of the angel in the "Second Vision" who made the "golden plates" available to him, designating him sometimes as "Nephi" and other times as "Moroni."[7] For more than twenty years *The Pearl of Great Price*, page 41,° identified the angel as "Nephi," as does Lucy Smith, Joseph's mother. It appears that even Joseph didn't know the identity of the angel. I believe that if Joseph did have any supernatural revelation, its author was certainly not the God of the Bible, because "God is not the author of confusion" (1 Corinthians 14:33).

We cannot underestimate the importance of the "First Vision," because it is the centerpiece in virtually all Mormon presentations of Smith's prophetic authority. The "First Vision" formed the basis for the key Mormon teaching relative to the nature of God (that the Father and the Son are two separate gods with flesh and bone bodies) as well as the doctrine that the Christian church was not on the earth in Smith's time, and that Smith was the designated prophet of the restoration of true Christianity. Smith's "First Vision" was also responsible for the Mormons' subsequent strong emphasis upon the condemnation of existing Christian churches, doctrines, and membership as "wrong," "abomination," and "corrupt."

The "First Vision" is extremely important to the Mor-

---

[7]See the *Millennial Star* 3:53, 71; and *Times and Seasons* 3:749, 753. Should any reader wonder whether Joseph Smith merely suffered an oversight or was ignorant of the articles published in *Times and Seasons*, Joseph said: "This paper commences my editorial career. I *alone* stand responsible for it" (Volume 3:710).

°1851 edition.

mon missionary and his efforts to spread Smith's gospel, and is apparently so vital that the Mormon missionary handbook paradoxically instructs the missionaries to emphasize common points of agreement with the people they are attempting to proselytize, buttressed by carefully selected "Vision" excerpts which carefully omit any mention of the following revealing statement:

> My object in going to inquire of the Lord was to know which of all the sects was right, that I might know which to join. No sooner, therefore, did I get possession of myself, so as to be able to speak, than I asked the Personages who stood above me in the light, which of all the sects was right—and which I should join.
>
> I was answered that I must join none of them, for they were all wrong; and the Personage who addressed me said that all their creeds were an abomination in his sight; that those professors were all corrupt; that: "they draw near to me with their lips, but their hearts are far from me, they teach for doctrines the commandments of men, having a form of godliness, but they deny the power thereof."
>
> *Pearl of Great Price*, Joseph Smith 2:18-19

The Only Church?

The Mormon Church considers itself *the* Church of Jesus Christ. It claims to be neither Protestant nor Catholic and, by its own admission, is at variance with "orthodox" Christianity as taught by historic Christian communions in the creeds of Christendom throughout the centuries. In this particular "revelation," God the Father and Jesus Christ allegedly told Joseph Smith, Jr., that all the "sects" of Christendom were wrong, that all their creeds were an abomination, and that all their professors were corrupt.

The Mormon Church would have us believe that Christianity had apostatized and disappeared from the face of the earth until Joseph Smith's "First Vision" and his subsequent unearthing of miraculous plates at the Hill Cumorah, later to be "translated" into what is known as *The Book of Mormon*. The arrogance of the claim deserves very little comment, since it is obvious to even the most nominal Christian that Jesus Christ's gospel, however imperfectly proclaimed by Christians throughout the ages from the first century to today, has been consistent in its claims and in the lives of those who are its true practitioners.

With one "special revelation" the Mormon Church expects its intended converts to accept the totally unsupported testimony of a fifteen-year-old boy that nobody ever preached Jesus Christ's gospel from the close of the apostolic age until the "restoration" through Joseph Smith, Jr., beginning in 1820! We are asked to believe that the church fathers for the first five centuries did not proclaim the true gospel—that Origen, Justin, Ireneaus, Jerome, Eusebius, Athanasius, Chrysostom, and then later Thomas Aquinas, Huss, Luther, Calvin, Zwingli, Tyndale, Wycliffe, Knox, Wesley, Whitefield, and a vast army of faithful servants of Jesus Christ all failed where Joseph Smith, Jr., was to succeed!

With one dogmatic assertion Joseph pronounced everybody wrong, all Christian theology an abomination, and all professing Christians corrupt—all in the name of God! How strange for this to be presented as restored Christianity, when Jesus Christ specifically promised that "the gates of hell" would not prevail against His church (Matthew 16:18)! In Mormonism we find God contradicting this statement in a vision to Joseph Smith, Jr., some eighteen centuries later!

Joseph had apparently not read the prophet Malachi: "I am the Lord, I change not" (Malachi 3:6). Nowhere does the Bible teach that the Christian faith will ever disappear from the earth and be in need of restoration by anybody. Even during the reign of the great Antichrist, who will suppress and persecute Christians as has never been known in all of Christian history (2 Thessalonians 2; Revelation 13:5-8), God's truth will survive. The message will continue unbroken, because for the Christian "greater is he that is in you than he that is in the world" (I John 4:4). The false prophets will come and go, along with the crowns and the thrones that will perish, as well as the kingdoms that will rise and wane, but, as history so clearly reveals, the church of Jesus "constant will remain."

Far from being a respecter of the sincerity and rights of other religious groups to maintain the integrity of their convictions concerning the historic gospel of our Lord, the Church of Jesus Christ of Latter-day Saints was racially bigoted for 149 years, and is harshly judgmental of others who do not accept the words of the Mormon prophet. It is not the Christian church that attacked Mormonism—it was Joseph Smith, Jr., who attacked all Christians, denouncing them, their beliefs, and all their churches, thus inviting the Christian church to respond to the charges and refute their "divine revelations."

The Blurred Vision

It would be possible to fill many pages discussing further the implications of the so-called "First Vision," but neither historical nor theological overkill are necessary. The facts speak for themselves. It is from *Mormon* sources that we derive the irreconcilable contradictions in Joseph Smith's story—not from anti-Mormon writers, as Smith's apologists try to assert. The cracks in the historic foundations of Mormonism are not the result of fanatical anti-Mormon researchers, but these cracks exist because of the basic untrustworthiness of the source—Joseph Smith, Jr. His polygamous immorality and fortune-telling activities reveal him for what he was—one of the false prophets of whom Jesus Christ warned His church to beware (Matthew 7:15). Smith's "First Vision" is so blurred by history that one wonders if Joseph himself did not suffer from aggravated spiritual astigmatism of the soul.

Anyone who had indeed experienced something as remarkable as Smith alleges would no doubt take his holy mission seriously. But not Joseph! In 1828, contrary to the vision which he claims he had, and contrary to the very words of God which he maintained he heard, Joseph Smith, Jr., sought to join the Methodist Church. He did this despite the fact that God had allegedly told him personally "not to join any of them, for they were all wrong," their creeds "abomination" and their professors "corrupt." Smith's name remained on the Methodist "class book" for six months, but was removed after the pastor and other church officials were informed of his treasure-hunting and spiritistic practices.[8]

Joseph Smith the Glass-Looker

It would be impossible to deal with the history of Mormonism without careful observation of the career of Joseph Smith, Jr., as a fortune-teller, peep-stone gazer, or "glass-looker." We have already seen that Smith's family was addicted to digging for treasure, but the methods which they used to arrive at the alleged location of the "treasures" is something the Mormon Church does not like to have discussed publicly in any detail. According to those who knew Smith (see Appendix D), he was in the habit of taking a particular stone, putting it inside his hat and looking into it, and then declaring at length that such and such was the location of the supposedly hidden treasure or object.

This was a common practice which sometimes involved occultic powers and with which we will deal in Chapter 8, Those who were involved in such pursuits were known as "glass-lookers," or today we might say "crystal gazers" or "fortune-tellers," and there is now irrefutable evidence that Smith belonged to this occultic confidence game. Smith himself, and his followers, vigorously denied this, along with the accusation that he was engaged in hunting for buried treasure. However, the testimony of Smith's own father-in-law refutes this denial.

---

[8]See the *Amboy Journal*, April 30, 1879, and June 11, 1879, for testimony verifying this.

I first became acquainted with Joseph Smith, Jr. in November, 1825. He was at that time in the employ of a set of men who were called "money diggers;" and his occupation was that of seeing, or pretending to see by means of a stone placed in his hat, and his hat closed over his face. In this way he pretended to discover minerals and hidden treasures. His appearance at this time, was that of a careless young man—not very well educated, and very saucy and insolent to his father. Smith, and his father, with several other 'money diggers' boarded at my house while they were employed in digging for a mine that they supposed had been opened and worked by the Spaniards, many years since. Young Smith gave the 'money diggers' great encouragement at first, but when they had arrived in digging, to near the place where he had stated an immense treasure would be found—he said the enchantment was so powerful that he could not see. They then became discouraged, and soon after dispersed. This took place about the 17th of November, 1825; and one of the company gave me his note for $12 68 for his board, which is still unpaid.

After these occurences, young Smith made several visits at my house, and at length asked my consent to his marrying my daughter Emma. . . .

> Isaac Hale (Joseph Smith's father-in-law)
> E. D. Howe, *Mormonism Unveiled.*
> (Painesville, Ohio: 1834), pages 262-3

Spokesmen for the Mormon Church have categorically denied that Smith was a convicted "glass-looker" or "fortune-teller," or that he was ever engaged in seeking for buried treasure. Some of their statements are well worth questioning in the light of the development of historical evidence from two dependable records, which prove beyond question that Joseph Smith, Jr., was arrested, tried, and convicted for the crime (misdemeanor) of "glass-looking" in the year 1826.

Whenever this charge has been made against Prophet Smith, it has been vigorously denied:

1. . . . previous to his obtaining the records . . . some very officious person complained of him (Joseph Smith) as a disorderly person, and brought him before the

authorities of the country; but there being no cause of action he was honorably acquitted.

> Oliver Cowdery, *Messenger and Advocate*, page 201

2. In . . . October 1825, I hired with . . . Josiah Stowel . . . Chenango County. . . . to dig for the silver mine, . . . Hence arose the very prevalent story of my having been a money digger.

> Joseph Smith, Jr., *History of The Church* 1:17

3. This alleged court record . . . seems to be a literary attempt of an enemy to ridicule Joseph Smith. . . . There is no existing proof that such a trial was ever held.

> Apostle John A. Widtsoe, in *Joseph Smith—Seeker After Truth* (Salt Lake City: 1951), page 78

4. If such a court record confession could be identified and proved, then it follows that his (Joseph Smith's) believers must deny his claimed divine guidance which led them to follow him.

> Francis W. Kirkham, *A New Witness for Christ in America* I:486-87

5. . . . if this court record is authentic it is the most damning evidence in existence against Joseph Smith.

> Dr. Hugh Nibley, *The Myth Makers*, page 142

The noted Mormon apologist Dr. Hugh Nibley is quite correct in his assessment of the fact that if it can be proven that Joseph was indeed a convicted "glass-looker," then his whole prophetic office is in question, and the words of the other Mormon spokesmen, including Oliver Cowdery, one of the "witnesses" to the authenticity of *The Book of Mormon*, stand completely refuted.

Although the 1826 Bainbridge court record was twice printed in the nineteenth century, it remained for Fawn Brodie, in her book *No Man Knows My History*, to give it wide attention. Immediately after her book appeared, the Mormon Church pronounced that record a forgery:

> . . . the alleged find is no discovery at all, for the pur-

ported record has been included in other books . . . after all her puffing and promise the author produces no court record at all, though persistently calling it such. . . . This alleged record is obviously spurious. . . . The really vital things which a true record must contain are not there, though there is a lot of surplus verbiage set out in an impossible order which the court was not required to keep.

This record could not possibly have been made at the time as the case proceeded. It is patently a fabrication of unknown authorship and never in the court records at all.

> Deseret News, Church Section,
> May 11, 1946

On the following page we have reproduced a photocopy of the actual 1826 document discovered in upper New York State on July 28, 1971, which shows that Joseph was indeed tried in the courtroom of Justice Albert Neely and fined the sum of $2.68 for "glass-looking."

The Reverend Wesley Walters, to whom we are indebted for uncovering the record of both Smith's conviction and the Palmyra revival hoax, also found the record of the constable (DeZeng) indicating that he had served warrant on Joseph Smith ("Serving warrant on Joseph Smith . . ."). The Reverend Mr. Walters also discovered a letter from Judge Joe Noble, Justice of the Peace in Colesville, New York. Justice Noble's letter, dated in 1842, not only records the fact that Smith was found guilty but states that he was "condemned"[9] for his glass-looking practices.[10]

The Mormon Church cannot prove that the account of Joseph's conviction was falsified. This account as it appeared in *Fraser's* Magazine (February 1873, pages 229-30) is completely vindicated by the 1971 discovery of the ori-

---

[9]Joseph, it was also reported, took "leg bail" (or in today's terminology "jumped bail") and returned a year later, claiming that the statute of limitations had run out.

[10]Turner Collection, the Illinois State Historical Library, Springfield, Illinois.

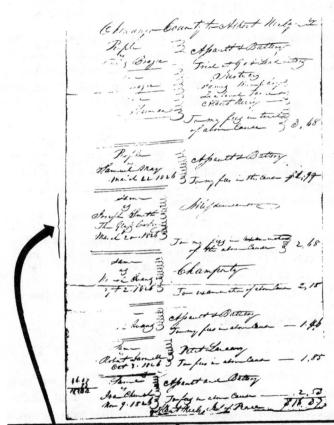

same
vs
Joseph Smith
The Glass looker
March 20, 1826

Misdemeanor

To my fees in examination
of the above cause   2.68

ABOVE IS A PHOTOGRAPH OF JUSTICE ALBERT NEELY'S BILL SHOWING THE COSTS INVOLVED IN SEVERAL TRIALS IN 1826. THE FIFTH ITEM FROM THE TOP MENTIONS THE TRIAL OF "JOSEPH SMITH THE GLASS LOOKER." WHEN THE LETTER "S" WAS REPEATED IN DOCUMENTS OF JOSEPH SMITH'S TIME, AS IN THE WORD "GLASS," THE TWO LETTERS APPEARED AS A "P" (SEE THE WORD "ASSAULT" IN ITEMS 1, 4, 7 AND 9). TO THE LEFT WE HAVE TYPED OUT THE PORTION OF THE BILL WHICH MENTIONS JOSEPH SMITH. THIS BILL PROVES THAT THE PUBLISHED COURT RECORD IS AUTHENTIC.

ginal bill. Therefore, following the Mormon Church's own logic and argument, Joseph's prophetic office as well as his character and truthfulness are hereby seriously impeached.

Lawsuits and Convictions

When one considers all of the material available on the subject of Joseph Smith's unsavory clashes with the law, the facts are simply overwhelming. Yet, from Brigham Young onward, the Mormon Church has attempted to suppress this damaging evidence. We need only listen to Prophet Young's own words:

> Joseph Smith had forty-seven lawsuits, and I was with him through the most of them, and never was the first thing proved against him; he was never guilty of the first violation of the law or of good order.
> *Journal of Discourses* 18:361

> Joseph, our Prophet, was hunted and driven, arrested and persecuted, and although no law was ever made in these United States that would bear against him, for he never broke a law. . . .
> *Journal of Discourses* 14:199

> Joseph Smith, in forty-seven prosecutions was never proven guilty of one violation of the laws of his country.
> *Journal of Discourses* 10:111

G. T. Harrison, a former Mormon and a practicing attorney who researched the legal background of Joseph Smith, Jr., comments authoritatively on Brigham Young's whitewash of the prophet:

> The above teachings are unreliable and untrue. The court records of the day show at least five convictions, and if the full records could be searched no doubt more would show up. Here are five times that Joseph Smith the Mormon prophet was found guilty and convicted.
> The earliest public document that mentions Joseph Smith, Jr. at all is a court record dated March 1826. . . .

Joseph Smith set up and operated the Kirtland Safety Bank or anti-bank contrary to the laws of Ohio. On February 8, 1837 Samuel D. Rounds made a formal complaint against Joseph Smith, and Joseph was arrested, tried and found guilty, and ordered to pay $1,000.00, penalty and costs (Courthouse Record, vol. U, page 362, Chardon, Geauga County, Ohio).

After the failure of the Kirtland Safety Bank, local non-Mormon creditors whom he could not repay brought a series of suits against the Prophet which the Geauga County, Ohio, court records show. Those records tell a story of trouble that would have overwhelmed a man of lesser gumption. Thirteen suits were brought against Joseph Smith between June 1837 and April 1839 to collect sums totalling nearly $25,000.00. The damages asked amounted to almost $35,000.00. Joseph Smith was arrested seven times in four months but was bailed out by members of the Church. Of the thirteen suits, only six were settled out of court. In the other seven suits the creditors either were awarded damages or won them by default.

On July 9, 1837, he was arrested on a complaint of Winthrop Eaton for a debt of $2,000.00 dated October 11, 1836. He was found guilty and damages were awarded to Mr. Eaton.

On March 25th, 1837, he was arrested on the complaint of Hezekiah Kelly for a debt of $3,000.00 dated December 1836. He was found guilty and damages were awarded to Mr. Kelly.

On complaint of T. Underwood, R. Bald, A. Spencer and S. Huffy, Joseph Smith was arrested for a debt of $2,000.00, for labor and services rendered to him in June 1837 and found guilty and damages were awarded complainants. (For references to the above three, see the Geauga County, Ohio, court records on the above dates.)

Mormonism Now and Then,
pages 295-96

The response of the Mormon prophet to legal actions is nowhere better exemplified than in the following statement, which also reveals Smith's concept of prophetic humility:

God is in the still small voice. In all these affidavits,

indictments, it is all of the devil—all corruption. Come on! ye prosecutors! ye false swearers! All hell, boil over! Ye burning mountains, roll down your lava! for I will come out on the top at last. I have more to boast of than ever any man had. I am the only man that has ever been able to keep a whole church together since the days of Adam. A large majority of the whole have stood by me. Neither Paul, John, Peter, nor Jesus ever did it. I boast that no man ever did such a work as I. The followers of Jesus ran away from Him; but the Latter-day Saints never ran away from me yet.

History of the Church 6:408-9

Unfortunately for Joseph, history has an ironic way of rising to haunt him. As the quotation indicates, Smith expected to "come out on top at last," obviously in the context a reference to lawsuits. Yet thirty days after he made this assertion he was assassinated in Carthage, Illinois. Joseph did not come out on top of his accusers—instead, he was taken down! In the last line of Joseph's boast he maintains that "the Latter-day Saints never ran away from me yet." But, in fact, the original three "witnesses" to the divine authenticity of *The Book of Mormon* had indeed run away from him, deserting the Church, and five of the first twelve apostles of the Latter-day Saint's Church had also left, along with his own private secretary, William Parrish.

Many prophecies made by Joseph Smith and his successors were subsequently violated by history. Today's Mormons might well ponder these things, along with Joseph's own opinion of himself in relation to the Mormon people:

God made Aaron to be the mouth piece for the children of Israel, and He will make me be god to you in His stead, and the Elders to be mouth for me; and if you don't like it, you must lump it.

Joseph Smith, *History of the Church* 6:319-20

The Seed of the Church

Joseph Smith, Jr., founded the city of Nauvoo in Illinois after his prophecy about the establishment of Zion in Independence, Missouri, miserably failed (*Doctrine and Covenants* 84:1-5; 97:19; 101:17-21; See also Appendix G). In Nauvoo Joseph's word was the last word, and he appropriated for himself the titles of "General" (despite no military training whatever), and "Chief Justice" of the municipal court of Nauvoo. Things appeared to be going well with the prophet, who by this time was avidly practicing polygamy, and the Mormon community of some 1600 was rapidly multiplying. Between the years 1831 and 1844 Smith issued 135 "revelations," including polygamy (*Doctrine and Covenants*, Section 132, which urged the Mormon people to practice polygamy; the penalty for abstaining was eternal damnation).

On June 27, 1844, a mob of some 200 persons (with faces blackened to avoid identification) stormed the Carthage jail and fatally shot Joseph and his brother Hyrum. The Mormons refer to this as Joseph's martyrdom, but, as history indicates, martyrs are people who willingly submit to death for their convictions, leaving the final justice to God. Such was not the case with Joseph Smith, Jr., who died with a gun in his hand,[11] returning the fire of his murderers! Self-defense is understandable, but hardly a qualification for martyrdom!

Brigham Young then took over the reins of prophetic control amidst great controversy and marched the fleeing Saints to the valley of the Great Salt Lake, where a horde of hungry seagulls consumed the locusts which were devouring the crops of the struggling Mormons. Here, isolated from all opposition, the Mormon Church under "Prophet" Young began its climb to religious and economic power.

Today Mormonism is thriving across the free world (now even in black Africa), and Mormon missionaries travel everywhere and preach incessantly the myth of Joseph

---

[11]*History of the Church* 6:617-18.

Smith's prophetic office and the supposed restoration of the Christian gospel through the Mormon religion.

As we have observed, Joseph Smith, Jr., laid the foundations of this polyglot faith with the assertion that God had established him as the prophet of the restoration, complete with revelations and alleged miracles, the greatest of which has come to be known as *The Book of Mormon*. History has revealed that Joseph Smith, Jr., was less a sainted martyr than an egotistical, self-ordained prophet who continues today through the Mormon hierarchy of General Authorities to suppress the truth about his shoddy past and prophetic failures. The words of the Bible are most apropos here.

> If there arise among you a prophet, or a dreamer of dreams, and giveth thee a sign or a wonder, and the sign or the wonder come to pass, whereof he spoke unto thee, saying, "Let us go after other gods, which thou hast not known, and let us serve them," thou shalt not hearken unto the words of that prophet, or that dreamer of dreams; for the Lord your God [testeth] you, to know whether ye love the Lord your God with all your heart and with all your soul. Ye shall walk after the Lord your God, and fear him, and keep his commandments, and obey his voice, and ye shall serve him, and cleave unto him. And that prophet, or that dreamer of dreams, shall be put to death, because he hath spoken to turn you away from the Lord your God, who brought you out of the land of Egypt, and redeemed you out of the house of bondage, to thrust thee out of the way which the Lord thy God commanded thee to walk in. So shalt thou put the evil away from the midst of thee (Deuteronomy 13:1-5).

Beyond doubt Joseph Smith fits the description Moses warned us of and has bequeathed to our country one of the greatest religioeconomic charades in the history of indigenous American cultism. The evidence is amply available for those who are willing to examine, weigh, and reach conclusions based upon facts. Such evidence demands a logical and rational verdict, free from the myths of Mormon historians and editors who add and subtract whatever they wish.

TWO

MORMONISM'S REVELATIONS
—
Divine Or Devilish?

According to Mormon history, Joseph Smith, Jr., was God's prophet sent to restore the gospel in our age. However, his office was aided considerably by the addition of three new "scriptures" to God's revelation previously given in the Bible. The Mormon Church maintains that there are four standard works which are revelations from God and which supposedly form the basis for all Mormon doctrine: *The Book of Mormon, Doctrine and Covenants, The Pearl of Great Price*, and the Bible, "in so far as it is correctly translated."

The earliest of these books, the Bible, is considered imperfect, having lost "many great and precious truths." *The Book of Mormon*, mentioned in Chapter 1 contains the history of the early migrants to the Western Hemisphere and the beginnings of Mormon doctrine. The second standard Mormon work, *Doctrine and Covenants*, is revelation contemporary with the fledgling Mormon Church. It contains revelations given through Joseph Smith (except for one by Brigham Young and the "Manifesto," to be discussed later) concerning administration of the Church, politics, economics, and spiritual and doctrinal matters.[1] Perhaps its most controversial "revelation" is the one revealing the necessity of polygamy (rescinded by the "Manifesto" given years later in Utah after the federal government declared polygamy illegal). *The Book of Abraham* is considered to be the translation of sacred writings that originally were in "reformed Egyptian hieroglyphics." It is contained in *The Pearl of Great Price*, the third standard Mormon work, and it introduces many of the heretical doctrines characterizing Mormonism. These four standard works, the Bible ("insofar as it is translated correctly"), *The Book of Mormon*, *The Pearl of Great Price*, and *Doctrine and Covenants*, are the foundation stones of the Mormon monolith.

In this chapter I will examine these so-called Scriptures of the Mormon Church, and their fraudulent nature will be clearly exposed for the objective reader. When one purports to have revelations from God, he must be able to defend those revelations and must prove that they are consistent with the nature of the true and living God.

The Bible

The Bible, consisting of 66 books of the Old and New Testaments, has been the infallible rule of faith and practice for the Christian church since it was written (the last book of the New Testament is considered to have been finished before 100 A.D.). Through the centuries before the time of our Lord, the Old Testament (commonly called by the Jews "the Law," "the Writings," and the "Psalms") was the final arbitrator in all disputes among God's people, the Jews (Romans 3:2). In it the God of the universe is

---

[1]The Reorganized Church of Jesus Christ of Latter-Day Saints does not accept the same form of Doctrine and Covenants as does the Utah Church. See Appendix A for a thorough discussion of this matter.

revealed. In it God's judgment, forgiveness, and righteousness are displayed through its history, prophecies, songs, and declarations.

Through the providence of God, His Word has remained true and constant in a world filled with change. The Bible was written over a period of roughly 1500 years, by many different men from many different backgrounds. And yet, through all of this there is no place in the whole canon of Scripture that contradicts any other portion. The God of the Old Testament is revealed as the same God of the New Testament. The truth of one book is the same as the truth of any other book within the Bible's covers.

On the trustworthiness of this Holy Book we may safely base our faith and lives, confident that God's Word is truth. Our Savior is revealed in all His glory in the Bible's pages, both before His incarnation and after. The Holy Bible is the witness of the Son; as He said, "Search the Scriptures, for in them ye think ye have eternal life, and they are they which testify of me" (John 5:39).

Sadly, those caught in the web of Mormon deceit have been taught that the Bible cannot give them assurance of God and His acts. Instead, they are taught that the Bible has been corrupted through the centuries (despite the completely contrary evidence of the precise science of textual criticism), and that its words today cannot be trusted. Why this unreasonable position by a sect which claims to "restore the gospel"?

In no uncertain terms, the Bible condemns the teachings of the Mormon Church. According to the Bible, there is only one true God. According to Mormonism, there are many gods, and Mormon males are told that they too may become gods! According to the New Testament, a man is to have but one wife. According to Mormonism, Smith was given a permanent commandment to take as many wives as could be supported!

This list of contradictions could be continued endlessly, for there is a strict dichotomy between the Bible and its God and the Mormon religion and its gods. There can be no harmony between the two. Faced with such contradictions, the Mormon Church can react in only one of two ways: to dismiss the Bible altogether, or to dismiss those portions of it which disagree with its preconceived ideology. The Mormon Church has chosen the latter course of action, nebulously teaching that the Bible is the Word of God "insofar as it is correctly translated." In practice, this means that wherever the Bible contradicts Mormonism, it must have been mistranslated!

Finally, the seeds of this degradation of God's Word can be traced to Smith's 1823 vision of the angel Moroni (or Nephi, as originally recorded). In this vision, supposedly an angel came to young Joseph and declared new revelations to him. Does the Bible have anything to say concerning this incident? Writing under inspiration of the Holy Spirit, the Apostle Paul directly addressed this type of situation in his warning to the gullible Galatians:

> . . . there be some that trouble you, and would pervert the gospel of Christ. But though we, or an angel from heaven, preach any other gospel unto you than that which we have preached unto you, let him be accursed.
> Galatians 1:7, 8

Smith's "angel" could hardly pass the test set by God in His Word! Is it any wonder that Mormonism quickly disavowed absolute fidelity to the Bible?

The Book of Mormon

The Mormon Church not only rests its faith on the trustworthiness of Joseph Smith, Jr., as a prophet, seer, and revelator, but also on *The Book of Mormon*, which purports to be a second witness to the truthfulness of the gospel of Jesus Christ. According to Joseph Smith, Jr., "I told the brethren that the *Book of Mormon* was the most correct of any book on earth, and the keystone of our religion, and a man would get nearer to God by abiding its precepts, than by any other book."[2] If it can be shown that *The Book of Mormon* is not what Joseph Smith and the Mormon Church represent it to be—"a divine revelation"—then the total foundation of Mormonism falls.

Joseph Smith maintained that in 1823 an angel named Moroni visited him at his home and instructed him to dig in a hill (later called Cumorah) in nearby Palmyra, New York, where he would find a remarkable record relating to the Bible and to the gospel of Jesus Christ itself. The zealous young seer purportedly dug up the record, which was written in "reformed Egyptian hieroglyphics." Since the young man could not read Egyptian, the plates were accompanied by the Urim and Thummin (supposed to be those referred to in Exodus 28:30 and Leviticus 8:8), miraculous stones "set in silver bows" to aid Joseph Smith in translation. According to Joseph, when he looked through the stones at the characters, they miraculously turned into English, and Smith had this recorded dutifully in what came to be known as *The Book of Mormon.*

The Book of Mormon is an unusual book indeed from the perspectives of theology, history, and science—particularly the science of archeology. This volume purports to be a history of three groups of people who migrated at different times from the Near East to Central and South America, finally migrating to North America. One of these groups was known as the Jaredites. The Jaredites, the story goes, did not want their language confounded at the Tower of Babel (*Book of Mormon*, Ether 1:34-37—unfortunately contradicting Genesis 11:7-9 in the Bible). Therefore, they journeyed to the New World uncorrupted in language, or, as one writer put it, "they continued to speak the pure language of Adam." The other two groups were Semites. The more important of these groups was said to be from the half-tribe of Manasseh, and was led by Lehi, a "visionary

---

[2]Joseph Smith, Jr., *History of the Church* 4:461 (Salt Lake City: Deseret Books).

man" from Jerusalem (1 Nephi 1:3). This group arrived in the Western lands around 589 B.C. The descendants of Lehi eventually split into two groups—the Lamanites and the Nephites. Wars plagued the descendants of Lehi, even as they had earlier destroyed the Jaredites, but not before the Nephite prophet, Mormon, hid the history of the peoples in the Hill Cumorah—not to be disturbed until Joseph Smith unearthed them in the nineteenth century.

The Jaredites traveled across the ocean in eight sealed barges while the descendants of Lehi traveled on a large ship guided by a primitive compass (1 Nephi 18:12). (The fact that the compass had not yet been invented fails to disturb the blindly faithful Mormons.) Both groups, according to The Book of Mormon, were instructed by Jesus Christ (before He was born in Bethlehem of Judea or given the name "Jesus"!—see Ether 3:14-15). Through the records of Lehi's descendants, Christ's appearance on the American continent is heralded as evidence of God's concern for the "lost tribes of Israel."

One of Lehi's sons, Nephi, was the principal righteous leader, and his descendants were known as Nephites. His brother, Laman, was unrighteous and his descendants were sinful and rebellious. The American Indians are considered by The Book of Mormon to be Lamanites, and their dark skin is considered to be evidence of a curse placed on them for their wickedness:

> And it came to pass that I beheld, after they had dwindled in unbelief they became a dark, and loathsome, and a filthy people, full of idleness and all manner of abominations.
>
> 1 Nephi 12:23
>
> And he had caused the cursing to come upon them, yea, even a sore cursing, because of their iniquity . . . .wherefore, as they were white, and exceeding fair and delightsome, that they might not be enticing unto my people the Lord God did cause a skin of blackness to come upon them.
>
> 2 Nephi 5:21

The Book of Mormon maintains that many great cities were reared by these civilizations. But descriptions of their possessions and accomplishments, while fascinating to Mormons, are fraudulent to competent archeologists.

This is the Mormon explanation of the coming of the first Mormon extrabiblical revelation, *The Book of Mormon*. How sad for the millions of faithful Mormons that it possesses not one shred of historicity! Even a cursory examination of *The Book of Mormon* and its fallacious claims reveals abundant evidence of its spurious and fictional origin.

Apart from the internal problems of *The Book of Mormon* (discussed below), and the external inconsistencies it raises (also discussed below), the manner in which it was translated by Smith should warn the careful Bible student immediately. In Chapter 8, which deals with the occultic nature of Mormonism, we discuss the occultic activities of both the Mormon Church and its founder, Joseph Smith. To Christians who are aware of the immense power of Satan, the god of this world (2 Corinthians 4:4), Smith's dabbling into occultic practices is enough to disqualify him as a man of God immediately. In the same vein, the use of occultic practices in translating *The Book of Mormon* is also totally at variance with God's methods of revelation, and effectively eliminates the Mormon "Golden Bible" from serious consideration as a word from God. (See Appendix C.)

Joseph Smith's father-in-law, Isaac Hale, maintained that Joseph was involved with

> . . . a set of men who were called money-diggers, and his occupation was that of seeing or pretending to see by means of a stone placed in his hat and his hat closed over his face. In this way he pretended to discover buried or hidden treasures. . . .
>
> . . . Smith stated to me that he had given up what he called glass-looking. . . . Soon after this I was informed that he had brought a wonderful book of plates with them. . . . The manner in which he pretended to read

and interpret was the same as when he looked for the money-diggers with the stone in his hat, and his hat over his face. . . .

New York Baptist Register, June 13, 1834

Substantiating Hale's testimony are the testimonies of David Whitmer and Martin Harris (two of the three witnesses of *The Book of Mormon*) as well as that of Joseph Smith's wife, Emma. Emma Smith declared:

In writing . . . I frequently wrote day after day, often sitting at the table close by him, he sitting with his face buried in his hat with the stone in it, and dictating hour after hour.

Reorganized Latter Day Saints, *Church History* 3:356

Martin Harris, one of the original witnesses to the "Golden Plates" story, and the man whose money financed the publishing of the first edition of *The Book of Mormon*, stated:

Joseph had a stone which was dug from the well of Mason Chase, . . . It was by means of this stone he first discovered these plates. . . . Joseph had had this stone for some time. There was a company there in the neighborhood, who were digging for money . . . and they took Joseph to look in the stone for them. . . . These things had all occurred before I talked with Joseph respecting the plates. But I had the account of it from Joseph, his wife, brothers, sisters, his father and mother. I talked with them separately, that I might get the truth of the matter. . . . Joseph said the angel told him he must quit the company of the money-diggers. . . .

Tiffany's Monthly, 1859, pages 163, 164, 167, 169

David Whitmer's testimony is as follows:

I will now give you a description of the manner in which the Book of Mormon was translated. Joseph would put the seer stone into a hat, and put his face in the hat, drawing it closely around his face to exclude the light; and in the darkness the spiritual light would shine. A piece of something resembling parchment would appear, and on that appeared the writing. One character at a time would appear, and under it was the interpretation in English. Brother Joseph would read off the English to Oliver Cowdery, who was his principal scribe, and when it was written down and repeated to Brother Joseph to see if it was correct, then it would disappear, and another character with the interpretation would appear. Thus the Book of Mormon was translated by the gift and power of God, and not by any power of man.

An Address to All Believers in Christ, page 12.

Internally, *The Book of Mormon* also fails the test as a new revelation of God. The book contradicts God's oldest attested revelation, the Bible, in numerous places. One of its more serious doctrinal errors is its mistaken view of the Trinity. *The Book of Mormon*, while affirming the existence of one God, identifies the person of the Father with the person of the Son, a revival of an ancient heresy known as modalism (Mosiah 15:1-5; 7:27; Ether 3:14).

And now Abinadi said unto them: I would that ye should understand that God himself shall come down among the children of men, and shall redeem his people.

And because he dwelleth in flesh he shall be called the Son of God, and having subjected the flesh to the will of the Father, being the Father and the Son—The Father, because he was conceived by the power of God; and the Son, because of the flesh, thus becoming the Father and Son—And they are one God, yea, the very Eternal Father of heaven and of earth. And thus the flesh becoming subject to the Spirit, or the Son to the Father, being one God. . . .

Mosiah 15:1-5a

Behold, I am he who was prepared from the foundation of the world to redeem my people. Behold, I am Jesus Christ. I am the Father and the Son.

Ether 3:14a

In addition, the Golden Bible has not withstood the test of history, as its Mormon proponents would have us believe. Since each word was allegedly translated miraculously by God through his "seer," Joseph Smith, Jr., it is logical for the Mormon Church to claim that it is "the most correct book on earth." This is precisely what is claimed for it. There could be no problems of translation and no errors of transmission, since God Himself was the agent of its production in English in the early 1800s.

However, the God of the Mormon kingdom is evidently not quite infallible when it comes to revelation. This "most correct" book, as published in 1830, has undergone more than *three thousand* changes in subsequent editions! Sometimes the changes are minor and were evidently made to compensate for Smith's poor command of English. (As Appendix C points out, some portions of *The Book of Mormon* are in quite good English—especially those parts copied verbatim from the King James Version of the Bible!) Perhaps we could allow the Mormon god a few mistakes in grammar, but many of the changes subsequent to the first edition of *The Book of Mormon* radically change the meaning of the text! Just a few of these changes graphically illustrate the fickle nature of the Mormon revelation:

Original (1830) Edition	*Modern Version*
. . .the mean man boweth down. . . .	. . .the mean man boweth not down. . . .
(page 87)	(page 74, v. 9)
. . .king Benjamin had a gift from God, whereby he could interpret such engravings. . . .	. . .king Mosiah had a gift from God, whereby he could interpret such engravings. . . .
(page 200)	(page 176, v. 28)
. . .Behold, the virgin which thou seest, is the mother of God. . . .	. . .Behold, the virgin whom thou seest is the mother of the Son of God. . . .
(page 25)	(1 Nephi 11:18)
. . .that the Lamb of God is the Eternal Father and the Saviour of the world. . . .	. . .that the Lamb of God is the Son of the Eternal Father. . . .
(page 32)	(1 Nephi 13:40)

It takes very little spiritual or intellectual discernment

after reading such changes to know that *The Book of Mormon* is not only unreliable but hopelessly confused in its own pronouncements!

Finally, *The Book of Mormon* is betrayed by external evidences. Two areas of external study show this clearly. Archeology has uncovered many of the errors in *The Book of Mormon* and removed it permanently from the ranks of reliable historical writing. In addition, an investigation into its origins has demonstrated that its prime author was more likely a retired Congregational minister-turned-novelist than an angel!

Archeology and the Book of Mormon

In a fascinating article by John Price (a former Mormon) which appeared in *The Indian Historian* (Vol. 7, no. 3, 1974),° the following comments on *The Book of Mormon* from an archeological and anthropological perspective appear. We are indebted to Mr. Price for a penetrating and revealing analysis.

> The *Book of Mormon* is a history of two migrant groups who came from the Near East to the Americas, the Jaredites (reported in the Book of Ether) and Lehi and his descendants (reported in the remaining books). A third group of migrants, who came "from Jerusalem at the time that Zedekiah, King of Judah, was carried away captive into Babylon," is also briefly mentioned. . . .
>
> The end to the Jaredites came with one war after another. In one battle "many thousands fell by the sword.". . .
>
> Finally, with "men, women, and children being armed with weapons of war, having shields, and breastplates, and headplates" they fought and killed each other off, except for Ether. Ether recorded the final chapter of his people's history and "hid them in a manner that the people of Limhi did find them.". . .

The following is a list of all the elements of identifiable material culture that are mentioned as having been possessed by the Jaredites.

1. Fruit, grain, cattle, oxen, cows, sheep, goats, swine, horses, asses, elephants, and the honey bee.
2. Houses, tents, spacious buildings, thrones, prisons with doors, and large barges.
3. Silks and fine linen.
4. Metallurgy of gold, silver, iron, steel, copper, and brass. Extensive mining that "cast up mighty heaps of earth to get ore."
5. Tools to plow, sow, reap, hoe, and thrash.
6. Swords of steel, shields, breastplates, and headplates.
7. Writings on engraved metal plates.

The second migration, of Lehi and his descendants, is more important for several reasons. Their history constitutes the bulk of the text. They are given the true priesthood and sacraments, although these are lost in time, just as they were lost in the Old World. . . . And a branch of these migrants, the Lamanites, survive to become the American Indians of contemporary times, but cursed with dark skins.

The Lord brought Lehi, a Jewish prophet, his family, their spouses, and other followers out of Jerusalem. . . . The Lord directed them in the construction of a ship and the sailing of it to the promised land, arriving about 589 B.C. "And it came to pass that after we sailed for the space of many days we did arrive at the promised land; and we went forth upon the land, and did pitch our tents . . . we did put all our seeds into the earth, which we had brought from the land of Jerusalem . . . we did find . . . that there were beasts in the forests of every kind, both the cow and the ox, and the ass and the horse, and the goat and the wild goat . . ."

Nephi, one of the sons of Lehi, kept the records of his people and founded one of the main branches of the new immigrants, to be called Nephites. . . .

". . . And it came to pass that the people of Nephi did till the land, and of fruit, and flocks of herds, and flocks of all manner of cattle of every kind, and goats, and wild goats, and also many horses."

One Nephrite [sic]*branch traveled to a land called Zara-

---

*All quotations in this book are reproduced exactly, including spelling and punctuation, as shown in the original documents.

hemla (south of the "narrow neck of land") where they met a people who had come "from Jerusalem at the time that Bedekiah, king of Judah, was carried away captive into Babylon." These people had an engraved stone which "gave an account of one Coriantumr, and the slain of his people." Later, the people of Lemhi discovered the engraved gold plates of the Jaredites and their swords and armor.

"They planted corn, wheat"

Zeniff and his people were given the lands of Lehi-Nephi and Shilom where they rebuilt walled cities; planted corn, wheat, barley, and fruits; kept flocks of animals; and made fine linen and "cloth of every kind.". . .

Mormon, who lived in the fourth century A.D., abridged the plates that had been made by the Nephite historians and buried them in a rock cairn in the Hill Cumorah before the battle of Cumorah. Later in A.D. 421 Moroni added some additional plates to the same cairn. Moroni was the son of Mormon, the last Nephrite survivor, and the protector of the plates. Fourteen hundred years later, in 1823-1837, the same Moroni appeared as an angel to Joseph Smith and turned the plates in the carn in the hill near Smith's house over to him for translation into English.

The following is a list of all the elements of identifiable material culture that are mentioned as having been possessed by the descendants of Lehi, and the people they met in Zarahemla.

1. Corn, wheat, barley, cows, oxen, horses, asses, sheep, goats, and swine. Grape wine and bread.
2. Tents, houses of wood and cement, gates, spacious buildings, towers, palaces, temples, prisons, dungeons, burial in a sepulchre, walled cities, highways, and large sailing ships.
3. Short skin girdles; clothes of silk, linen, and "homely" cloth; and coats.
4. Metallurgy of gold, silver, iron, steel, copper, and brass. Coins of gold and silver. Ringlets and bracelets of gold.
5. Axes, chains, a compass, seer stones, tools to till the ground, ladders, cups, and cords.
6. Bows and arrows, quivers, darts, javelins, swords, daggers, clubs, slings; metal armor of breastplates, arm-shields, and head-shields; horse drawn war chariots; fortifications of earth works, timber walls, and towers

for the defense of cities and in a great defensive line between Nephrites and Lamanites.

7. Writings in "reformed Egyptian" on engraved plates of gold, written engravings on stone, and written correspondance in the form of epistles.

8. Sacrificial and burnt offerings of the first of flocks.

Anthropological Prehistory

An impressive feature of New World prehistory is the extent to which it developed independently of the Old World. The massive weight of evidence points to separate spheres of cultural history. The aboriginal New World did not have wheat, barley, cows, oxen, horses or elephants (after about 5,000 B.C.), asses, sheep, or domesticated goats or swine. No Native Americans made grape wine or wheat bread. Instead, native plants and animals were domesticated: corn, beans, squashes, potatoes, tomatoes, manioc, turkeys, llamas, etc. The New World lacked the wheel (and therefore chariots); silk and linen; metallurgy of iron, steel, and brass; and metal coins, chains, and armor. The Juredites and Nephrites are portrayed as having had plow agriculture of wheat and barley and pastoralism of sheep and cattle, but nothing remotely resembling this kind of culture has ever been found, either archaeologically or ethnographically, in the aboriginal New World. The *Book of Mormon* portrays courts of judges ruling in terms of written laws, a seven day week with a day of rest on the final day, and people paid wages in gold and silver coinage where they are employed. Again, nothing like this has ever been found in the aboriginal New World.

"There is no evidence"

There is evidence for rare New World landfalls by Old World sailing peoples prior to Columbus but these were very recent (mostly after A.D. 1000) and usually of no significant cultural influence. . . . This was not plow agriculture, the animal drawn plow was absent in the pre-Columbian world. It was hand horticulture of corn or manioc or potatoes, not wheat and barley.

There are simply no gaps in the record of archaeological surveys and excavations large enough to admit of the possible existence of Near Eastern style societies anywhere in the New World. It is simply ridiculous today to claim that major Near Eastern style wars were fought by hundreds of thousands of people in upper state New York with metal swords and armor and horse drawn chariots. Not only is there no evidence for such phenomena, but there is extensive evidence in that area for an indigenous shift from hunting to simple horticultural societies, after they received corn, beans, squash, and other domesticates from neighboring societies *Go back to lesson*

Joseph Smith as an Archaeologist

Amateur archaeology in the early 1800's in rural upper state New York focused on explaining the existence of hundreds of large burial mounds in the region. They were filled with skeletons and artifacts of pottery, stone, and occasionally of copper or even silver. There were eight of these within twelve miles of the Smith farm.[6] It appeared that the workmanship of the pottery and copper artifacts was finer than that of the local Iroquois, so it was felt that the Moundbuilders must have been an earlier and greater civilization. Since the major evidence was burials, it was believed that the whole region from western New York to Ohio had been the scene of a terrible war that brought an end to an entire society, buried now in the mounds.

. . .In the early 1800's the *Palmyra Register* and *Palmyra Herald*, the newspapers of Joseph Smith's home town, discussed how the civilized arts of the Moundbuilders were much greater than other Indians. It was held that they were peaceful farmers who had been exterminated by savage hunters, who were the ancestors of the modern Indians. It was common at the time to speculate about this local prehistory.

Joseph Smith's mother wrote that when her son was still in his teens (before 1824) he would create stories about the American aborigines. "During our evening conversation, Joseph would occasionally give us some of the most amusing recitals that could be imagined. He would describe the ancient inhabitants of this continent, their dress, mode of travelling, and the animals upon which they rode; their cities, their buildings, with every particular; their mode of warfare, and also their religious worship. This he would do with as much ease, seemingly, as if he had spent his whole life with them."[7]

---

[6]Fawn N. Brodie, *No Man Knows My History: The Life of Joseph Smith the Mormon Prophet.* (New York, Knopf, 1945), p. 19.
[7]*Ibid.*, p. 35.

The forts and burial mounds described in the *Book of Mormon* are, in fact, like those of the Iroquois . . . .

In the course of his digging Smith apparently found a large copper breastplate. "It was concave on one side and convex on the other, and extended from the neck downwards as far as the centre of the stomach of a man of extraordinary size." He also acquired the seer stones that he referred to as the Urin and Thummin, described by his mother as "two smooth three-cornered diamonds set in glass and the glasses set in silver bows." One local story prior to the writing of the *Book of Mormon* told that a history of the Indians had been found in Canada at the base of a hollow tree. Another story, reported in a Palmyra paper in 1821, told of how diggers on the Erie Canal found engraved "brass plates," along with skeletons and fragments of pottery. Smith apparently knew of Alexander von Humboldt's accounts of ruins in Central America because he later cited them to support the authencicity of the *Book of Mormon* story. For many of his ideas it appears that Smith drew heavily from *View of the Hebrews; or the Ten Lost Tribes of Israel in America* by Ethan Smith, published in 1823. He later cited this work as well for support. He had his own convictions about such matters of current religious controversy as infant baptism, the trinity, and church government. He knew the Moundbuilder civilization theory and the currently popular theory that the Americas had been settled by lost tribes of Israel. He then put all of these ideas together in what has turned out to be the most widely sold and influential book on American prehistory ever written.

Price's astute analysis of the archeological travesty committed by *The Book of Mormon* is confirmed by virtually every competent archeologist who has ever undertaken to examine, even in a cursory fashion, the wild claims of the quasihistorical *Book of Mormon.* Even the National Museum of Natural History of the Smithsonian Institution in Washington, D.C., and *National Geographic* Magazine have disavowed any truth to Mormonism's assertion of the archeological accuracy of *The Book of Mormon!*

References for the quotations used by Mr. Price in his article are as follows: Omni 1:15; Ether 14:4; 15:15; 15:33;

1 Nephi 18:23-25; Enos 1:21; Mosiah 10:5; and Heleman 6:13.

The True Author of The Book of Mormon?

Widespread publicity accompanied the 1977 release of a book examining the origins of *The Book of Mormon* and has caused considerable consternation within the Mormon Church. *Who Really Wrote the Book of Mormon?* by researchers Howard Davis, Wayne Cowdrey, and Donald Scales, has produced substantial evidence to support the claim that *The Book of Mormon* actually was plagiarized from an unpublished novel which had been written before 1816 by Solomon Spalding, a retired minister who occupied his leisure time with composing stories and two novels.

When Mormonism first began its growth in the early 1830s, heated controversy arose concerning the origin of its sacred book. Its followers, standing behind their prophet, Joseph Smith, Jr., sided with him in declaring *The Book of Mormon* to be a new Bible, God's Word to man. Its opponents refused to believe such a story, and an investigation was undertaken in order to ascertain the true roots of the book. Spalding had died before this time (in 1816) and was unable to defend his novel himself. However, his friends, relatives, and acquaintances were very familiar with his second novel, *Manuscript Found*, and, upon hearing *The Book of Mormon* being read by Mormon preachers, immediately recognized it as essentially the long-lost *Manuscript Found*. Dozens of affidavits were gathered from Spalding's acquaintances and family attesting that Spalding was the source of the poorly revised tale which Smith broadcast as *The Book of Mormon*. Additional affidavits were gathered which confirmed the Spalding claim and which were sworn to by relatives and acquaintances of Smith and other early Mormon leaders.

However, with poor communication and little organization, the publication of these testimonies was sporadic. A massive Mormon campaign to counter the facts, combined with a lack of organized rebuttal, caused the Spalding controversy to die down before the end of the century. Many people still referred to Spalding's novel as the possible source of *The Book of Mormon*, but few people had the time or means of access necessary to compile all the necessary information.

Almost thirty years ago, when I was first researching Mormonism, I examined a copy of Spalding's *first* novel, *Manuscript Story*, which is still in existence and in the possession of Oberlin College in Ohio. From a careful comparison of that work with *The Book of Mormon*, I was convinced that Solomon Spalding was their common author. As a painter's strokes are unique, and identify each of his varying pictures, so the author's strokes of style and personal mannerisms uniquely identify each of his works. There was no denying that the two books were somewhat different, but there was also strong evidence that the same author had originated both.[3] However, I did not have the time necessary to exhaustively research the theory, and could only pray that someone with the time and resources could do what needed to be done on this important project.

Then in 1976 I was approached by three young men who had spent three years of their lives in an intensive study of this very puzzle. Not only had they been the first to compile almost all of the testimonies relating to the Spalding affair, but they had also traced the relationship between Smith and Spalding in the person of Sidney Rigdon, one of Smith's closest confidants and a former sojourner in Pittsburgh at the same time Spalding was living there. Their work was astounding, their conclusion apparently inescapable.

---

[3] See Mormon historian B.H. Roberts' analysis of parallels between *The Book of Mormon* and *Manuscript Story* at Oberlin College.

As the crowning touch to their work, part of Spalding's original manuscript of his *second* novel, which had been lost since around 1828, and which was in Spalding's own handwriting, has evidently resurfaced! Twelve pages of manuscript writing has been examined by careful handwriting analysis and attested to be in the handwriting of Solomon Spalding himself, <u>and is a word-for-word portion of *The Book of Mormon*</u>! The bitter irony to the Mormon Church is that these pages have been preserved all these years by the Mormon Church itself as a portion of the original *Book of Mormon*. No Church official had been able to positively identify the handwriting of that section with the handwriting of Smith or any of his known associates. And of course this would hardly have been possible if it were actually the handwriting of Solomon Spalding! The Mormon Church has issued denials of this identification but prohibits further examination of the documents in question.

A complete discussion of the Spalding origin of *The Book of Mormon* can be obtained by reading *Who Really Wrote the Book of Mormon?* I have included here a copy of two of the handwriting experts' testimonies identifying a portion of *The Book of Mormon* handwriting as that of Solomon Spalding. I have also included a chronology concerning Sidney Rigdon and his association with both Spalding and Smith (see following pages). Although Rigdon claimed that he knew nothing of Mormonism before he was approached by Mormon missionaries in late 1830, the evidence shows that he knew Smith long before that, was one of the primary instigators in the development of *The Book of Mormon* and the new religion, and was probably the person who took Spalding's novel from the printshop in which it lay before 1816. It was that manuscript (written by Solomon Spalding) which was added to and revised religiously and then ultimately presented as *The Book of Mormon*.

At least ten people testified that Rigdon knew Smith before the beginning of Mormonism (Stephen H. Hart, Rev. S. F. Whitney, Rev. Darwin Atwater, Adamson Bent-

Henry Silver
QUALIFIED HANDWRITING EXPERT
EXAMINER OF QUESTIONED DOCUMENTS

June 4, 1976

Report to Howard Davis: Re: Questioned handwriting on
                                           parts of manuscripts.

Exhibits A - Four photocopies of parts of manuscript bearing the
              questioned handwriting of the deceased known as
              Solomon Spalding.

Exhibits B - Photocopies of 12 pages of manuscript known to have been
             written around 1810 by the person known as Solomon
             Spalding, so bearing his known handwriting.

             Photocopies of two pages of a letter written to an un-
             identified friend, also bearing the known handwriting or
             or exemplars of the deceased known as Solomon Spalding.

             And photocopy of a Deed, dated Jan., 1811, bearing the known
             handwriting, including the known signature of the person,
             deceased, known as Solomon Spalding.

In comparing the said questioned handwriting in Exhibits A with the said
known handwriting or exemplars in Exhibits B, I find the following:

1. The peculiarity of form of the capital letters in the questioned
   handwriting, Exs. A, are definitely similar to that of the corresponding capitals in the said known handwriting or exemplars, Exs. B.

2. The peculirarity of forms of the small letters in the questioned
   handwriting, Exs. A, are definitely similar to that of the corresponding small letters in the exemplars, Exs. B.

3. The proportionate heights of the capital to small letters in the
   questioned handwriting, Exs. A, are definitely similar to that of
   the capital to small letters in the exemplars, Exs. B.

4. The forms of the links connecting the letters within words of the
   questioned handwriting, Exs. A, are definitely similar to the letter
   links connecting corresponding letters within corresponding words in
   the exemplars, Exs. B.

5. The width of spaces between letters of words in the questioned handwriting, Exs. A, are definitely similar to the width of spaces
   between corresponding letters in corresponding words in the exemplars,
   Exs. A.

6. The base pattern or lineage of writing of the questioned handwriting,
   Exs. A, is definite similar to the base pattern or lineage of

Page 2.

writing of the exemplars, Exs. B.

7. The forms of ending strokes of words of the questioned handwriting, Exs. A, are definitely similar to that of the ending strokes of corresponding words of the exemplars, Exs. B.

    It is seen that the writer of the ending d's of words, of the questioned handwriting, Exs. A, habitually made the ending strokes of the said d's so that they ended ~~turned high~~ with high upward strokes that turned leftward at their ends - the similar ending of d's at the ends of words is seen in the exemplars, Exs. B.

8. The angles of letter slants of the questioned handwriting, Exs. A, are definitely similar to the angles of letter slants of corresponding letters in corresponding words of the exemplars, Exs. B.

CONCLUSION:

    Owing to the predominating number of definite similiarities, pointed out under the preceeding 8 points, between the said questioned handwriting in Exhibits A and the said known handwriting or exemplars, in Exhibits B, It is my definite opinion that all the questioned handwriting in Exhibits A were written by the same writer, known as Solomon Spalding, who wrote his known handwriting in Exhibits B.

                                    Henry Silver
                                    Handwriting Expert
                                    Examiner of Questioned Documents

William Kaye
Examiner of Questioned Documents
Special Document Photographs for Demonstration

September 8, 1977

Wayne Cowdrey
Donald Scales
Howard Davis
c/o 1550 So. Anaheim Blvd. Suite C
Anaheim, Ca. 92805

Re: Questioned handwriting of
Book of Mormon manuscript

Gentlemen:

Pursuant to your assignment to me, I have been examining
the Mormon documents (Unidentified Scribe Section, Kimball Acqui-
sition, Original Dictated Book of Mormon Manuscript) and the
Spalding documents (Conneaut Creek--Manuscript Story manuscript,
and assorted deeds and letters in his known hand) with a view to
determining whether or not the two sets of documents were written
by one and the same hand.

I have examined the original Spalding documents in Ohio
supplied by Oberlin College. In addition, I have examined the
original Mormon documents supplied by the Mormon Church in Salt
Lake City, Utah. I have also examined photostatic copies of both
sets of documents provided me by Oberlin College and the Mormon
Church. I have spent dozens of hours on the project and herewith
present a summary of my studies:

I have found numerous similarities between the Mormon documents that relate significantly to those I have found in the
Spalding documents. While a detailed report would require many
more hours of writing and comparison studies (for example, to
date I have carefully studied over 2500 letter "T's" in the two
sets of documents alone), my present opinion stands on my hours
of examination to this point. There are many similarities in
regard to certain letters and words that are present in the
Solomon Spalding manuscript and in the Book of Mormon manuscript.

It is my considered opinion and conclusion and I believe that
my examination to this point of the original documents concurs
with my first report (which was based on photocopies originally
provided me) and shows unquestionably that the questioned handwriting in the above named Mormon documents and the known handwriting in the above named Spalding documents undoubtedly have
all been executed by the same person.

Sincerely,

William Kaye

ley, Thomas J. Clapp, Alexander Campbell, Dr. S. Rosa, Mr. Almon B. Green, John Rudolph, and Lorenzo Saunders). One of Lorenzo Saunders' testimonies is quoted here as an example of the extensive evidence in our possession concerning this period in Smith's and Rigdon's lives:

HILLSDALE COUNTY, State of Michigan.

Lorenzo Saunders being duly sworn deposes and says: That I reside in Reading, Hillsdale County, State of Michigan; that I was born in the town of Palmyra, Wayne County, State of New York, on June 7, A.D. 1811, and am now seventy-six years of age. That I lived in said town of Palmyra until I was forty-three years of age. That I lived within one mile of Joseph Smith at the time said Joseph Smith claimed that he found the "tablets" on which the "Book of Mormon" was revealed. That I went to the "Hill Comorah" on the Sunday following the date that Joseph Smith claimed he found the plates, it being three miles from my home, and I tried to find the place where the earth had been broken by being dug up, but was unable to find any place where the ground had been disturbed.

That my father died on the 10th day of October, A.D. 1825. That in March of 1827, on or about the 15th of said month I went to the house of Joseph Smith for the purpose of getting some maple sugar to eat, that when I arrived at the house of said Joseph Smith, I was met at the door by Harrison Smith, Jo's brother. That at a distance of ten or twelve rods from the house there were five men that were engaged in talking, four of whom I knew, the fifth one was better dressed than the rest of those whom I was acquainted with. I inquired of Harrison Smith who the stranger was? He informed me his name was Sidney Rigdom [sic] with whom I afterwards became acquainted and found to be Sidney Rigdon. This was in March 1827, the second spring after the death of my father. I was frequently at the house of Joseph Smith from 1827 to 1830. That I saw Oliver Cowdery writing, I suppose the "Book of Mormon" with books and manuscript laying on the table before him; that I went to school to said Oliver Cowdery and knew him well. That in the summer of 1830, I heard Sydney Rigdon preach a sermon on Mormonism. This was after the "Book of Mormon" had been published, which took about three years from the time that Joseph Smith claimed to have had his revelation.

[Signed.] LORENZO SAUNDERS.
[Seal.]

Sworn and subscribed to before me this 21st day of July, A.D. 1887.

LINUS S. PARMELEE,
Justice of the Peace of Reading, Mich.

Chronology

1812	Spalding moved to Pittsburgh, Pennsylvania.
	Sidney Rigdon moved to Pittsburgh.
1814	Spalding moved to Amity, Pennsylvania, and left manuscript of second novel at printshop.
	Rigdon's close friend worked at same print shop.
1822	Rigdon (Baptist pastor in Pittsburgh) showed Spalding manuscript to Dr. Winter.
1823	Rigdon expelled from Baptist Church.
1823-30	Rigdon served as evangelist for Disciples of Christ.
	Rigdon baptized as a Mormon on November 14.
1827 (February)	Gap in Rigdon's itinerary.
1827 (March)	Gap in Rigdon's itinerary.
	Lorenzo Saunders testifies to seeing Smith and Rigdon together.
1827 (April)	Gap in Rigdon's itinerary.
1827 (June)	Gap in Rigdon's itinerary.

	Mrs. Eaton establishes that Smith and Rigdon were together.
1827 (August)	Gap in Rigdon's itinerary.
1827 (October)	Gap in Rigdon's itinerary. Lorenzo Saunders says Smith and Rigdon were together. Abel D. Chase saw Smith and Rigdon together for the first time in 1827.
1828 (June)	Gap in Rigdon's itinerary. Pomeroy Tucker says Rigdon appears at Smith's when 118 pages of manuscript were missing. *Doctrine and Covenants*, Sec. 3, states that 116 pages are missing.
1828 (August)	Gap in Rigdon's itinerary. Lorenzo Saunders says Rigdon and Smith were together.
1828 (October)	Gap in Rigdon's itinerary.
1829 (January)	Gap in Rigdon's itinerary.
1829 (May)	Gap in Rigdon's itinerary. *Doctrine and Covenants*, Sec. 11-13: baptism by John the Baptist.
1829 (June-July)	*Doctrine and Covenants*, Sec. 14-18: three heavenly witnesses, etc. David Whitmer says Smith and someone looking like Rigdon were together. Gap in Rigdon's itinerary.
1829 (November -December)	Lorenzo Saunders sees Smith and Rigdon together.
1830 (January -March)	Gap in Rigdon's itinerary. *Doctrine and Covenants*, Sec. 19: command for printer of *Book of Mormon* to be paid.
1830 (April-June)	Gap in Rigdon's itinerary. *Doctrine and Covenants*, Sec. 20-23:

	April 6, church established.
	Mr. Pearne saw Smith and Rigdon "often" together.
1830 (August -November)	Gap in Rigdon's itinerary.
	Lorenzo Saunders heard Rigdon preach on Mormonism in summer.
	Mrs. S. F. Anderick says Smith and Rigdon were seen together several times during warm weather.
	August and September—*Doctrine and Covenants*, Sec. 27: talks of heavenly messenger.
	September—*Doctrine and Covenants*, Sec. 28-31: talks of church conference.
	October—*Doctrine and Covenants*, Sec. 32-33: commands missionaries to go west, where they find and "convert" Sidney Rigdon.
1830 (November)	November 14: Sidney Rigdon baptized into Mormon Church by Oliver Cowdery.

The world is now in a position to judge *The Book of Mormon* on three different levels. First, the book does not correspond to what we know God has already said in His Word. Second, its internal inconsistencies, thousands of changes, and persistent plagiarization of the King James Bible decidedly remove it from serious consideration as a revelation from God.[4] Finally, its external inconsistencies

---

[4]A few of the more prominent plagiarisms are as follows:

1 Nephi 20, 21	— Isaiah 48, 49
2 Nephi 7, 8	— Isaiah 50, 51
2 Nephi 12-24	— Isaiah 2-14
Mosiah 14	— Isaiah 53
3 Nephi 12-14	— Matthew 5-7
3 Nephi 22	— Isaiah 54
3 Nephi 24, 25	— Malachi 3, 4

not only expose its misuse of archeology, science, history, and language, but actually allow us to investigate its true origin, where we find it to be nothing more than a plagiarized alteration of a romantic novel by a poor retired minister.[5] Surely the honest reader must admit that Mormonism has failed utterly in substantiating the divine authenticity of its most important sacred work.

Doctrine and Covenants

The Doctrine and Covenants is the second sacred book of the Mormon religion. It is a more or less complete collection of revelations given through Joseph Smith concerning all aspects of the Mormon Church, and includes such mundane revelations as the order to pay the printer for printing the first edition of *The Book of Mormon*.

The first revelations were taken down by Joseph's scribes as they fell from the lips of the "inspired" prophet. They were compiled, printed, and entitled *The Book of Commandments*. Later, when the Mormons were driven from Missouri, the existing printing presses were destroyed.

In 1835 the "revelations" were changed, added to, and again printed. There are conservatively 65,000 changes between *The Book of Commandments* and *The Doctrine and Covenants*.

The Doctrine and Covenants also contains many of the Mormon theological aberrations which clearly show the strict separation between Mormonism and the historic Christian faith. Its most famous revelation, however, concerns polygamy and Smith's wife's initial revulsion of the practice. Section 132 is supposedly God's commandment to

---

[5]For at least 150 years up to and including Joseph Smith's time, many authors had believed that the American Indians might have had Hebrew origins. However, since that time this theory has been thoroughly disproven by reputable archeological and anthropological studies.

Emma Smith, wife of the prophet, to accept all those additional wives given to Joseph or else face the eternal wrath of almighty God. This seems rather incredible, since *The Book of Mormon* states:

> Behold, David and Solomon truly had many wives and concubines, which thing was abominable before me, saith the Lord (Jacob 2:24).

After *The Book of Mormon* was published, Joseph allegedly inquired of the Lord if he could have more than one wife, and received permission in contradiction to the earlier revelation of the same subject recorded in *The Book of Mormon*!

In later years, Emma Smith declared that her husband Joseph had never had any other legal wives—that she was his only legal wife. That was quite true. The rest were illegal when viewed from the monogamous stance of the United States, based on the clear revelation of monogamy in the New Testament.

When one reads of the terrible persecution and suffering, the rivalry and heartache endured by the multiple wives in early Mormonism, one cannot conceive that a holy and just God had commanded such an evil. Reports of the Mormon families in Utah who were without mothers because the poor women went insane or committed suicide rather than endure any more degradation are heartrending. God declared that a man should leave his mother and his father and cleave unto his *wife*, and that the *two* should become *one*, (Genesis 2:24).

Fortunately for the poor women of Mormonism (and those moral men who hated polygamy but believed that God had revealed it to the prophet), a later president of the Church, Wilford Woodruff, was more sensible. When the federal government threatened the Mormons with exile to Mexico because of their polygamy, Woodruff received a "Divine Manifesto" (now called a "revelation") which rescinded the "everlasting" decree of plural marriage and relegated polygamy to a "celestial" state, to be enjoyed in the flesh only in the future life!

Doctrine and Covenants is not God's revelation to man or to the Church. It is a compilation of some of the worst deceptions ever foisted on unsuspecting and innocent people, who have been deceived into believing in a god who is not consistent but changes with every whim of his emotions. The Bible confirms to us, however, that the eternal God never changes (Malachi 3:6) and that His Son, the perfect spiritual image of the invisible Father (Colossians 1:15) is also the same yesterday, today, and forever (Hebrews 13:8).

The Pearl of Great Price

The Pearl of Great Price was the third extrabiblical "revelation" added to the Mormon canon of scripture. This compilation of different types of literature differs markedly from the consistent revelation of the Bible and even from the historical narrative form of *The Book of Mormon*. It is a compilation of several different types of work from several different time periods: supposedly ancient Hebrew Scripture (*The Book of Abraham*); roughly emended Biblical material (*The Book of Moses*, Smith's own translation of portions of the Bible); latter day revelations (*The Articles of Faith* and the *History of Joseph Smith the Prophet*, plus two "visions" voted by the Assembly at the Mormon Church Conference of October 1976). This volume lends itself to extensive investigation in several areas. Our treatment of *The Pearl of Great Price* will be brief, however, since its most controversial book, *The Book of Abraham*, comes under our close scrutiny in Chapter 6 ("Mormonism's Racism—The Fraud of the Book of Abraham").

The Articles of Faith are still strictly adhered to by the Mormon Church. These are the statements of belief on the most central areas of Mormon religious practice. It is in this unusual work that we find the Bible relegated to a position far inferior to *The Book of Mormon* (and, necessarily, other Mormon revelations). In the famous Article 8, we are told by the authority of the Mormon Church that the Bible can be trusted only as far as it is "translated correctly," but that *The Book of Mormon* is the Word of God without reservation. On the basis of our brief previous exposé of *The Book of Mormon* and its fraudulent nature, this is truly degrading to God and unworthy of anyone who would sincerely declare himself a Christian!

As we would expect, we do not have to go far to find out what the Mormon Church considers "correctly" translating the Bible, because *The Pearl of Great Price* also contains a portion of Joseph's Bible-translating efforts. His translation methods here are no more reliable than those he supposedly used for *The Book of Mormon*. Flying in the face of all respectable Biblical scholarship, Smith drastically changed the words of Scripture to fit his own theology and ego without one shred of linguistic or textual evidence for it. For example, in his "translation" of the Book of Genesis, Smith added a prophecy of his own coming! The passage reads, "And that seer will I bless . . . and his name shall be called Joseph, and it shall be after the name of his father . . . for the thing which the Lord shall bring forth by his hand shall bring my people unto salvation" (Genesis 50:33, *Holy Scriptures, Inspired Version*, by Joseph Smith, Jr.).

The Pearl of Great Price also contains the "prophetic credentials" of Joseph Smith, Jr. As we have just seen in our examination of the actual origin of *The Book of Mormon*, and in our detailed examination of Smith's life in Chapter 1, these "credentials" are not worth the paper they have been printed on. The history of Joseph Smith is certainly not the history of a prophet of God! It would be more accurately titled, "The History of Joseph Smith, the Glass-Looker and Pretended Prophet."

In conclusion, *The Pearl of Great Price* is certainly not

from God, and could never either add to or supplant the Bible, which it flatly contradicts. For a thorough discussion of *The Book of Abraham* portion of *The Pearl of Great Price*, see Chapter 6.

The three standard works of Mormonism (other than the Bible) are not what the God of the Bible has revealed. His Word cannot be picked apart or added to at the whim of self-styled prophets who are uncomfortable with some of its pronouncements. The Bible is the infallible Word of God, the only rule of faith and practice for those who love Christ's coming. The three added Mormon "revelations" are not revelations at all, but are the works of men who have arrogated to themselves positions of grandeur and leadership which God in His wisdom pointedly withheld. These works contradict themselves, but, more important, they contradict what God has already said and what has been verified through both history and the changed lives of men and women.

THREE

THE GODS
OF MORMONDOM
—
Polytheism Returns

The very core of the Judeo-Christian religion is the doctrine of God, or, as expressed in the classical Jewish affirmation of faith, the *shema*: "Hear, O Israel: the Lord our God is one Lord" (Deuteronomy 6:4). This is, of course, a key issue when we approach Mormon theology because, as we shall see in this chapter and in Chapter 4, the Mormons have erected an almost subcultural language barrier which permits them to speak of believing in "God the Father and His Son, Jesus Christ, and in the Holy Spirit" without ever defining the meaning of those terms within the historic context of the New Testament or the history of the Christian church and its creedal statements.

If one sentence could be used to sum up the difference between Mormonism and Christianity, it could be said without fear of contradiction that Mormonism is polytheistic and Christianity is monotheistic. Historic Christian theology has always affirmed that "within the nature of the one Eternal God there are three Persons: the

Father, the Son, and the Holy Spirit." Literally hundreds of volumes from theological libraries would confirm this belief beyond a question of a doubt, and even the encyclopedias *Britannica* and *Americana* clearly set forth what Christianity has stated in this area.

This notwithstanding, the Mormon Church defines the doctrine of the Trinity as actually a belief in *three separate gods*,[1] which is not monotheism but tritheism. This view has been condemned not only by the historic Christian church but also by *The Book of Mormon*, as shown previously (Chapter 2).

While it is true that the nature of God, because He is infinite, transcends the comprehension of man, and that God is beyond our logical capacities to comprehend fully, He is not *illogical*, nor has He left Himself without a witness. The Bible, which Mormonism maintains it honors as "the Word of God," most explicitly declares the doctrine of monotheism, as opposed to all polytheistic structures. Even the great Jewish philosopher Martin Buber understood what Christian theologians were attempting to set forth in the doctrine of the Trinity and was willing to acknowledge that it was not basically contradictory to so speak of the "oneness" of the Divine Nature.

The True God

There can be no doubt that the New Testament sets forth the thesis that there are three separate Persons in the Deity, known as the Father, the Son, and the Holy Spirit, and each of these is affirmed to be Eternal God (2 Peter 1:17; John 1:1; Acts 5:3, 4). At the same time, the New Testament declares that there is only one God (1 Timothy 2:5). We are led inexorably to the conclusion that the three distinct Persons *are* the one God, though the finite mind of man may not be able to grasp the depth of this revelation of the divine character.

---

[1]Joseph Smith, Jr., *History of the Church* 6:474.

As a matter of record, classic Judaism condemned the worship of so-called "gods" as idolatry and blasphemy (Exodus 20:1-3), a fact amplified by the Apostle Paul in 1 Corinthians 8:4-6. The Apostle was the greatest authority in the New Testament on Hebrew law (apart from the Master Himself), and his credentials cannot be challenged. He clearly meant what he said—that though there are beings that are *called* gods in the heavens or on earth, there is for Judaism and Christianity only one God.

When Jesus Christ was asked what the first and greatest commandment of the law was, He stated in Mark 12:29-31:

> Hear, O Israel: The Lord our God is one Lord; and thou shalt love the Lord thy God with all thy heart, and with all thy soul, and with all thy mind, and with all thy strength: this is the first commandment. And the second is like, namely this, Thou shalt love thy neighbor as thyself. There is none other commandment greater than these.

Paul once again underscores this in Galatians 3:20, where he declares, "God is one," and makes the very important point in Galatians 4:8 that, though the Galatians had worshipped "other gods" when they were the servants of Satan, they were really worshipping what by nature was not Deity at all.

In Biblical theology the nature of God is eternal (Psalm 90:2; Malachi 3:6; Exodus 3:14, 15; and particularly Isaiah 43:10). Isaiah is most careful to affirm the fact that there is only one God (43:10), and he goes out of his way to quote the Lord as stating, "Before me there was no god formed, neither shall there be after me." If we needed any further proof of God's eternity and uniqueness, Isaiah 44:6 would suffice:

> Thus saith the LORD the King of Israel, and his Redeemer the LORD of hosts: I am the first, and I am the last, and beside me there is no God.

It is only necessary to trace the usage of the terms "Alpha" and "Omega" (the first and last letters in the Greek alphabet) through the Book of Revelation to identify the "first" and the "last." Chapters 1, 21, and 22 identify Jesus Christ as being in eternal union with His Father, while the writer of the Epistle to the Hebrews reminds us that it was this same Christ who offered Himself "through the eternal Spirit" (9:14).

It cannot be debated that "other gods" are mentioned in the Bible (for example, Moses in the eyes of Pharaoh, and Satan, who is designated "the god of this world" [Exodus 7:1; Psalm 82:6; and 2 Corinthians 4:4]), but none of the so-called "gods" or "lords" specified in Scripture were *by nature* God, or Deity, since a god is simply the object of an individual's worship. Pharaoh believed that Moses was a god because of the enormous power released through him, and the judgment of the Lord which came upon the land of Egypt. It would be perfectly natural for a pagan king who was a polytheist to believe that miracles such as these would authenticate a man as being a god. (The judges of Israel were called "gods" derogatorily—see Psalm 82; Jeremiah 5:28-31; John 10:34, 35). Satan is worshipped by his followers, and men who serve him become his servants and he becomes their god, whether they are aware of it or not. It is apparent from the record that Moses was only a man and that Satan is but a fallen angel (Isaiah 14:12-15; Ezekiel 28:15).

We may adore anything we choose, whether it be money, power, status, family, business, sex, various earthly possessions, or even alien spirits, but the fact that this practice is acknowledged in history does not mean that those things which are worshipped are Diety. Jeremiah the prophet rises to haunt the gods of Mormonism: (Jeremiah 10:10, 11) "But the LORD is the true God; He is the living God and the everlasting King. At His wrath the earth quakes, and the nations cannot endure His indignation. Thus you shall say to them, 'The gods that did not make the heavens and the earth shall perish from the earth and from under the heavens.'" True Deity is all-powerful (Revelation 1:8), true Diety is all-knowing (1 John 3:20), and true

Deity is both omnipresent (Psalm 139:7-10; Acts 17:24-28; Jeremiah 23:23, 24) and eternal (Psalm 90:2; Hebrews 13:8).

Satanic Polytheism

The Bible fully recognizes that men worship idols and fall down before tree stumps and arts designed by their own hands (Ezekiel 20; Isaiah 44:9-20). We see this in the structure of the Old Testament's criticism of the Gentiles and Paul's reinforcement of it: ". . .the things which the Gentiles sacrifice, they sacrifice to devils, and not to God; and I would not that ye should have fellowship with devils" (1 Corinthians 10:20).

Everything, then, which is opposed to the true, eternal, living God is in reality drawing its power from Satanic sources, from the one whom Jesus Christ described as "the prince of this world" (John 14:30). Regardless of Mormon objections and arguments for their polytheistic structure, it is obvious that they have wrested the texts of the Old and New Testaments out of their contexts, contrary to the whole tenor of Biblical revelation. It is only necessary for us to understand that the God of the Bible is pure Spirit, that He must be worshipped in spirit and in truth (John 4:24), and that He appeared once as true man in the Person of Jesus Christ (John 1:1, 14, 18). Jesus of Nazareth had no inhibitions about declaring His identity (see John 8:58; 10:30), and He did not hesitate to say, "If ye believe not that I am [Greek *ego eimi*, Christ's expression for His eternal Deity], ye shall die in your sins," for "whither I go, ye cannot come" (John 8:24, 21; cf. John 8:58; Exodus 3:14, 15).

The Apostle John testified that the Lord Jesus was "making himself equal with God" (John 5:18), and the Apostle Thomas worshipped Him as the living God in human flesh (John 20:28). The personality and deity of the Holy Spirit is also unchallenged by any serious student of New Testament theology, because He repeatedly speaks as a person and as God (see Acts 13:2; Acts 5:3, 4; and His personal prophecy to the Apostle Paul through Agabus, as found in Acts 21:10, 11).

What admittedly escapes our intellectual comprehension emerges as starkly realistic and with a clear ring of truth: there is only one true God (Isaiah 46:9). Mormonism claims that it acknowledges only one god for *this* earth, but the very fact that it teaches the existence of other gods and that its male followers themselves hope to become gods demands that the Christian church classify this cult as polytheistic. It is logically impossible to be a polytheist and a Christian, and the gods of Mormondom disqualify its adherents from truly being what they claim to be—"*the Church of Jesus Christ of Latter-day Saints.*"

Mormon theologians are fond of pointing to various passages in the Bible which describe God as having hands, feet, eyes, ears, nose, mouth, head, and hair, and affirming that man is created in His image (Genesis 1:26, 27), supposedly proving that God has a body and is only a big man! This particular assertion will not survive the standard scholarly tests of interpretation when compared with Psalm 91:4, where God is described as having wings and feathers, and in the New Testament, where Jesus Christ is proclaimed as "the true vine," "the living bread," "the way," and "the door," all of which are literary devices designed to portray in human terms something of the character of the Eternal God in understandable form.

Mormon missionaries are not eager to discuss their view of what George Arbaugh (author of *Revelation and Mormonism*) has termed "the romance of the gods," and they would have us believe that *Christianity* is polytheistic! But, as the next section of this chapter will demonstrate (from primary Mormon sources, including Joseph Smith, Brigham Young, official Church publications, Apostles, and theologians of the Mormon Church), the Mormon doctrine of God is both anti-Christian and an outright perversion of the Christian gospel concerning the nature and character of God. We shall, however, let the record speak for itself, with complete confidence that when the gods of Mormonism are seen for what they are, and Mormonism's doctrine of "exaltation" is exposed, even the most nominally oriented Christian cannot help but be repulsed by its crassly unbiblical nature.

The Mormon Church relies upon considerably more material for its teachings than its so-called "four standard works," and it is hoped that the references which follow will be remembered by the reader and applied to any individuals who may wish to challenge the sources used.

Polytheism Returns

As the reader peruses the following documentation from historic Mormon theology, he should remember that the Mormon Church today does not hesitate to contradict Joseph Smith or Brigham Young, but, when challenged, vigorously denies the contradiction. (See *Church News*, week ending June 5, 1965, editorial page: "One of the most important things we may learn about our religion is that God is unchangeable, the same yesterday, today and forever" [page 16].) However, the following quotations speak for themselves.

1. God himself was once as we are now, and is an exalted man, and sits enthroned in yonder heavens!
    . . . I am going to tell you how God came to be God. We have imagined and supposed that God was God from all eternity. I will refute that idea, and take away the veil, so that you may see . . . . It is the first principle of the gospel to know for a certainty the character of God, and to know that we may converse with him as one man converses with another, and that He was once a man like us; yea, that God himself, the Father of us all, dwelt on an earth, the same as Jesus Christ himself did; and I will show it from the Bible. . . .

    Here, then, is eternal life—to know the only wise and true God; and you have got to learn how to be gods yourselves, and to be kings and priests to God, the same as all gods have done before you, namely, by going from one small degree to another, and from a small capacity to a great one; from grace to grace, from exaltation to exaltation, until you attain to the resurrection of the dead, and are able to dwell in everlasting burnings, and to sit in glory, as do those who sit enthroned in everlasting power. . . .

> Joseph Smith, Jr., *History of the Church* 6:305-6

2. A. I will preach on the plurality of Gods. I have selected this text for that express purpose. I wish to declare I have always and in all congregations when I have preached on the subject of the Deity, it has been the plurality of Gods. It has been preached by the Elders for fifteen years.

I have always declared God to be a distinct personage, Jesus Christ a separate and distinct personage from God the Father, and that the Holy Ghost was a distinct personage and a Spirit: and these three constitute three distinct personages and three Gods. If this is in accordance with the New Testament, lo and behold! we have three Gods anyhow, and they are plural: and who can contradict it?

> Joseph Smith, Jr., *History of the Church* 6:474

B. The head God organized the heavens and the earth. I defy all the world to refute me. In the beginning the heads of the Gods organized the heavens and the earth. . . .

The heads of the Gods appointed one God for us; and when you take [that] view of the subject, it sets one free to see all the beauty, holiness and perfection of the Gods. All I want is to get the simple, naked truth, and the whole truth.

Many men say there is one God; the Father, the Son and the Holy Ghost are only one God! I say that is a strange God anyhow—three in one, and one in three! It is a curious organization. . . . All are to be crammed into one God, according to sectarianism. It would make the biggest God in all the world. He would be a wonderfully big God—he would be a giant or a monster.

> Joseph Smith, Jr., *History of the Church* 6:475-76

3. The Father has a body of flesh and bone as tangible as man's; the Son also; but the Holy Ghost has not a body of flesh and bones, but is a personage of Spirit. . . .

Doctrine and Covenants 130:22

4. How many Gods there are, I do not know. But there never was a time when there were no Gods and worlds. . . .

Brigham Young, *Journal of Discourses* 7:333

5. Each of these Gods, including Jesus Christ and his Father, being in possession of not merely an organized spirit, but a glorious immortal body of flesh and bones. . . .

Parley P. Pratt, *Key to the Science of Theology,* Tenth edition, page 44

6. Mormon prophets have continuously taught the sublime truth that God the Eternal° Father was once a mortal man who passed through a school of earth life similar to that through which we are now passing. He became God—an exalted being through obedience to the same eternal Gospel truths that we are given opportunity today to obey.

Milton R. Hunter, *The Gospel Through the Ages,*(1945 edition) page 104.

7. My next sermon will be to both Saint and sinner. . . . Our God and Father in heaven, is a being of tabernacle, or, in other words, He has a body, with parts the same as you and I have; . . . I will tell you how it is. Our Father in Heaven begat all the spirits that ever were, or ever will be, upon this earth; and they were born spirits in the eternal world.

Brigham Young, *Journal of Discourses* 1:50

8. Now hear it, O inhabitants of the earth, Jew and Gentile, Saint and sinner! When our father Adam came into the garden of Eden, he came into it with a *celestial body,* and brought Eve, *one of his wives,* with him. He helped to make and or-

---

°Emphasis theirs.

gel, the ANCIENT OF DAYS! about whom holy men have written and spoken—*HE is our* FATHER *and our* GOD, *and the only God with whom* WE *have to do.* Every man upon the earth, professing Christians or non-professing, must hear it, and *will know it sooner or later.* °

. . .Now, let all who may hear these doctrines, pause before they make light of them, or treat them with indifference, for they will prove their salvation or damnation.

. . .In the Bible, you have read the things I have told you to-night; but you have not known what you did read. I have told you no more than you are conversant with; but what do the people in Christendom, with the Bible in their hands, know about this subject? Comparatively nothing.

Brigham Young, *Journal of Discourses* 1:50-51

9. *Daniel in his seventh chapter speaks of the Ancient of Days: he means the oldest man, our Father Adam, Michael,†* he will call his children together and hold a council with them to prepare them for the coming of the Son of Man. He (Adam) is the father of the human family, and presides over the spirits of all men, and all that have had the keys must stand before him in this grand council. This may take place before some of us leave the stage of action. The Son of Man stands before him, and there is given him glory and dominion. Adam delivers up his stewardship to Christ, that which was delivered to him as holding the keys of the universe, but retains his standing as head of the human family.

Joseph Smith, Jr., *History of the Church* 3:386-87

Undoubtedly Joseph Smith was unique in applying the term "Ancient of Days" to Adam, since theologians down through the centuries have been quite consistent in identifying the "Ancient of Days" with Almighty God. It is apparent that Joseph Smith's concept of God was the same as Brigham Young's.

° Emphasis theirs.
† Emphasis ours.

The reader should also take note of the following statement by Joseph Smith:

> In vision Daniel witnessed the enactment of a drama of magnificent splendor as the Mighty God, to whom the title of the Ancient of Days is given, presents to His Son, Jesus Christ, a Kingdom so that all people, nations and languages may serve Him.
>
> *Destiny* December 1953, page 1

What makes the last quotation so fascinating is that the term "Mighty God" is given to Jesus Christ (*El Gibbor*) in Isaiah 9:6, and in Isaiah 10 it is declared that Jacob will return to the Mighty God (verse 21). The only Mighty God that Jacob could return to is "the God of Abraham, Isaac, and Jacob," who is the Eternal God (Exodus 3:6). If Michael is the Ancient of Days, as classic Mormon theology maintains, then this *Destiny* article conclusively demonstrates that he is the father of Jesus Christ. Isaiah certainly intended to convey the idea of the deity of the Messiah (9:6) by the use of the term "Mighty God." The contradiction among *Journal of Discourses* 1:50-51, the *Destiny* article, and the Bible fairly leaps into the open here. This becomes even more obvious when the Bible describes Christ with the same terms that are used of the Ancient of Days (Revelation 1:12-16; cf. Daniel 7:9).

10.   . . .How much unbelief exists in the minds of the Latter-day Saints in regard to *one particular doctrine which I revealed to them, and which God revealed to me—namely that Adam is our father and God**—I do not know, I do not inquire, I care nothing about it. Our Father Adam helped to make this earth, it was created expressly for him, and after it was made he and his companions came here. He brought one of his wives with him, and she was called Eve, because she was the first woman upon the earth. . . .

Where is the mystery in this? We say that Father Adam came here and helped to make the earth. *Who is he? He is Michael, a great prince, and it was said to him by Eloheim [sic], "Go ye*

*Emphasis ours.

and make an earth.° What is the great mystery about it? He came and formed the earth. Geologists tell us that it was here millions of years ago. How do they know? They know nothing about it. But suppose it was here, what of it? Adam found it in a state of chaos, unorganized and incomplete. . . .Adam came here and got it up in a shape that would suit him to commence business. What is the great mystery about it? None, that I have seen. The mystery in this, as with miracles, or anything else, is only to those who are ignorant. Father Adam came here, and then they brought his wife. "Well," says one, *"Why was Adam called Adam?"* *He was the first man on the earth, and its framer and maker. He, with the help of his brethren, brought it into existence. Then he said, "I want my children who are in the spirit world to come and live here. I once dwelt upon an earth something like this, in a mortal state,*° I was faithful, I received my crown and exaltation. I have the privilege of extending my work, and to its increase there will be no end. *I want my children that were born to me in the spirit world to come here and take tabernacles of flesh,*° that their spirits may have a house, a tabernacle or a dwelling place as mine has, and where is the mystery?

Brigham Young, *Deseret News*,
June 18, 1873, page 308

11. ADAM, THE FATHER AND GOD OF THE HUMAN FAMILY. The above sentiment appeared in *Star* No. 48, a little to the surprise of some of its readers; and while the sentiment may have appeared blasphemous to the ignorant, it has no doubt given rise to some serious reflections with the more candid and comprehensive mind. A few reasonable and Scriptural ideas upon this subject may be profitable at the present time.

Then Adam is really God! And why not? If there are Lords many and Gods many, as the Scriptures inform us, why should not our Father Adam be one of them? . . .

. . .No wonder Father Adam fell, and ac-

°Emphasis ours.

companied the woman, sharing in all the miseries of the curse, that he might be the father of an innumerable race of beings who would be capable of becoming Gods.

With these considerations before us, we can begin to see how it is that we are under obligations to our father Adam, as to a God. He endured the sufferings and the curse that we might *be*; and we are, that we might become Gods. Through him the *justice* of God was made manifest.°

> *Millennial Star* 15:801,
> December 10, 1853

12. OUR FATHER ADAM.—The extract from the *Journal of Discourses* may startle some of our readers, but we would wish them to recollect that in this last dispensation God will send forth, by His servants, things *new* as well as *old*, until man is perfected in the truth.°

> *Millennial Star* 15:780,
> November 26, 1853

13. This is the hope of all Saints who have a just conception of the future; and why should we not be willing for father Adam to inherit all things, as well as for ourselves? He is the *first*, the Father of all the human family, and his glory will be above all, for he will be God over all, necessarily, standing as he will through all eternity at the head of those who are the redeemed of his great family. Though all the sons should, through their faithfulness, become Gods, they would still know that the Son was not greater than the Father.

. . .It is upon this foundation that the throne of Michael is established as Father, Patriarch, God; and it is for all his children who come into this world, to learn and fully understand the eternity of that relationship.°

> *Millennial Star* 15:802,
> December 10, 1853

14. I have learned by experience that there is but one God that pertains to this people, and He is the God that pertains to this earth—the first man. That first man sent his own Son to redeem the

---

° Emphasis theirs.

world, to redeem his brethren; his life was taken, his blood shed, that our sins might be remitted.

> Heber C. Kimball, *Journal of Discourses* 4:1, June 29, 1856

15. . . .some of the officers have not met in council for three years. They are lacking faith on one principle—the last 'cat that was let out of the bag.' Polygamy has been got over pretty well, that cloud has vanished away, but they are troubled about Adam being our Father and God. There is a very intelligent person investigating our principles, and who has been a great help to the Saints; he has all the works, and can get along very well with everything else but the last 'cat,' and as soon as he can see that clearly, he will become a 'Mormon.' I instructed him to write to Liverpool upon it.

> *Millennial Star* 16:482

16. ELDER JAMES A LITTLE— . . . I believe in the principle of obedience; and if I am told that Adam is our Father and our God, I just believe it.

> *Millennial Star* 16:530

17. . . .If, as Elder Caffall remarked, there are those who are waiting at the door of the Church for this objection to be removed, tell such, *the Prophet and Apostle Brigham has declared it, and that it is the word of the Lord.*°

> *Millennial Star* 16:534

18. . . .every knee shall bow, and every tongue confess that he is the God of the whole earth. Then will the words of the Prophet Brigham, when speaking of Adam, be fully realized—"He is our Father and our God, *and the only God with whom WE have to do.*"°

> *Millennial Star* 17:195

19. Friday 9th April 1852 . . . Another meeting this evening. President B. Young taught that Adam was the father of Jesus and the only God to us.[102] That he came to this world in a resur[r]ected body &c more hereafter.

> *Diary of Hosea Stout* 2:435

20. 102. This speech on the "Adam-God" theory gave rise to much later discussion, some of which con-

---

°Emphasis theirs.

tinued into the 1920's. It is not now accepted as
L.D.S. Church doctrine.

Juanita Brooks' footnote to
Diary of Hosea Stout 2:435

21. Some years ago, I advanced a doctrine with
regard to Adam, being our father and God, that
will be a curse to many of the Elders of Israel
because of their folly. With regard to it they yet
grovel in darkness and will. It is one of the most
glorious revealments of the economy of heaven,
yet the world hold it in [derision]. Had I revealed
the doctrine of baptism from the dead instead [of]
Joseph Smith there are men around me who
would have ridiculed the idea until dooms day.
But they are ignorant and stupid like the dumb
ass.

Brigham Young, October 8, 1864,
Misc. Sermons of Brigham Young,
Church Archives

22. Some have grumbled because I believe our God to
be so near to us as Father Adam. There are many
who know that doctrine to be true.

Brigham Young,
Journal of Discourses 5:331

23. The Lord told me that Adam was my father and
that He was the God and Father of all the inhabitants of this earth.

Heber C. Kimball,
Memorandum, April 30, 1862;
Sacred History,
Solomon F. Kimball,
Church Archives

24. Is there in the heaven of heavens a leader? Yes,
and we cannot do without one and that being the
case, whoever his is may be called God. Joseph
said that Adam was our Father and God.

Brigham Young, May 14, 1876
Journal History,
Church Archives

25. Adam is Michael the Archangel and he is the
Father of Jesus Christ and is our God and Joseph
taught this principle.

Brigham Young, December 16, 1867
Wilford Woodruff Journal,
Church Archives

26.   Some has thought it strange what I have said concerning Adam. But the period will come when this people if faithful will be willing to adopt Joseph Smith as their Prophet, Seer, Revelator, and God, but not the Father of their spirits, for that was our Father Adam.

Brigham Young, December 11, 1869
Wilford Woodruff Journal,
Church Archives

27.   There is one revelation that this people are not generally acquainted with. I think it has never been published. . . .It is given in questions and answers. . . . "What is the name of God in the pure language?" . . . "Ahman." "What is the name of the Son of God?" Answer, "Son Ahman—the greatest of all the parts of God excepting Ahman." . . . "What is the name of angels in the pure language?" "Anglo-man."

This revelation goes on. . . . What is the conclusion to be drawn from this? It is, that these intelligent beings are all parts of God, and that those who have the most of the parts of God are the greatest, or next to God, and those who have the next greatest portions of the parts of God, are the next greatest, or nearest to the fulness of God; . . .

Orson Pratt, *Journal of Discourses* 2:342

28.   . . .Adam is our God. Who his God & Father may be I have no knowledge.

A. F. MacDonald, June 8, 1868
"Minutes of the School
of the Prophets,"
Provo, Utah

29.   Oct. 6th attend Conference, a very interesting Conference. . . . President Brigham Young said thus . . . that Adam and Eve were the natural father and mother of every spirit that comes to this planet, or that receives, tabernacles on this plannet [sic]. . . . we are brothers and sisters, and

> that Adam was, God our Eternal Father. . . . Or-
> son Prat[t] told me he did not believe it he said he
> could prove by the Scriptures it was not cor-
> rect. . . . I feared lest he should apostetize
> [sic]. . . .
>
> Joseph Lee Robinson, *Journal
> and Autobiography*, page 62
> of typed copy

30.   The doctrine preached by Prest [sic] Young for a
       few years back wherein he says that Adam is our
       God—the God we worship—that most of the peo-
       ple believe this . . . Amasa Lyman stumbled on
       this he did not believe it—he did not believe in
       the atonement of Jesus—Orson Pratt has also told
       the Prest that he does not believe it—this is not
       the way to act—we should not suffer ourselves to
       entertain one doubt—we are not accountable on
       points of Doctrine if the President makes a state-
       ment it is not our prerogative to dispute it.

                   "Minutes of the School of
                   The Prophets," under date
                   June 8, 1868, Provo, Utah,
                   1868-71, p. 38 of typed
                   copy at Utah State
                   Historical Society

A Non-Christian Cult

As observed from the above quotations, Mormonism ex-
poses itself as a non-Christian cultic system on the basis of
its doctrine of God alone. We should, however, pay extremely close attention to what the LDS Church apologists
have now tried to term "the Adam-God myth." In a
hopeless attempt to redeem the tangled non-Christian concepts of Joseph Smith and Brigham Young about the nature
of God, they have accused those who point out these facts of
attempting to injure the reputation of President Young and
the Mormon people.

They also maintain, contrary to all the evidence, that
"an honest reading of . . . reported discourses of President
Brigham Young prove that the great second President of the

Church held no such views as have been put into his mouth in the form of the Adam-god myth."[2]

A good example of Mormon doubletalk is found in their authoritative statements:

> Cultists and other enemies of the restored truth, for their own peculiar purposes, sometimes try to make it appear that Latter-day Saints worship *Adam* as their Father in heaven. In support of their false assumptions, they quote such statements as that of President Brigham Young to the effect that Adam is our father and our god and the only god with whom we have to do.
> Bruce R. McConkie,
> *Mormon Doctrine*, page 18

> We hear a lot of people talk about Adam passing through mortality and the resurrection on another earth and then coming here to live and die again. Well that is a contradiction of the word of the Lord . . . President Brigham Young is quoted—in all probability the sermon was erroneously transcribed! . . . If the enemies of the Church who quote this wished to be honest, they could not help seeing that President Brigham Young definitely declares that Adam is Michael the Archangel, the Ancient of Days, which indicates definitely that Adam is *not* Elohim, or the God whom we worship, who is the Father of Jesus Christ.
>
> Further, they could see that President Young declared that Adam *helped* to make the earth. . . .
> Joseph Fielding Smith,
> *Doctrines of Salvation* 1:91, 96

Brigham Young also declared Adam to have helped make and organize the world. (Joseph Fielding Smith, *Doctrines of Salvation* 1:96)

The question we are faced with is, who is the Creator? Let's look at the words of the Bible, the oldest revelation and one that is recognized even by the Mormon Church:

> In the beginning God created the heaven and the earth.
> Genesis 1:1

---

[2]John A. Widtsoe, *Evidences and Reconciliations*, pages 68-71.

> In the beginning was the Word, and the Word was with
> God, and the Word was God. . . . All things were made
> by him. . . .
>
> John 1:1, 3

> (The Father, speaking to the Son): Thou, Lord, in the
> beginning hast laid the foundation of the earth; and the
> heavens are the works of thine hands.
>
> Hebrews 1:10

> Thus saith the LORD, thy Redeemer, and he that
> formed thee from the womb, I am the LORD that
> maketh all things, that stretcheth forth the heavens
> alone, that spreadeth abroad the earth by myself.
>
> Isaiah 44:24

The verdict of the Bible is that there is only one God,
who created all things. Within the nature of that one eternal God there are three distinct persons—the Father, the
Son, and the Holy Spirit. Neither historic Mormonism,
whose founding prophets taught that Adam was God, nor
the current church, which tries to avoid the Adam-God
issue, is right. Almighty God is our only Creator and the
only One deserving of worship.

In order to expose this bit of subterfuge (advanced with
utter contempt against the facts of history) it is only necessary to analyze the following facts.

Brigham Young, as previously cited, identified Adam
with the Creator or Father of all the spirits "that ever were
or ever will be upon this earth" (compare *Journal of
Discourses* 1:50 with the *Deseret News*, June 18, 1873). In
this same discourse, Brigham Young went out of his way to
declare:

> . . . How much unbelief exists in the minds of the Latter-
> day Saints in regard to one particular doctrine which I
> revealed to them, and which God revealed to
> me—namely, that Adam is our Father and God. . . ."

When this is viewed within the context of the previously
cited reference, we can clearly see that Brigham's God was
Adam, and that he got this doctrine from Joseph Smith, Jr.
(see documentation above). No one with the facts should

deny Brigham's affirmation of this doctrine, his refusal to back down, and the understanding of his contemporaries that this was a revelation. The absolute Mormon authority of Brigham Young, as demonstrated in Chapters 1 and 4, should lay to rest forever the Mormon Church's claim that "Brigham Young and others may have taught this doctrine." It is not a question of whether Smith and Young *may* have taught it—they *did* teach it, and the Mormon Church *did* teach it.

The Church even recommended that Brigham Young's sermons, as published in England and in the United States, were to be believed as doctrine proceeding from God. To remove all doubt in this area, the following quotation is of extreme importance:

> . . . And we would here take occasion to remark, that it would be well if all our readers would secure a copy of the *Journal of Discourses* as it is issued, and also of every standard work of the Church; and not only secure these works but attentively read them and thoroughly study the principles they contain. Those of the Saints who fail to obtain the standard publications of the Church will not be likely to prove very intelligent Saints. . . . Without the intelligence that comes through the Holy Priesthood, the Saints cannot gain salvation and this intelligence is given in the various publications of the Church. Who then will endanger his salvation by being behind the times? Not the wise, certainly.
>
> Editorial, *Millennial Star* 15:780

There is no mistaking what Brigham intended, and his sermons (compiled from the *Millennial Star*, the *Times and Seasons*, the *Deseret News*, and other publications) were endorsed by this official Church editorial. Logically, then, if one ignored such of Brigham Young's teachings as the Adam-God doctrine, he would "endanger his salvation." The introduction to the *Journal of Discourses* confirms this high view of its reliability:

... these Sermons will be most valuable, as a guage of doctrine, a rule of rectitude, and a square to life, furnishing at the same time an extensive repository of historical information.

Introduction to *Journal of Discourses*,
First Edition, page vii

LETTER FROM THE FIRST PRESIDENCY.

Great Salt Lake City, Utah Territory, June 1, 1853.

Elder Samuel W. Richards, and the Saints abroad.

Dear Brethren—It is well known to many of you, that Elder George D. Watt, by our counsel, spent much time in the midst of poverty and hardships to acquire the art of reporting in Phonography, which he has faithfully and fully accomplished; and he has been reporting the public Sermons, Discourses, Lectures, &c., delivered by the Presidency, the Twelve, and others in this city, for nearly two years, almost without fee or reward. Elder Watt now proposes to publish a *Journal* of these Reports, in England, for the benefit of the Saints at large, and to obtain means to enable him to sustain his highly useful position of Reporter. You will perceive at once that this will be a work of mutual benefit, and we cheerfully and warmly request your co-operation in the purchase and sale of the above-named *Journal*, and wish all the profits arising therefrom to be under the control of Elder Watt.

BRIGHAM YOUNG,
HEBER C. KIMBALL, } First Presidency of the Church of
WILLARD RICHARDS, } Jesus Christ of Latter-day Saints.

Joseph Smith stated:

> And this is the ensample unto them, that they shall speak as they are moved upon by the Holy Ghost. And whatsoever they shall speak when moved upon by the Holy Ghost shall be scripture, shall be the will of the Lord, shall be the mind of the Lord, shall be the word of the Lord, shall be the voice of the Lord, and the power of God unto salvation.
>
> Joseph Smith, *Doctrine and Covenants* 68:3, 4

Brigham Young, second president of the Church of Jesus Christ of Latter-day Saints and successor to Joseph Smith, Jr., the murdered Mormon prophet, was the man who led the Latter-day Saints from Nauvoo to the Valley of the Great Salt Lake and quite literally ruled Mormonism unchallenged until his death in 1877.

It is of tremendous significance that the Church of Jesus Christ of Latter-day Saints today is doing virtually everything within its power to deprive both Brigham Young and Joseph Smith of absolute authority in all areas of theology by simply stating that they recognize as authoritative only "*The Book of Mormon, The Doctrine and Covenants, The Pearl of Great Price*, and the Bible, insofar as it is correctly translated." This they are attempting to do because it is a continuous embarrassment to them to have to defend some of the statements of their founding prophets, particularly since the Church today is vainly attempting to extricate itself from their blunders.

A most interesting illustration of this comes from the declaration of a Mormon attorney responding for the Church in a lawsuit brought in California.

> . . . It is the position of the Church that the Bible, *The Book of Mormon*, the *Doctrine and Covenants*, and *The Pearl of Great Price* are the standard works of the Church and are the only books officially accepted as Scripture. The books, writings, explanations, expositions, views, theories of even the wisest and greatest men, either in or out of the Church, do not rank with the standard works. Even the writings, teachings and opinions of the prophets of God are acceptable only to the extent that they are

in harmony with what God has revealed and what is recorded in the standard works. It is an error to suppose that every utterance made by brethren holding the Priesthood, even the General Authorities of the Church, is to be received as authorized doctrine. It is not admitted nor claimed by the Church that any of the writings contained in the Journal of Discourses is an accurate reflection of statements actually made by the persons represented to be the source thereof.[3]

The most significant thing about this particular authoritative statement (under oath) is that the Mormon Church is, in effect, saying that everything they have ever published and circulated to their people in their entire history is not to be relied upon and cannot be considered authoritative unless it agrees with the four standard works. It is unfortunate that *within this sworn statement there appears the declaration, new in the history of Mormonism, that they do not even acknowledge that some of the materials contained in the Journal of Discourses and other so called nonstandard works of the Church can be attributed to the persons whose names have appeared on them since their initial publication by the Mormon Church!*

What is being said in effect is that "we disclaim anything which disagrees with our current theological position, without saying we reject the authority of the people who made the statements." Why, then, publish the *Journal of Discourses?* Why publish *Millennial Star?* Why publish *Deseret News?* Why publish *The Discourses of Brigham Young* and promote them as authoritative publications of the Church? The beginning of the *Journal of Discourses* (first edition) published in England (see reproduced letter on page 94), clearly carries the imprimatur or the official

---

[3]Martin vs. Johnson, Corporation of the Presiding Bishop, Corporation of the President, California Anaheim Mission, Santa Ana Institute of Religion, Fountain Valley First Ward, Costa Mesa First Ward, Costa Mesa Institute of Religion, and Irvine Institute of Religion. The Superior Court of the State of California for the County of Orange, January 22, 1976, pages 1 and 2.

statement of Brigham Young and his counselors to the effect that what is contained therein is to be regarded as reliable where Church doctrine is concerned. Yet today the Mormon Church, in an effort to escape the theological aberrations and contradictions of its early founders, want both the Church and the public to believe that they have consistently held the same positions both doctrinally and in regard to their "Scriptures" as they always have in the past and still do today.

However, the only consistency we actually see in the Church on this matter is that it has repeatedly affirmed the divine sanction on many so-called nonstandard works and utterances.

According to *The Latter-day Saints' Biographical Encyclopedia* (January 5, 1901, Number 1, Volume 1, pages 11, 13, and 14), an official publication of the Mormon Church, Brigham Young was described in the following terms:

> In a revelation given to the Prophet, Joseph Smith, January 19, 1841, the Lord says: "I give unto you my servant, Brigham Young, to be a president over the Twelve Travelling Council, which Twelve hold the keys to open up the authority of my kingdom upon the four corners of the earth and after that to send my word to every creature."
> The Quorum of Twelve stands next in authority to the presidency of the church, and in the case of the decease of the prophet, the Twelve preside over the church with their president at the head, and thus was brought to the front Brigham Young, the man whom God designed should succeed the prophet Joseph Smith. . . . When the Twelve were sustained as the presiding authority of the church, Brigham Young arose to speak and in the presence of the multitude was transfigured by the spirit and power of God so that his form, size, and countenance and voice appeared as those of the martyred prophet. Even non-members were struck with amazement and expected to see and hear the departed Seer. From that moment doubt and uncertainty were banished from the hearts of the faithful; they were fully assured that the mantle of Joseph Smith had fallen upon

Brigham Young. After the martyrdom of Joseph and Hyrum, persecution did not cease; the prophets were slain but truth did not die. The man who stood at the earthly head was taken away, but the authority he held had been conferred upon others. . . . During his administration of thirty years as president of the church, he made frequent tours accompanied by his associates in the priesthood. . . . Though he did not utter so many distinct prophecies, he builded faith fully upon the foundation laid through the prophet Joseph Smith, and all his movements and counsels were prophetic, as fully demonstrated by subsequent events. He was a prophet, statesman, pioneer and colonizer.

The above statement declares the Church's position on Brigham Young and acknowledges the fact that he did indeed utter "prophecies"—and in fact "all his movements and counsels were prophetic."

Many instances could be cited to support Brigham Young's authority in the Church and in the areas of revelation and theology as he taught the Mormon people. In the interest of historical validity, a few references from fully recognized and accepted Mormon sources will serve to outline the position he held in the Church. Since authority holds such a high place in Mormon teaching, and in fact is the source of their entire mythological priesthood (see Chapter 5), the following evidence is of great value.

I wonder if some one won't go away and say that brother Kimball and the authorities were misinformed. I can tell you they are not; for those men who stand at the head of affairs have the light of heaven with them all the time; they have the power of the Spirit and the visions of the heavens with them always, and they can read men and women from head to foot.

After this, I don't want anybody to go away from the meeting and say, "I guess they were mistaken." Don't let us hear any more of it, brethren; never let such a thing be spoken, that a Prophet of God is mistaken. I ask this congregation, and I adjure you in the name of the Lord to speak, if ever you heard brother Brigham, brother Kimball, brother Jedediah, or brother Wells say anything that was not strictly true. I answer, you never did.

John Young, *Journal of Discourses* 5:25, 26

Statements by Brigham Young

I know just as well what to teach this people and just what to say to them and what to do in order to bring them into the celestial kingdom, as I know the road to my office. It is just as plain and easy. The Lord is in our midst. He teaches the people continually. I have never yet preached a sermon and sent it out to the children of men, that they may not call Scripture.

Journal of Discourses 13:95, *Deseret News*, January 29, 1870

I will make a statement here that has been brought against me as a crime, perhaps, or as a fault in my life. Not here, I do not allude to anything of the kind in this place, but in the councils of the nations—that Brigham Young has said "when he sends forth his discourses to the world they may call them Scripture." I say now, when they are copied and approved by me they are as good Scripture as is couched in this Bible, and if you want to read revelation read the sayings of him who knows the mind of God. . . .

Journal of Discourses 13:264

When I have spoken by the power of God and the Holy Ghost, it is the truth, it is scripture, and I have no fears but that it will agree with all that has been revealed in every particular.

Deseret Weekly News 26:27A

What I know concerning God . . . I have received from the heavens, not alone through my natural ability, and I give God the glory and the praise.

Journal of Discourses 16:46

As if the preceding quotes were not enough to establish President Young's own concept of his divinely inspired authority as a prophet of God when he delivered a lecture, corrected it, and permitted it to be published, the following confirms how Young's contemporaries understood his position and authority in matters of doctrine.

There are Mormons today, and some who spoke after Young's death, who disagree with him but would not proclaim that he was wrong. The case of Apostle Orson Pratt, who rejected Brigham's doctrine of "Adam-God" and the attitude of the Church with Young at its head, is proof that Young would not accept criticism of his revelations or doctrine. Apostle Pratt also disagreed with Young on the subject of progression of the gods after death, and the attitude of the Church indicates that Brigham still could accept no opposition to his revelations. Pratt was denounced in the statement signed by the First Presidency of the Church and certain members of the Quorum of Twelve in an article appearing in the *Millennial Star* (Volume 27, pages 657-63, October 21, 1865). Pratt was condemned for certain statements which he made in *The Life of Joseph Smith*, by Lucy Smith (which he published) and in his *Great First Cause* as well as *The Seer*. Pratt's criticism sprang from Young's advancing doctrines and theories declared to be out of harmony with the Church, and "self-confounding."

Further confirmation of Brigham Young's wrath when opposed is found in the testimony of Samuel Richards, prominent Mormon spokesman and for many years editor and publisher of the official Mormon paper, the *Millennial Star*:

> Evening with the Regency in the upper room of the President's office, . . . A very serious conversation took place between President B. Young and Orson Pratt upon doctrine. O. P. was directly opposed to the President's views and very freely expressed his entire disbelief in them after being told by the President that things were so and so in the name of the Lord. He was firm in the position that the President's word in the name of the Lord, was not the word of the Lord to him. The President did not believe that Orson Pratt would ever be Adam, to learn by experience the facts discussed, but every person in the room would be if they lived faithful.
>
> March 11, 1856, *History of Samuel W. Richards*, page 15

The Accuracy of Brigham Young's Discourses

The Mormon Church today, embarrassed by some of the doctrines "revealed" by "Prophet Young," has not hesitated to insinuate that his published statements in the *Journal of Discourses* were inaccurately reported. Such subterfuge cries out for refutation. In the preface of *The Discourses of Brigham Young*, John A. Widtsoe, a Mormon theologian, states:

> This book was made possible because Brigham Young secured stenographic reports of his addresses. As he traveled among the people, reporters accompanied him. All that he said was recorded. Practically all of these discourses (from December 16, 1851 to August 19, 1877) were published in the *Journal of Discourses*, which was widely distributed. The public utterances of few great historical figures have been so faithfully and fully preserved.

Brigham himself stated:

> We do not wish incorrect and unsound doctrines to be handed down to posterity under the sanction of great names, to be received and valued by future generations as authentic and reliable, creating labor and difficulties for our successors to perform and contend with, which we ought not to transmit to them. The interests of posterity are, to a certain extent in our hands. Errors in history and in doctrine, if left uncorrected by us who are conversant with the events, and who are in a position to judge of the truth or falsity of the doctrines, would go to our children as though we had sanctioned and endorsed them. Such a construction could very easily be put upon our silence respecting them, and would tend to perplex and mislead posterity, and make the labor of correction an exceedingly difficult one for them. We know what sanctity there is always attached to the writing of men who have passed away, especially to the writings of Apostles, when none of their contemporaries are left, and we, therefore, feel the necessity of being watchful upon these points. Personal feelings and friendships and associations ought to sink into comparative insignificance, and have no weight in view of consequences so momentous to the people and kingdom of God as these.
>
> *Millennial Star* 27:659

It is readily discernible that neither Brigham Young, his counselors, nor the general authorities of the Church were about to have any "unsound doctrines" "handed down to posterity," and that they wanted what was revealed to them through Joseph Smith and Brigham Young to be considered by future generations "as authentic and reliable." Brigham felt that what was transmitted to posterity should be accurate:

> Errors in history and in doctrine, if left uncorrected by us who are conversant with the events, and who are in a position to judge of the truth or falsity of the doctrines, would go to our children as though we had sanctioned and endorsed them. Such a construction could very easily be put upon our silence respecting them, and would tend to perplex and mislead posterity, and make the labor of correction an exceedingly difficult one for them.

It is folly, therefore, to think that Brigham Young or his contemporaries thought anything other than what they plainly stated regarding their own authority or that of Joseph Smith.

The photographic reproduction from the 1854 first edition of the *Journal of Discourses*, published in England under the supervision of Elder George Watt, should eliminate doubt completely.

We are told by Brigham Young and his associates, Heber C. Kimball and Willard Richards, that Elder George Watt accurately recorded "the public sermons, discourses, lectures, and etc. delivered by The Presidency, The Twelve and others in this city for nearly two years, almost without fee or reward. . . ." This *Journal of Discourses*, we are further told, was "for the benefit of the Saints at large, and to obtain means to enable him [Watt] to sustain his highly useful position of Reporter."

President Young, Elder Widtsoe, and a number of others knew full well the authority of Brigham Young. Brigham stated that he edited his sermons before they were released to the world, so there is no doubt about the accuracy of what he intended:

In printing my remarks, I often omit the sharp words, though they are perfectly understood and applicable here; for I do not wish to spoil the good I desire to do. Let my remarks go to the world in a way the prejudices of the people can bear, that they may read them, and ponder them, and ask God whether they are true.

Journal of Discourses 5:99, 100

Those who printed Brigham's sermons in the *Millennial Star* and in the *Deseret News*, from which the bulk of the *Journal of Discourses* is derived, never questioned what Prophet Young declared as authoritative. But it remains for President Wilford Woodruff to have the final word:

I have read the sermons Brigham Young published in the *Journal of Discourses*—some of them—they're in my library, and I presume are considered correct as published. They are published by the Church of which I am President. They are correct insofar as every man had a chance to correct his own discourses or should do so if he has a chance. Sermons reported by G. D. Watt, one of the official reporters, were considered reported correctly, and when they are found in the *Journal of Discourses* they are considered correct. Some of my own sermons are published there, and they are correct.

Complainant's Abstract of Pleading and Evidence, Temple Lot Case, page 309

So sure was Prophet Young that his words were divinely inspired that he did not hesitate to state:

In my doctrinal teachings I have taught many things not written in any book, ancient or modern, and yet notwithstanding the many things I have told the people, I have never looked into the Bible, the *Book of Mormon* or the *Doctrine and Covenants* or any of our Church works to see whether they agreed with them or not. When I have spoken by the power of God and the Holy Ghost it is the truth, it is Scripture and I have no fears but that it will agree with all that has been revealed in every particular.

Deseret Weekly News 26:274

How strange it is now to see that the Church of Jesus Christ of Latter-day Saints is not willing to claim that "... any of the writings contained in the *Journal of*

Discourses is an accurate reflection of statements actually made by the persons represented to be the source thereof"! It appears that they will even deny their own prophet, if necessary, when he proclaims what can be unimpeachably established as "church doctrine." In their denials, the Mormon Church says, ". . . writings, teachings, and opinions of the prophets of God are acceptable only to the extent they are in harmony with what God has revealed and what is recorded in the standard works," but they have conveniently omitted mention of the word "revelation" or "revelations" given by "prophets of God." These they are forced to accept as Church doctrine, even though some of them do not appear in "the standard works." This has been noted but certainly bears repetition within the context of Brigham Young's authority as recognized in Mormon history and classic Mormon theology. Despite contemporary Mormon protests, we have seen that Brigham Young and his contemporaries had no doubts that God had put His stamp of approval upon what they were proclaiming as revelation.

Joseph Smith, Jr., preached a "plurality of gods." He rejected the Christian doctrine of the Trinity quite bluntly as "a strange God, anyhow" (Joseph Smith, Jr., *History of the Church* 6:476). Therefore it is not necessary to dwell at great length upon the depth of his errors in theology. Joseph maintained, and the Mormon Church still maintains (by so-called "revelation") that God the Father is a changeable being, as are Jesus Christ and the Holy Spirit; in fact, that *all* the gods are changeable and are constantly progressing. It is therefore refreshing to read in Hebrews 13:8 that Jesus Christ is "the same yesterday, and today, and forever." The Mormon Church's polytheistic pantheon of polygamous patriarchs, who seem "ever learning but never able to come to a knowledge of the truth," is a far cry from the affirmation of Jesus Christ: "*I* am the truth" (John 14:6).

The Mormon Church wants us to believe in many gods, and that each male member of its Priesthood may progress eventually to godhood. In this exalted condition he will be an immortal resurrected being who sexually procreates children with the wives he has been sealed to in the Mormon Temples while on earth. But the uniqueness of the true God is found in far too many places in the Bible for people to be taken in by the gods of Mormondom, and to confirm this one would be wise to carefully study 1 Chronicles 17:20; 1 Timothy 2:5; Isaiah 45:5, 6, 18, 21, 22; Mark 10:18; Ephesians 4:4-6; Psalm 86:10; Deuteronomy 32:39; 5:7.

Both *The Book of Mormon* and the Bible contradict Joseph Smith in many places, as we have already noted in Chapter 2. For example, *The Book of Mormon* declares the oneness of God, the unchangeable nature of God (Moroni 8:18), and the holy Trinity (Alma 11:26-29; 3 Nephi 11:27, 36)—just three of the many inadvertent slips of the prophetic pen!

The Mormon Church must never be permitted to ignore such contradictions, nor the important fact that Adam is called by Brigham Young and Joseph Smith the first man, the first of the human family, who begat all the spirits that ever were or ever will be upon this earth.[4] Elohim, they say, was Adam's Creator, but Elohim also had a Creator—so the regression of the gods is infinite in the muddle of Mormon mythology. As we approach in the next chapter the doctrine of the Person of Christ as reflected in classic Mormon theology and the revelations of Joseph Smith and Brigham Young and their successors, the "Adam-God" doctrine will be seen to be of great importance because of its intensely corrupt nature.

---

[4]*Doctrine and Covenants* 84:16; Moses 1:34; *History of the Church* 4:207; *Journal of Discourses* 1:50; *Deseret News*, June 18, 1873.

FOUR

BRIGHAM YOUNG AND THE "JESUS" OF THE MORMONS

In the preceding chapter we have clearly seen the fact that Mormonism is a polytheistic religion and cannot be classified as Christian. Although Mormonism embraces some Christian practices and some of the ethical and moral structure of the Christian gospel, it is at its heart vigorously anti-Christian, denying as it does the Christian doctrine of the Trinity as well as the sole authority of Scripture, and adding extrabiblical revelations which contradict classic Biblical theology of both the Old and New Testaments.

In this chapter we shall be dealing specifically with what the Apostle Paul referred to in 2 Corinthians 11:3, 4, 13-15:

> But I am afraid that just as Eve was deceived by the serpent's cunning, your minds may somehow be led astray from your sincere and pure devotion to Christ. For if someone comes to you and preaches a Jesus other than the Jesus we preached, or if you receive a different spirit from the one you received, or a different gospel from the one you accepted, you put up with it easily enough.

. . . For such men are false apostles, deceitful workmen, masquerading as apostles of Christ. And no wonder, for Satan himself masquerades as an angel of light. It is not surprising, then, if his servants masquerade as servants of righteousness. Their end will be what their actions deserve. (NIV)

The Counterfeit Jesus

It is evident from the Apostle's warning that a counterfeit Jesus, a counterfeit Holy Spirit, and a counterfeit gospel exist in this world, and it is important for us to understand the nature of the "other Jesus," and how we may differentiate between him and the Eternal Word made flesh (John 1:1, 14).

When we use the word "Jesus," the understanding of who He is depends upon the listener's definition of the term. For example, the word "Jesus" to a Jehovah's Witness means Michael the Archangel, the first and greatest creation of Jehovah God, who became a man, died, and rose spiritually (not bodily) from the dead.

When one is speaking with a Christian Scientist, the word "Jesus" becomes Jesus *and* Christ, Jesus being the illusion of physical or material reality as manhood, and Christ being the true divinity of all men. The same is true with the Unity School of Christianity, Metaphysics, Religious Science, Divine Science, and most of the other "mind science" groups.

When one is speaking to a follower of Herbert Armstrong and his cult (the Worldwide Church of God), Jesus is specifically identified as God, but as one progresses into their theology it becomes very apparent that, for the Armstrong cult, that is the goal of all true believers, so that man at last becomes God!

When one utilizes the term "Jesus" with Theosophists or Rosicrucians or followers of Edgar Cayce's cult (Association for Research and Enlightenment), we find that they believe that the "cosmic consciousness" existed in all ages as the "Christ," but as "Jesus" in only the so-called Christian era.

The cult of Spiritism, on the other hand, has no hesitation in referring to Jesus as "an advanced medium in the sixth sphere," while Unitarians regard Him as merely an extremely good man whom His mistaken followers unfortunately deified after His alleged resurrection.

An analysis of the Unification Church of Reverend Sun Myung Moon reveals that their Jesus was supposed to start a perfect family the first time, but unfortunately committed errors which led to His crucifixion. It remains for Mr. Moon to actually fulfill what Jesus failed to do, and his followers are taught that the second advent of Jesus Christ took place at the time of Moon's birth in Korea in 1920.

It would be possible to go on and on, showing the redefinitions which have taken place relative to the name "Jesus," but it is obvious that when the Apostle Paul said there was "another Jesus" he made direct reference to just such semantic redefinitions.

Along with the counterfeit Jesus, there is also a counterfeit of the Holy Spirit, who counterfeits the fruits and the gifts of God's genuine Spirit, not excluding the miraculous.

The Counterfeit Disciples

That there are counterfeit gospels is unchallengeable; if in every area of your theological structure you are essentially accurate but you have a corrupt concept of God and of the Person of Jesus Christ, God's anointed Savior, then everything else becomes a hollow sham, a worthless counterfeit. The Second Letter to the Corinthians (11:13-15) tells us who the ones are who preach another Jesus, another spirit, and another gospel: Paul informs us that they are counterfeit apostles, deceitful workers who transform themselves to appear as ministers of Christ but are in fact representatives of Satan. Lucifer is designated, by the very nature of his name, as "lightbearer," but the apostle warns us that the light that he brings through any counterfeit Jesus, spirit, or gospel is for the purpose of deception. This is clearly pointed out by Paul's use of the word "masquerade."

In this important instance the Apostle Paul, under the guidance of the Spirit of God, made a very important differentiation when he spoke of the disciples of the "other Jesus." The apostle chose the Greek term *metaschematizo* rather than the term *metamorphoo*, and to any student of New Testament Greek, the reason is immediately apparent. The first word means, according to Vine's *Expository Dictionary of New Testament Greek Words*, "to fashion oneself . . . to transform," and is used specifically to designate "Satan and his human ministers, false apostles" (page 80 under FASHION).

Dr. Vine also declared that *metaschematizo* refers to "change in fashion or appearance" and differs from *metamorphoo* in that this word, derived from *morphe*, lays stress on the inward change. "*Schema* . . . lays stress on the outward" (page 148 under TRANSFIGURE).

The other Jesus and his disciples, therefore, have an outward transformation which does not alter their inward nature, in contrast to the Christian, who is *transformed* by the power of God (Romans 12:2; *metamorphoo*—Greek). Through the process of regeneration by the Holy Spirit, constituting the redemption of the soul, the true Christian is then transformed outwardly by the power of the Holy Spirit, who now indwells the believer and molds his or her life into the image of the Lord Jesus Christ inwardly (after His true nature).

It is because of this that Christians may be spoken of as "partakers of the divine nature" (2 Peter 1:4)—*not* because they become part of God, but because they are "transformed" into the reflection of God ("His image") through Jesus Christ, who is the perfect "image of the invisible God, preeminent over all creation" (Colossians 1:15, literal translation). This is a lifelong process for the Christian, and is designated in Christian theology and in the New Testament in numerous instances as "sanctification," or the divine setting apart of the individual in mature growth. The Lord weeds out of the garden of the soul those things which displease Him, as we progressively yield to His Spirit's presence and power. With Satan the transformation only *looks* like the genuine, for underneath there has been no basic change at all in the nature of his children. "We know that we are of God, and the whole world lieth in wickedness [or 'the wicked one']" (1 John 5:19).

Thus we are not paranoid if we affirm the cosmic conspiracy of Satan to imitate the church, Jesus Christ, the Holy Spirit, the gospel, and His apostles. Rather, we are truly sane when we take God at His Word and recognize that the nature of the enemy appears as light, but, seen through the divine filter of Biblical revelation, is the ultimate in darkness.

Mormons have fallen victim to this Satanic "transformation" and imagine themselves disciples of the real Jesus, possessors of the genuine Holy Spirit, and purveyors of the true gospel. They are totally unaware that it is they, rather than those of the historic Christian church, who are deceived.

The theologian Karl Barth once said, "Show me your Christology and I will tell you what you are." Dr. Barth meant to convey the fact that if one does not possess the genuine Jesus, His Spirit, and His gospel, this lack alone is sufficient to violate the Biblical faith and exclude a person from the kingdom of heaven. The most important question of all is, "What think ye of Christ? Whose son is he?" (Matthew 22:42). The answer to that question was given by the Apostle Peter, who declared, "Thou art the Christ, the Son of the living God" (Matthew 16:16). To this declaration of faith the Lord Jesus responded, "Blessed art thou, Simon Bar-jona, for flesh and blood hath not revealed it unto thee, but by my Father which is in heaven" (Matthew 16:17).

Christ not only accepted the title "Son of God," which in Jewish theology was a direct reference to oneness with the Father and hence deity (see John 10:30ff; cf. Proverbs 30:4), but He identified the source of Peter's information about His identity by stating that it was *God the Father* who revealed this to Peter, and *not* any human being (Matthew 16:17).

With these things clearly in focus, we may now approach the "Jesus" of Mormonism. We must go to their primary sources—Joseph Smith, Jr., Brigham Young (whose Mormon authority has been clearly established in Chapter 3), and noted Mormon theologians and writers, well-recognized by the Church and never repudiated in their analysis of the Mormon doctrine. We shall be paying particular attention in this analysis to the revelations and teachings of the Prophet Brigham Young, who succeeded Joseph Smith and claimed to derive his authority from both Smith and God for his revelations and teachings.

We now have the basics necessary to understand the source of the Mormon Church's teachings about Jesus. Is the Jesus of Mormonism the Jesus of the Bible? Or is he the "other" Jesus we discussed at the beginning of this chapter?

The Jesus of Mormonism

In our study of the Mormon doctrine of God we learned that Jesus Christ was considered to be a second god, created by Eloheim (Mormon spelling), and that Michael or Adam was a god separate from Him (see Chapter 3). It is important not to overlook this affirmation by Brigham Young, because it was he (leaning heavily upon Joseph Smith, Jr.) who declared the doctrine of Adam-God and sustained it vigorously, along with his contemporaries. Though the Jesus of historic Mormon theology was called Jehovah, He was not recognized as the Eternal God, even though the divine name from which the English transliteration "Jehovah" is derived was applied to Jesus by Himself (John 8:58, Greek; cf. Septuagint translation of Exodus 3:14; Christ is the great I AM, eternal God). Contemporary Mormon theology attempts to hide Joseph Smith's and Brigham Young's doctrine concerning the identity of Jesus Christ and His virgin birth.

Brigham Young and the Virgin Birth

Following his predecessor, Joseph Smith, Jr., who stated, "It is the first principle of the gospel to know for a certainty the character of God" (King Follett Discourse, *History of the Church* 6:305; *Times and Seasons* 5:614; *Journal of Discourses* 6:3), Brigham Young had some intriguing "revelations" from God concerning the Person of Jesus Christ. In one of his most famous discourses Brigham Young declared:

> My next sermon will be to both Saint and sinner. One thing has remained a mystery in this kingdom up to this day. It is in regard to the character of the well-beloved Son of God, upon which subject the Elders of Israel have conflicting views. . . .The question has been, and is often, asked, who it was that begat the Son of the Virgin Mary. . . . I will tell you how it is. Our Father in Heaven begat all the spirits that ever were, or ever will be, upon this earth; and they were born spirits in the eternal world. Then the Lord by His power and wisdom organized the mortal tabernacle of man. We were made first spiritual, and afterwards temporal.
>
> Now hear it, O inhabitants of the earth, Jew and Gentile, Saint and sinner! When our father Adam came into the garden of Eden, he came into it with a *celestial body*, and brought Eve, *one of his wives*, with him. He helped to make and organize this world. He is MICHAEL, *the Archangel*, the ANCIENT OF DAYS! about whom holy men have written and spoken—HE *is our* FATHER *and our* GOD, *and the only God with whom* WE *have to do*. Every man upon the earth, professing Christians or non-professing, must hear it, and *will know it sooner or later*. . . . When the Virgin Mary conceived the child Jesus, the Father had begotten him in his own likeness. He was *not* begotten by the Holy Ghost. And who is the Father? He is the first of the human family; and when he

took a tabernacle, it was begotten by *his Father* in heaven, after the same manner as the tabernacles of Cain, Abel, and the rest of the sons and daughters of Adam and Eve. . . . Jesus, our elder brother, was begotten in the flesh by the same character that was in the garden of Eden, and who is our Father in Heaven. Now, let all who may hear these doctrines, pause before they make light of them, or treat them with indifference, for they will prove their salvation or damnation. . . .

Now, remember from this time forth, and for ever, that Jesus Christ was not begotten by the Holy Ghost.*

Brigham Young,
Journal of Discourses 1:50-51

Brigham Young reiterated this twenty-one years later. (See chapter 3, pages 84-85.)

When this quotation is cross-referenced with the King-Follet Discourse, one of the last sermons preached by Joseph Smith, it cannot be missed that Smith was the source of Brigham Young's teaching concerning both Adam-God and the doctrine of the non-virgin birth. Joseph said at that time:

It is the first principle of the Gospel to know for a certainty the character of God and to know that we may converse with Him as one man converses with another, and that He was once a man like us; yea, that God himself, the Father of us all, dwelt on an earth, the same as Jesus Christ Himself did.

Joseph Smith, Jr.,
Journal of Discourses 6:3;
Times and Seasons 5:614;
History of the Church 6:305

The careful student will note that Brigham quoted Joseph: "God himself, the Father of us all, dwelt on an earth the same as Jesus Christ did" (cf. *Deseret News,* June

---

*Emphasis theirs.

18, 1873, where Young describes Adam by divine revelation as saying that "I once dwelt upon an earth something like this in a mortal state, I was faithful, I received my crown and exaltation").

This parallels Smith's statement concerning exaltation, where he commanded Mormon males:

> . . . you have got to learn how to be Gods yourselves, and to be kings and priests to God, the same as all Gods have done before you,—namely, by going from one small degree to another, and from a small capacity to a great one,—from grace to grace, from exaltation to exaltation, until you attain to the resurrection of the dead, and are able to dwell in everlasting burnings and to sit in glory, as do those who sit enthroned in everlasting power.
>
> *Journal of Discourses* 6:4;
> *History of the Church* 6:306;
> *Times and Seasons* 6:614;
> *Teachings of the Prophet*, pages 346-47

From the April 3, 1977, edition of the *Salt Lake City Tribune*, a Church-owned newspaper, President Kimball is quoted as telling "members of his faith Saturday night that they can attain godhood if they continue to perfect their lives."

He continued by saying that "What man is, God has been, and what God is, man seeks to become."

The above statements were made in the Tabernacle as part of the Church's 147th General Conference.

Brigham Young faithfully taught Joseph Smith's doctrine of exaltation to godhood and his identification of Adam as the Father of the human race, the god of this earth, the Ancient of Days, the first man, the first of the human family, and the father of Jesus Christ. This is what historic Mormon theology means when it refers to the "miraculous conception of Jesus the Christ"!

According to the *Millennial Star* 14:356, "President Young preached several sermons on various subjects, the Holy Ghost resting upon him in great power, while he revealed some of the precious things of the kingdom." This was particularly concerning Young's sermon (quoted above), which stated, "Now, remember from this time forth, and for ever, that Jesus Christ was not begotten by the Holy Ghost." In this same discourse Brigham said:

> Treasure up these things in your hearts. In the Bible, you have read the things I have told you to-night; but you have not known what you did read.
> Brigham Young,
> *Journal of Discourses* 1:51

Brigham Young claims that the Bible confirms what he is teaching in this discourse, and yet the Bible vigorously contradicts him in Matthew 1:18 and 20b:

> Now the birth of Jesus Christ was on this wise: When as his mother Mary was espoused to Joseph, before they came together, she was found with child of the Holy Ghost . . . that which is conceived in her is of the Holy Ghost.

When this passage of God's Word is contrasted with Luke 1:35, we learn that Mary was told by the angel of the Lord precisely how she would conceive the Child Jesus:

> The Holy Ghost shall come upon thee, and the power of the Highest shall overshadow thee; therefore also that holy thing which shall be born of thee shall be called the Son of God.

In both instances of the divine record Jesus Christ is declared to have been conceived by the Holy Spirit, yet Brigham Young contradicts this. Mary, it will be recalled, asked, "How shall this be, seeing I know not a man?" (Luke 1:34—literally from the Greek "I am a virgin"). The angelic response indicates special creation by the Holy Spirit, but this is not so in Brigham Young's theology or in the theology of classic Mormonism.

The Argument of Subterfuge

We have noted throughout this presentation the documentation establishing that classic Mormon theology, as believed and practiced by Mormons for more than 124 years, is a blasphemy of the doctrine of the virgin birth and the character of the Lord Jesus. However, when presenting this to disciples of the Mormon Church (many of whom are unfamiliar with a great deal of the documentation here), they give the standard answer of the Mormon Church: Brigham Young "*may* have taught" the doctrine of Adam-God and other Mormon leaders may have gone along with it.

Today, while picking and choosing the doctrine they wish to accept from the infamous "Adam-God" sermon, the Mormons totally accept the idea that Jesus was *not* begotten by the Holy Spirit while denying that Adam is God. They condemn those who simply take Brigham Young at his word as people who "desire to malign and misrepresent." Joseph Fielding Smith wrote, "Another ambiguous statement from President Brigham Young . . . is torn from its context and used by enemies of the truth to make it appear that he believed something entirely different from the whole burden of all his other teachings" (*Doctrines of Salvation*, 1:101, 102).

One statement to which this alludes is in *Journal of Discourses* 1:50-51, which Smith attempts to explain away on the grounds that Brigham Young really meant that the Creator God (Elohim) ". . . is our Father; that men are of the same race—the race called humans; . . . it is a doctrine common to the Latter-day Saints, that God, the Great Elohim, is the First, or Creator, of the human family" (*Doctrines of Salvation* 1:103).

John A. Widstoe, in his book *Evidences and Reconciliations*, pages 68-71, attacks critics of Brigham Young's peculiar theology by stating:

> He spoke of Adam as the great patriarch of the human race, a personage who had been privileged and able to assist in the creation of the earth, who would continue his efforts on behalf of the human family, and through whom many of our needs would be met. . . . Nowhere is

it suggested that Adam is God, the Father whose child Adam himself was. . . . . The dishonest inference has been drawn and advertised widely that President Young meant that Adam was the earthly father of Jesus Christ. This deduction cannot be made fairly in view of the context or of his other published utterances on the subject. . . .

The perspective of years brings out the remarkable fact that, though the enemies of the Latter Day Saints have had access in printed form to the hundreds of discourses of Brigham Young, only half a dozen statements have been useful to the columniators of the founder of Utah. Of these, the sermon of April 9, 1852, which has been quoted most frequently, presents no errors of fact or doctrine if read understandingly and honestly.

It is of great significance to observe that none of these apologists for Mormon doctrine have effectively dealt with Brigham Young's statement in the *Journal of Discourses*, as cross-referenced to the *Deseret News* (see pages 84-85, 112-113) and some of the other materials which we have already examined. All the materials refute these fabricated explanations, but Mormon apologists do not give up easily. It is not uncommon to find them citing Brigham Young in a sermon preached by him on February 8, 1857 (*Journal of Discourses* 4:216), in which he stated:

I want to tell you, each and every one of you, that you are well acquainted with God our heavenly Father, or the great Eloheim.

From this statement Mormon apologists attempt to prove that when Brigham referred to "our heavenly Father" he meant Elohim, and not Michael or Adam. Therefore, when he declared that Jesus Christ was begotten "by the same character that was in the Garden of Eden and is our Father in heaven" (*Journal of Discourses* 1:51) he could not possibly have meant Adam! Unfortunately, they once again ignore Brigham's clear statements.

As we have already seen, in the early part of this chapter, as well as in Chapter 3, Elohim has "a body of flesh and bones as tangible as man's," according to Joseph Smith, Jr.

If the Mormon contention is to be accepted at face value, then they are no better off with Elohim having sexual relations with the Virgin Mary than they are if it is Adam! Either way, Christ was begotten because Mary became God's wife or concubine. An article in the *Salt Lake City Tribune* (Sunday, April 8, 1973, page A8, column 7) detailing the Spring Conference of the Mormon Church dismisses all speculation:

Apostle's Humor Draws Laughter

Outburst after outburst of delighted laughter filled the tabernacle Saturday afternoon as the fourth session of the 143rd annual Conference of the Church of Jesus Christ of Latter-day Saints drew to a close.

The speaker was Elder LeGrand Richards of the Council of Twelve Apostles, well-known for its missionary activities.

Describing an experience he once had in the mission field, Elder Richards told of speaking to a large gathering of clergymen.

"I explained to them the difference between reformation and restoration," Elder Richards said. "Then, when I finished my remarks, one of them stood up and said, 'Mr. Richards, we've been told you believe God had a wife. Would you please explain this?'

"I think he thought he had me," said Elder Richards. The audience in the tabernacle began to chuckle. "I retorted that I didn't see how God could have a son if he didn't have a wife."

The Tabernacle audience's chuckle grew to a full roar of laughter as Elder Richards turned to President Harold B. Lee, seated near the podium, to ask if this was a proper answer.

President Lee nodded.

Apostle Richards in 1973 confirmed what Brigham Young said in 1873! It is significant that then-President Lee nodded in agreement. How strange to the ears of true Christians is the statement that God could not have a son if he did not have a wife!

Going on with "present-day revelation," Mormon prophet Spencer W. Kimball affirmed:

". . . when we sing in that doctrinal hymn and anthem of affection, 'O My Father,' we get a sense of the ultimate in maternal modesty, of the restrained, queenly elegance of our Heavenly Mother, and knowing how profoundly our mortal mothers have shaped us here, do we suppose her influence on us as individuals to be less if we live so as to return there?"

"Church News," *Deseret News*,
General Conference Issue, week ending
April 8, 1978, page 4

In Mormonism, "Heavenly Father" and "Heavenly Mother" begat all the spirits that ever were. This is a flagrant disregard of Holy Scripture and even of the Mormons' own sacred writings, for in them a Heavenly Mother is not even alluded to.

The Book of Genesis clearly states that God created Adam and Eve from the dust of the earth and breathed into their nostrils the breath of life. Adam was created first, and then Eve was created from his inner substance (Genesis 2:7, 21-23). The Apostle Paul confirms this fact in 1 Corinthians 11:8, 9. It should be carefully noted that God did *not* have a wife with whom He had sexual relations in order to produce Adam.

The interested student of the Bible will notice, in reading Brigham Young, that he did not believe the Biblical record of the creation of Adam. He categorically stated:

You believe Adam was made of the dust of this earth. This I do not believe, though it is supposed that it is so written in the Bible; but it is not, to my understanding.
Journal of Discourses 2:6.

Again, dealing with this particular issue, Brigham stated:

Though we have it in history that our father Adam was made of the dust of this earth, and that he knew nothing about his God previous to being made here, yet it is not

so; and when we learn the truth we shall see and understand that he helped to make this world, and was the chief
manager in that operation. . . . You may read and believe
what you please as to what is found in the Bible. Adam
was made from the dust of an earth, but not from the dust
of this earth. He was made as you and I are made, and no
person was ever made upon any other principle.

Journal of Discourses 3:319

Another reason for Brigham Young referring to Elohim
as "our heavenly Father" is found in the fact that Young
himself had stated, and continued to state, that the gods in-
finitely progressed. When referring to Adam, he declared:

Whether Adam is the personage that we should consider
our heavenly Father, or not, is considerable of a mystery
to a good many. I do not care for one moment how that
is; it is no matter whether we are to consider Him our
God, or whether His Father, or His Grandfather, for in
either case we are of one species—of one family—and
Jesus Christ is also of our species.

Journal of Discourses 4:217

Thus in the theology of classic Mormonism, Elohim also
had a father, and his father had a father, and all of them
were continuously progressing, reaching for perfection.
Elohim, for Brigham, was the Creator of Adam and the
Father of his spirit, most likely from another earth
(*Discourses of Brigham Young*, pages 104-5). As such Adam
was the Creator of all the spirits upon *this* earth. Brigham's
sermon (*Deseret News*, June 18, 1873), as we will see, confirms this.

Mormon apologists have yet to honestly come to grips
with this, and from the nature of the case it is understandable that they are reluctant to try!

The Bible nowhere states, as Brigham Young affirms,
that "When our Father Adam came into the Garden of
Eden he came into it with a celestial body and brought Eve,
one of his wives, with him." Genesis 2:7, 21-23 and
1 Corinthians 15:46 contradict Young's assertion that "we
were made first spiritual and afterwards temporal" (*Journal
of Discourses* 1:50). From his discourse of February 8, 1857

(*Journal of Discourses* 4:218), Brigham identifies God as "the same species as ourselves" and enunciates the classic Mormon position of the progression of the gods. Brigham Young stated:

> "Well," says one, "Why was Adam called Adam?" He was the first man on the earth, and its framer and maker. He, with the help of his brethren, brought it into existence. Then he said, "I want my children who are in the spirit world to come and live here. I once dwelt upon an earth something like this, in a mortal state. I was faithful, I received my crown and exaltation. I have the privilege of extending my work, and to its increase there will be no end. I want my children that were born to me in the spirit world to come here and take tabernacles of flesh, that their spirits may have a house, a tabernacle or a dwelling place as mine has, and where is the mystery?"
>
> *Deseret News*, June 18, 1873, page 308

> I have frequently thought of mules, which you know are half horse and half ass, when reflecting upon the representations made by those divines. I have heard sectarian priests undertake to tell the character of the Son of God, and they make him half of one species and half of another, and I could not avoid thinking at once of the mule, which is the most hateful creature that ever was made, I believe. You will excuse me, but I have thus thought many a time. . . .
>
> It is all here in the Bible; I am not telling you a word but what is contained in that book.
>
> Things were first created spiritually; the Father actually begat the spirits, and they were brought forth and lived with Him. . . .
>
> When the time came that His first-born, the Saviour, should come into the world and take a tabernacle, the Father came Himself and favoured that spirit with a tabernacle instead of letting any other man do it. The Saviour was begotten by the Father of His spirit, by the same Being who is the Father of our spirits, and that is all the organic difference between Jesus Christ and you and me.
>
> *Journal of Discourses* 4:217, 218

Brigham's reference to the Incarnation as an analogy to "half horse and half ass" gives an insight into his "knowledge" of the holy and of his spiritual perception. To even think of Jesus Christ in this category is sufficient to exclude Young from the ranks of Christians and from the prophets of God. Brigham Young makes a claim to Biblical authority, but the question should be asked at this point, "Where does he find this in the Scriptures?" and the answer must be, "He doesn't, because it does not exist there."

We have, however, learned valuable things from all of these quotations. We have learned that in Mormonism Adam was the first man on "this" earth. We have read that they teach he preexisted in the spirit world before he arrived here with Eve, one of his celestial wives. We have been told by the Prophet that Adam is the father of all the spirits that were created to live on this earth and that he himself came from another earth, where he apparently had been created by *his* father, Eloheim (*Deseret News*, June 18, 1873). It has been revealed to the Mormons that Jesus Christ was not begotten by the Holy Spirit but was instead the product of sexual relations between the god of this planet (Adam) and the Virgin Mary. Historic Mormon theology has told us that "Jesus, our elder brother, was begotten in the flesh by the same character that was in the garden of Eden, and who is our Father in Heaven" (*Journal of Discourses* 1:51). To refer to Brigham again: "And who is the Father? He is the first of the human family; and when he took a tabernacle, it was begotten by *his Father* in heaven, after the same manner as the tabernacles of Cain, Abel, and the rest of the sons and daughters of Adam and Eve; . . ." (*Journal of Discourses* 1:50).

We recognize that the tabernacles (bodies) of Cain and Abel were begotten by sexual intercourse, and, according to historic Mormon theology (including Brigham Young and subsequent Mormon prophets), this was done in the same manner as "the rest of the sons and daughters of Adam and Eve." Brigham Young understood the language he was using, but what he taught was not the Virgin Birth but was instead what the Mormons today call the "miraculous conception of Jesus the Christ."

For Brigham the words of Joseph Smith were his authority for teaching both the doctrine of Adam-God and the blasphemous dogma that Jesus Christ was the product of a sexual union between "a mortal mother and of an immortal, or resurrected and glorified, Father," as James Talmage phrased it in his *Articles of Faith* (ed. 1977, page 473). It was Joseph Smith who wrote, "Commencing with Adam, who was the first man, who is spoken of in Daniel as being the "Ancient of Days," or in other words, the first and oldest of all . . . ." (*Millennial Star* 18:164; *History of the Church* 4:207; *Teachings of the Prophet Joseph Smith*, page 167).

The first of the human family, or the first man, was to them a god who came from another planet, was a polygamist before he arrived, and was identified as ". . . father Adam, who was the first man" (*Doctrine and Covenants* 84:16). There are still other references to his identity: ". . . the first man, who is Adam, our first father. . . ." (Abraham 1:3), and ". . . the first man of all men have I called Adam, which is many" (Moses 1:34). The evidence is overwhelming, and both the logic and the facts are irrefutable.

Corroborating Data

Adam and Eve are the parents of all pertaining to the flesh, and I would not say that they are not also the parents of our spirits.

Brigham Young, *Journal of Discourses* 7:290

Some may think what I have said concerning Adam strange, but the period will come when the people will be willing to adopt Joseph Smith as their Prophet, Seer and Revelator and God! but not the father of their spirits, for that was our Father Adam.

Brigham Young, School of the
Prophets, December 11, 1869; *Journal
History of Brigham Young*, page 1313;
also *Journal of Wilford Woodruff*,
same date

Brigham Young's secretary and one of his closest associates was L. John Nuttall. His journal, therefore, is evidence concerning Brigham Young's understanding of the identity of "the Father:"

Adam was an immortal being when he came on this earth. He had lived on an earth similar to ours, he had received the Priesthood and the Keys thereof, and he had been faithful in all things and gained his resurrection and his exaltation and was crowned with glory, immortality and eternal lives and was numbered with the Gods for such he became through his faithfulness. And *he had begotten all the spirits that were to come to this earth. And Eve, our common mother, who is the mother of all living, bore these spirits in the Celestial world, and then this earth was organized by Elohim, Jehovah, and Michael, who is Adam, our common Father.*° Adam and Eve had the privilege to continue the work of progression, consequently came to this earth and commenced the great work of forming tabernacles for those spirits to dwell in.

L. *John Nuttall Journal,*
February 7, 1877, 1:19, as recorded
in *Michael/Adam* by Ogden Kraut

Wilford Woodruff was a president of the Mormon Church and the man under whose leadership polygamy was abolished. His personal journal entry, recorded the very next day after Brigham Young's well-known Adam-God sermon, therefore constitutes important testimony:

Some have said that I was very presumptuous to say this Brother Brigham was my God and Saviour, Bro. Joseph was his God and one that gave Joseph the keys of the kingdom was his God which was Peter. Jesus Christ was his God *and (the) Father of Jesus Christ was Adam.*°
Journal of Wilford Woodruff,
April 10, 1852

°Emphasis ours.

The preceding Mormon quotations demonstrate the concept, popular at the time, of Adam being the Father of the spirit children to whom he gave earthly tabernacles for the ultimate purpose of their exaltation. But other evidence, hidden from the average Mormon, identifies the Lord Jesus as the *son* of Adam, precisely as Brigham enunciated it:

> The man Joseph, the husband of Mary, did not, that we know of, have more than one wife, but Mary the wife of Joseph had another husband. . . . That very babe that was cradled in the manger, was begotten, not by Joseph, the husband of Mary, but by another Being. Do you inquire by whom? He was begotten by God our heavenly Father.
>
> Brigham Young, *Journal of Discourses* 11:268

> The Savior comes to the Father, the Ancient of Days, and presents to the Father the kingdoms of this world all in a saved condition—except the sons of perdition. And he says, "Here, Father; here they are, and I with them." Then he is prepared to go forth and fill up his kingdom, and so he goes on.
>
> *Brigham Young in St. George,*
> 1877, by L. John Nuttall,
> from *Michael/Adam* by Ogden Kraut

It must not be missed at this point that Brigham Young calls the Father "the Ancient of Days" (see Chapter 3), a direct reference to Joseph Smith's comment identifying the Ancient of Days with Adam, who is the Father of all the spirits who have ever lived or will live on this planet. The Adamic parentage of Jesus Christ is affirmed and attested to in other places:

> Father Adam's oldest son, "Jesus the Savior," who is the heir of the family, is Father Adam's first begotten in the spirit world, who according to the flesh is the only begotten as it is written.
>
> In his divinity, he having gone back into the spirit world, and come in the spirit to Mary, and she conceived; for when Adam and Eve got through with their work in this

earth, they did not lay their bodies down in the dust, but returned to the spirit world from whence they come.

Brigham Young, *L. John Nuttall Journal* 1:21

As noted above, the Mormons are no better off with "Eloheim" [sic] as the Father of Jesus than they are with Adam. Either way, a resurrected man progresses to Godhood and has sexual relations with the Virgin Mary. According to classic Mormon theology, Mary would have been Adam-God's spirit-daughter in the "preexistence." This is nothing less than incest among the gods. (See quotation 10 by Brigham Young on pages 84-85 of this book.) Joseph Fielding Smith, tenth Prophet to the Mormon Church, wrote:

CHRIST NOT BEGOTTEN OF HOLY GHOST . . . Christ was begotten of God. He was not born without the aid of Man and *that Man was God!*

Doctrines of Salvation 1:18

Apostle Bruce R. McConkie also states:

. . . Christ was begotten by an Immortal Father in the same way that mortal men are begotten by mortal fathers.

Mormon Doctrine, page 547

The majority of Mormon people do not know that Mormonism teaches the *non*-virgin birth of Christ, and are often shocked when they learn that this is accepted Church doctrine. To add further to the confusion, Spencer W. Kimball made this remark at the April, 1978, Conference of the Mormon Church:

. . . the mission of Christ was foretold centuries before His birth, and was seen in vision by many prophets and Mary, His eternal mother.

Deseret "Church News" Section, April 8, 1978, page 3

In the "preexistence," was Mary the mother or sister of the Mormon Jesus? Was she the wife or daughter of a Mormon god? Who *really* was the father of Jesus—Adam or "Eloheim"? This is part of the maze of Mormonism!

The Additional Evidence

There is one more piece of evidence which shows that the Jesus of historic Mormon theology is indeed "another Jesus."

In accordance with classic Mormon theology, the counterfeit Jesus foisted upon the Mormons by Joseph Smith, Jr., Brigham Young, and the succeeding hierarchy of the Church is affirmed to be "the spirit brother of Lucifer" (*Journal of Discourses* 13:282) and a polygamist who was married to at least Mary Magdalene, Mary the sister of Lazarus, and Martha—and who procreated children (*Journal of Discourses* 2:82).

The following quotations will substantiate the matter and should be carefully analyzed:

1. One of the Father's spirit sons was to be chosen to create the earth and redeem its inhabitants. When the Father, Elohim, inquired, "Whom shall I send?" there were two who volunteered to go. Because the Father selected the first, the second became angry and did not keep his first estate; and in his rebellion there were many who followed after him. These facts, only, Abraham records; and statements from other scriptures are necessary to fill in the details.

   Hyrum L. Andrus, *Doctrinal Commentary on The Pearl of Great Price*
   Salt Lake City:
   Deseret Book Company, 1967, page 107

2. Of Lucifer, who instituted the rebellion and thereby became Satan, God said:
   . . . he came before me, saying—Behold, here am I, send me, I will be thy son, and I will redeem all mankind, that one soul shall not be lost, and surely I will do it; wherefore give me thine honor.

   But, behold, my Beloved Son, which was my Beloved and Chosen from the beginning, said unto me—Father, thy will be done, and the glory be thine forever.

   Wherefore, because that Satan rebelled against me, and sought to destroy the agency of man, which I, the

Lord God, had given him, and also, that I should give
unto him mine own power; by the power of mine
Only Begotten, I caused that he should be cast down;

And he became Satan, yea, even the devil, the father
of all lies, to deceive and to blind men, and to lead
them captive at his will, even as many as would not
hearken unto my voice.

> *Ibid.*, pages 108-9
> Moses 4:1-4

3. It will be borne in mind that once on a time, there was
a marriage in Cana of Galilee; and on a careful
reading of that transaction, it will be discovered that
no less a person than Jesus Christ was married on that
occasion. If he was never married, his intimacy with
Mary and Martha, and the other Mary also whom
Jesus loved, must have been highly unbecoming and
improper to say the best of it.

I will venture to say that if Jesus Christ were now to
pass through the most pious countries in Christendom with a train of women, such as used to follow
him, fondling about him, combing his hair, anointing
him with precious ointment, washing his feet with
tears, and wiping them with the hair of their heads
and unmarried, or even married, he would be
mobbed, tarred, and feathered, and rode, not on
an ass, but on a rail. . . .

At this doctrine the long-faced hypocrite and the
sanctimonious bigot will probably cry, blasphemy! . . . Object not, therefore, too strongly
against the marriage of Christ. . . .

> Brigham Young, *Journal of
> Discourses* 4:259-60

4. I discover that some of the Eastern papers represent
me as a great blasphemer, because I said, in my lecture on Marriage, at our last Conference, that Jesus
Christ was married at Cana of Galilee, that Mary,
Martha, and others were his wives, and that he begat
children.

All that I have to say in reply to that charge is
this—they worship a Savior that is too pure and holy
to fulfil the commands of his Father. I worship one
that is just pure and holy enough "to fulfil all righteousness;" not only the righteous law of baptism, but

the still more righteous and important law "to mul-
tiply and replenish the earth." Startle not at this! for
even the Father himself honored that law by coming
down to Mary, without a natural body, and begetting
a son; and if Jesus begat children, he only "did that
which he had seen his Father do."

Orson Hyde, *Journal of
Discourses* 2:210

5. When Mary of old came to the sepulchre on the first
day of the week, instead of finding Jesus she saw two
angels in white, "And they say unto her, Woman, why
weepest thou? She said unto them, Because they have
taken away my Lord," or husband, "and I know not
where they have laid him."

Orson Hyde, *Journal of
Discourses* 2:81

6. The grand reason of the burst of public sentiment in
anathemas upon Christ and his disciples, causing his
crucifixion, was evidently based upon polygamy. . . .
A belief in the doctrine of a plurality of wives caused
the persecution of Jesus and his followers. We might
almost think they were "Mormons."

Jedediah Grant, *Journal of
Discourses* 1:346

7. The birth of the Saviour was as natural as are the
births of our children; it was the result of natural action. He partook of flesh and blood—was begotten of
his Father, as we were of our fathers.

Brigham Young, *Journal of
Discourses* 8:115

8. In relation to the way in which I look upon the works
of God and his creatures, I will say that I was naturally
begotten; so was my father, and also my Saviour Jesus
Christ. According to the Scriptures, he is the first
begotten of his father in the flesh, and there was
nothing unnatural about it.

Heber C. Kimball, *Journal
Discourses* 8:211

9. "I retorted that I didn't see how God could have a son
if He didn't have a wife."

The Tabernacle audience's chuckle grew to a full roar

of laughter as Elder Richards turned to President Harold B. Lee, seated near the podium, to ask if this was a proper answer.

President Lee nodded.

"Apostle's Humor Draws Laughter",
Salt Lake City Tribune,
April 8, 1973, page A8, column 8.

On the same note as we began the chapter, so we conclude it. The verdict of the Word of God is that the Mormon "Jesus" is just one god among *many* gods; he is not the Eternal Word of God made flesh, which is the redeeming Christ of New Testament revelation.

FIVE

THE MYTH OF MORMONISM'S PRIESTHOOD

From the earliest days of Mormonism the LDS Church has made a special claim about its authority to preach the "restored" gospel of Jesus Christ. This claim rests upon the alleged possession of the Aaronic and Melchizedek Priesthoods. In the theology of Mormonism the Priesthood occupies a position of tremendous importance and exercises authority over every male member of the Church above the age of twelve. Therefore, no analysis of Mormonism would be complete without examining the history and alleged theological validity of the Mormon claims to authority. No less an authority than Joseph Smith, Jr., proclaimed the doctrine when he maintained that he and Oliver Cowdery were the recipients of the Aaronic Priesthood at the hands of John the Baptist (May 15, 1829).[1] He further claimed that the Priesthood of Melchizedek was conferred later, during the appearance of Peter, James, and John.

---

[1]Joseph Smith, *Pearl of Great Price* 2:68-73.

Historic, theological, and logical necessity call for a closer examination of the Mormon Church's teaching. *The Book of Commandments* (which later was retitled *Doctrine and Covenants*) in the edition of 1833 does not even mention Peter, James, John, or the Priesthood, an unfortunate oversight which Joseph "corrected" in *Doctrine and Covenants*, the edition of 1835.[2] However, there is no "revelation" given that declares the date or relates the circumstances in which this greater priesthood was allegedly bestowed upon Smith.

More than thirteen verses have been added to the initial "revelation" of 1833, which, when added to the general confusion of Mormon theology, introduces the first of many irreconcilable contradictions. John the Baptist (who had the authority to baptize—Matthew 3:13-16) should have baptized Joseph and Oliver in accordance with the Mormon regulations of the "restored" gospel. This "other" gospel requires that one be baptized before one obtains the Priesthood.[3] However, John merely conferred the Aaronic Priesthood on them, even though, according to Mormonism, they were unregenerate at the time, not having been baptized in water for remission of their sins. Consequently, the water baptisms which Joseph Smith and Oliver Cowdery later performed on each other were also invalid. This is because Mormon theology teaches that only a valid priest may baptize, and, according to Joseph's "Lord" in a revelation given November, 1831, "no man has a legal right to this office, to hold the keys of this priesthood, except he be a literal descendant and the first-born of Aaron."[4] As we have

---

[2]*Book of Commandments*, 1833, Chapter 28; and *Doctrine and Covenants*, 1835, Section 27. There is no way to know for certain the exact dates of the first 65 "revelations," for when they were reprinted in 1835 (as mentioned above and previously in Chapter 2), many of the dates changed as "new" revelations were added in the middle of the "old," changing the numbering sequence of chapters and verses. See photocopy opposite.
[3]*Doctrine and Covenants*, Section 20.
[4]*Doctrine and Covenants* 19:31, 20:25, 37, 68; 68:18.

60

CHAPTER XXVIII.

1 *A Commandment to the church of Christ, given in Harmony, Pennsylvania, September 4, 1830.*

LISTEN to the voice of Jesus Christ, your
Lord, your God and your Redeemer, whose
word is quick and powerful.
2 For behold I say unto you, that it mattereth
not what ye shall eat, or what ye shall drink, when
ye partake of the sacrament, if it so be that ye do
it with an eye single to my glory;
3 Remembering unto the Father my body which
was laid down for you, and my blood which was
shed for the remission of your sins:
4 Wherefore a commandment I give unto you,
that you shall not purchase wine, neither strong
drink of your enemies:
5 Wherefore you shall partake of none, except it
is made new among you, yea, in this my Father's
kingdom which shall be built up on the earth.
6 Behold this is wisdom in me, wherefore marvel
not, for the hour cometh that I will drink of the fruit
of the vine with you, on the earth, and with all those
whom my Father hath given me out of the world:
7 Wherefore lift up your hearts and rejoice, and
gird up your loins and be faithful until I come:
~~even so.~~ Amen.

(W.D.)

AND YE SHALL BE CAUGHT UP, THAT WHERE I AM YE SHALL BE ALSO. —W.A.

AND TAKE UPON YOU MY WHOLE ARMOR, THAT YE MAY BE ABLE TO WITHSTAND THE EVIL DAY, HAVING DONE ALL, THAT YE MAY BE ABLE TO STAND. STAND, THEREFORE, HAVING YOUR LOINS GIRT ABOUT WITH TRUTH, HAVING ON THE BREASTPLATE OF RIGHEOUSNESS, AND YOUR FEET SHOD WITH THE PREPARATION OF THE GOSPEL OF PEACE, WHICH I HAVE SENT MINE ANGELS TO COMMIT UNTO YOU; TAKING THE SHIELD OF FAITH WHEREWITH YE SHALL BE ABLE TO QUENCH ALL THE FIERY DARTS OF THE WICKED; AND TAKE THE HELMET OF SALVATION, AND THE SWORD OF MY SPIRIT, WHICH I WILL POUR OUT UPON YOU, AND MY WORD WHICH I REVEAL UNTO YOU, AND BE AGREED AS TOUCHING ALL THINGS WHATSOEVER YE ASK OF ME, —W.A.

MORONI, WHOM I HAVE SENT UNTO YOU TO REVEAL THE BOOK OF MORMON, CONTAINING THE FULNESS OF MY EVERLASTING GOSPEL, TO WHOM I HAVE COMMITTED THE KEYS OF THE RECORD OF THE STICK OF EPHRAIM; AND ALSO WITH ELIAS, TO WHOM I HAVE COMMITTED THE KEYS OF BRINGING TO PASS THE RESTORATION OF ALL THINGS SPOKEN BY THE MOUTH OF ALL THE HOLY PROPHETS SINCE THE WORLD BEGAN, CONCERNING THE LAST DAYS; AND ALSO JOHN THE SON OF ZACHARIAS, WHICH ZACHARIAS HE (ELIAS) VISITED AND GAVE PROMISE THAT HE SHOULD HAVE A SON, AND HIS NAME SHOULD BE JOHN, AND HE SHOULD BE FILLED WITH THE SPIRIT OF ELIAS; WHICH JOHN I HAVE SENT UNTO YOU, MY SERVANTS, JOSEPH SMITH, JUN., AND OLIVER COWDERY, TO ORDAIN YOU UNTO THE FIRST PRIESTHOOD WHICH YOU HAVE RECEIVED, THAT YOU MIGHT BE CALLED AND ORDAINED EVEN AS AARON; AND ALSO ~~ELIJAH~~ UNTO WHOM I HAVE COMMITTED THE KEYS OF THE POWER OF TURNING THE HEARTS OF THE FATHERS TO THE CHILDREN, AND THE HEARTS OF THE CHILDREN TO THE FATHERS, THAT THE WHOLE EARTH MAY NOT BE SMITTEN WITH A CURSE; AND ALSO WITH JOSEPH AND JACOB, AND ISAAC, AND ABRAHAM, YOUR FATHERS, BY WHOM THE PROMISES REMAIN; AND ALSO WITH MICHAEL, OR ADAM, THE FATHER OF ALL, THE PRINCE OF ALL, THE ANCIENT OF DAYS; AND ALSO WITH PETER, AND JAMES, AND JOHN, WHOM I HAVE SENT UNTO YOU, BY WHOM I HAVE ORDAINED YOU AND CONFIRMED YOU TO BE APOSTLES, AND ESPECIAL WITNESSES OF MY NAME, AND BEAR THE KEYS OF YOUR MINISTRY AND OF THE SAME THINGS WHICH I REVEALED UNTO THEM; UNTO WHOM I HAVE COMMITTED THE KEYS OF MY KINGDOM, AND A DISPENSATION OF THE GOSPEL FOR THE LAST TIMES; AND FOR THE FULNESS OF TIMES, IN THE WHICH I WILL GATHER TOGETHER IN ONE ALL THINGS, BOTH WHICH ARE IN HEAVEN, AND WHICH ARE ON EARTH; AND ALSO WITH —W.A.

just discussed, Joseph Smith and Oliver Cowdery were not valid priests.

After they baptized each other they ordained each other to the Aaronic Priesthood, which they supposedly possessed, but which they actually held invalidly. No matter which way the matter was finally resolved, they would have no need of ordaining each other to a priesthood which they had already received at the hand of John the Baptist.

Additionally, in Mormon theology, the gift of the Holy Spirit is communicated by the laying on of hands. But even a superficial study of the documents in question reveals that this was not possible in the case of the priesthood conferred by John the Baptist on Joseph Smith and Oliver Cowdery. John the Baptist is said to have told them that the priesthood which they had received from him "had not the power of the laying on of hands for the gift of the Holy Ghost."[5] This did not deter Smith, however, for three verses later he affirms that the Holy Ghost fell upon Oliver Cowdery when he was baptized by Joseph Smith, and that Smith himself was "filled with the Holy Ghost" along with "the spirit of prophecy" after his baptism by Cowdery.

True and False Priesthoods

Peter, James, and John's appearances to confer upon Joseph Smith the priesthood of Melchizedek (as we have noted earlier, there is no revelation to confirm this) is another example of the contradictions between Mormonism and the Bible. In Hebrews 5:6, 10 we read about Christ: "As he saith also in another place, Thou art a priest forever after the order of Melchisedec . . . called of God a high priest after the order of Melchisedec." The English word order is determined by the Greek term *taksin*, which refers to manner, nature, or quality. Greek lexicons confirm the fact that Jesus Christ was a priest after the Mel-

---

[5]*Pearl of Great Price*, Joseph Smith, 2:70.

chizedek "manner." That is, His condition (as the one who lives "after the authority of the endless life") establishes His position as unique. The writer of Hebrews chose a unique word, *akatalutou*, to describe Christ's position and authority. The word appears only once in New Testament Greek, at Hebrews 7:16, where our Lord is described as possessing indestructible, imperishable, or indissoluble life.

Since Jesus Christ continues to live by resurrection, He holds the Melchizedek priesthood, according to Hebrews 7:24, "inviolate" or "without successors" (*aparabaton*—see Vine's *Expository Dictionary of New Testament Words*). The late Greek scholar Edgar Goodspeed (along with A. T. Robertson, one of the world's greatest scholars in New Testament Greek) translated the word as "untransferable," demolishing Mormonism's claim that Joseph Smith could have received it or could have had authority to transmit it. It is interesting to observe that *Doctrine and Covenants* 84:21-22 tells us a person cannot see the face of God without the Priesthood and live. Smith claimed to have seen God in 1820, nine years *prior* to his receiving the priesthood!

The Aaronic priesthood, we are told in Hebrews, terminated its function at the cross, when Jesus Christ, the Lamb of God (1 Peter 2:24) "bore in his own body our sins upon the tree." At that particular point the veil of the Temple barring the entrance to the Holiest of All was torn in two (Matthew 27:51).

Christ became both priest and offering, thus effecting what the writer of Hebrews calls a "change" in both the law and the priesthood (Hebrews 7:12). The Aaronic order was done away with at the cross, for "it is not possible that the blood of bulls and goats should take away sins" (Hebrews 10:4), and it is equally clear that Jesus Christ appeared at the end of the age to take away sin. Hebrews chapter one reminds us that Christ "When he had by himself purged our sins, sat down on the right hand of the Majesty on high" (Hebrews 1:3). The Holy Spirit declares that the

Aaronic priesthood was changed (Greek, *metatithemi*), as was the law itself, having reached its fullness or consummation in the Lord Jesus Christ. Paul tells us that Christ is the "end" of the law for righteousness, or, to be more accurate in the Greek text itself, He is the "purpose" or the "goal" (Greek, *telos*) of the law (Romans 10:4).

The Son of God, who has ascended into heaven to make intercession for us according to the will of God (Hebrews 4:14-16), possesses the Melchizedek priesthood and authority by Himself, and He holds it "inviolate" and "untransferable." In Galatians Paul underscores this by pointing out that the function of the law was to act as a schoolmaster (3:24) to lead us to Christ, so that we would be justified by faith. Now that faith (Jesus) has arrived we are no longer under the schoolmaster, but we are under grace, which works through love.

The attempt of Mormon theology to reestablish what God has formally terminated by fulfillment in His Son is a comedy of Biblical and historical error; it strikes at the heart of the gospel. The Mormons have no priesthood; it is pure mythology, concocted by unlearned men ignorant of Biblical theology. It has survived only because it has never really been exposed for what it is—a pretension interposed by Joseph Smith between the true believer and his Savior. But never underestimate the importance of the Priesthood in Mormonism:

> This authoritative Priesthood is designed to assist men in all of life's endeavors, both temporal and spiritual. Consequently, there are divisions or offices of the Priesthood, each charged with definite duties fitting especially the need.
>
> J. A. Widtsoe, *Priesthood and Church Government*, page 107

The Prophet Joseph Smith once said that all priesthood is Melchizedek, that the Melchizedek Priesthood embraces all offices and authorities in the priesthood. This is stated in *Doctrine and Covenants* 107:5: "All other authorities or offices in the Church are appendages to this Priesthood." The Aaronic Priesthood, therefore, is comprehended within the framework of the Melchizedek Priesthood (see Smith's statement in *Doctrine and Covenants* 84:17). Smith maintained that through the authority of this priesthood alone "laymen speak and act in the name of the Lord for the salvation of humanity." He also stated:

> The Priesthood was first given to Adam; he obtained the First Presidency, and held the keys of it from generation to generation. He obtained it in the Creation, before the world was formed. . . . He had dominion given him over every living creature. He is Michael the Archangel, spoken of in the Scriptures. Then to Noah, who is Gabriel; he stands next in authority to Adam in the Priesthood. . . .
>
> *History of the Church* 3:385-86

All Mormon theology rests upon Joseph Smith's assertion as to the authority of the Melchizedek Priesthood. But the Epistle to the Hebrews alone destroys this claim. The Bible nowhere says that Jesus conferred authority upon people by the laying on of hands, or by ordaining them to any priesthood, or that anyone in the New Testament church held either priesthood.

The Church of Jesus Christ of Latter-day Saints claims that the entire structure of its priesthoods is based on the revelation of Joseph Smith, along with that of Peter, James, and John (who are alleged to have derived it from the Lord Jesus Christ). But Christ continues to live, and He does not pass His priesthood on to anyone. The Bible, then, passes judgment on Joseph and his doctrine by proclaiming, "Let God be true, and every man a liar" (Romans 3:4).

The Priesthood and Authority

Martin Luther once declared that there is in the church of Christ "a priesthood of all believers." By this he meant that all those indwelt by the Spirit of God are partakers of the blessings which God prepared for us in Christ before the ages began.

The Apostle Peter stated it most eloquently:

> You are the chosen race, the royal priesthood, the conse-
> crated nation, his own people so that you may declare the
> virtues of Him who has called you out of darkness into
> His wonderful light; you, who were once no people but
> are now God's people, once unpitied but now pitied in-
> deed. . . .
>
> 1 Peter 2:9, 10 *Goodspeed*

Peter's words receive added impact from John, who proclaimed:

> Blessings and peace to you from Him who is, and was,
> and is coming, and from the seven spirits before His
> throne, and from Jesus Christ, the trustworthy witness,
> the firstborn of the dead, the sovereign of the kings of the
> earth. To Him who loves us, and has released us from our
> sins by His own blood—He has made us a kingdom of
> priests for His God and Father—to Him be the glory and
> power forever.
>
> Revelation 1:4-6 *Goodspeed*

The Lord Jesus Christ is our Mediator, our Intercessor
in the presence of the Father. He has made us a kingdom of
priests to serve God. We are to offer to Him acceptable
sacrifices, such as praise (Jeremiah 33:11; Hebrews 13:15),
our bodies (Romans 12:1), and prayer (Proverbs 15:8). The
"kingdom of priests" was established many centuries
before 1829. It was the body of Christ, the church, and not
once in Scripture is the church ever designated as possessing either the Aaronic or Melchizedek priesthoods, as
noted above. Mormon theologians claim that the Mormon
Church has ongoing revelations from God, but we are instructed in 1 Thessalonians 5:21 to "test all things and to
hold fast to that which is good" (literal translation). That
which is good is that which is in conformity to what we
know to be the Word of God, Holy Scripture. The "revelations" that Joseph Smith and his followers have brought
forth are in contradiction with that revelation and there-

fore deserve to be rejected for what they are—spiritual counterfeits.

Scores of documents could be appended to illustrate the contradictions about the priesthoods which the Mormons claim to hold (see the close of this chapter for a sample), but the matter of authority must also be mentioned. Mormon missionaries say, "Where do you get your authority?" They are referring to your authority to baptize and/or speak in the name of the Lord Jesus Christ. Christians should refer them to John 1:12 at this point, where the Scripture says:

> But as many as received him, to them gave he power to become the sons of God, even to them that believe on his name.

The King James Version uses the word "power" instead of "authority" or "right" in this particular verse, but the Greek word *eksousia* is clear in establishing the *authority* of the believer as a child *(teknon)* of God. Christians are also members of a royal priesthood and are a kingdom of priests called to serve God. If Mormonism insists on maintaining the fiction of its priesthood, it should be pointed out that, although John the Baptist allegedly bestowed the Aaronic Priesthood, and Peter, James, and John bestowed the Melchizedek Priesthood, the Gospel of John declares that Jesus Christ bestows an authority and priesthood which surpass any other concept of authority.

The Mormon Church also emphasizes "the laying on of hands." It would be foolish to maintain that there was no such practice in the New Testament (see Acts 6:1-6; 9:12; 8:14-19). The laying on of hands was symbolic of healing, the impartation of spiritual gifts, blessing, or the bestowal of responsibility. However, the laying on of hands was never used as the Mormon Church interprets it.

True authority is given by the power of the Lord Jesus Christ, and He gave both power and authority to the church to proclaim the gospel to the ends of the earth. Matthew 28:19 is a classic illustration of this. This "great commission" says:

Go ye therefore, and teach all nations, baptizing them in the name of the Father and of the Son and of the Holy Ghost. . . .

The Apostles also claimed authority over disease in the New Testament. Peter, for example, effected the healing of a crippled man in the Temple at Jerusalem (Acts 4:7-12). Peter did the same in praying for Dorcas (Acts 9:36-41).

The Christian church has absolute authority in the words of the Lord Jesus and Holy Scripture, but not in some mythical priesthood based on the testimony of Joseph Smith, Jr., and his misguided witnesses, whose character and credentials are impeached. Let us be careful to understand the credentials of *our* Great High Priest and the authority which He has bestowed upon those who are His disciples. Let us in Christian love point out the historical and theological discrepancies which exist between Mormon revelation and Biblical revelation. Let us resist any attempt by Mormonism to equate its priesthoods with the true priesthood and authority, which originate only in Jesus Christ.

Additional Conflicting Documentation

The following documentation will give the reader an understanding of the mass of contradictory material abounding in historical Mormon records concerning the priesthood. (The photocopy which appears earlier in this chapter shows the original "revelation" regarding the conferring of the Aaronic Priesthood upon Joseph Smith and Oliver Cowdery, along with later additions to the revelations totaling over 470 words.)

The important details that are missing from the "full history" of 1834 are likewise missing from the the *Book of Commandments* in 1833. The student would expect to find all the particulars of the Restoration [of the Melchizedek Priesthood] in this first treasured set of 65 revelations, the dates of which encompassed the bestowals of the two Priesthoods, but they are conspicuously absent. . . . The notable revelations on Priesthood in the *Doctrine and Covenants* before referred to, Sections 2 and 13, are missing, and Chapter 28 gives no hint of the Restoration which, if actual, had been known for four years. More than four hundred words were added to this revelation of August, 1829 in Section 27 of the *Doctrine and Covenants*, the additions made to include the names of heavenly visitors and two separate ordinations. The *Book of Commandments* gives the duties of Elders, Priests, Teachers, and Deacons and refers to Joseph's apostolic calling but there is no mention of Melchizedek Priesthood, High Priesthood, Seventies, High Priests, nor High Council[l]ors. These words were later inserted into the revelation on Church organization and government of April, 1830, making it appear that they were known at that date, but they do not appear in the original, Chapter 24 of the *Book of Commandments* three years later. . . .

There seems to be no support for the historicity of the Restoration of the Priesthood in journals, diaries, letters, nor printed matter prior to October, 1834. . . .

LaMar Petersen, *Problems in Mormon Text*, pages 7, 8

David Whitmer was one of the three witnesses to *The Book of Mormon*, and, although he later apostatized from the Mormon Church, Mormon authorities still consider his testimony valid for authentication. The following is his opinion of the Melchizedek Priesthood and its High Priests of the Church, taken from his *Address to All Believers in Christ*:

You have changed the revelations from the way they were first given and as they are to-day in the Book of Commandments, to support the error of Brother Joseph in taking upon himself the office of Seer to the church. You have changed the revelations to support the error of high priests. You have changed the revelations to support the error of a President of the high priesthood, high counselors, etc. You have altered the revelations to support you in going beyond the plain teachings of Christ in the new covenant part of the Book of Mormon.

Page 49

High Priests were only in the church before Christ; and to have this office in the "Church of Christ" is not according to the teachings of Christ in either of the sacred books: Christ himself is our great and last High Priest. Brethren—I will tell you one thing which alone should settle this matter in your minds; it is this: you cannot find in the New Testament part of the Bible or Book of Mormon where one single high priest was ever in the Church of Christ. . . . It is a grievous sin to have such an office in the church. As well might you add to the teachings of Christ—circumcision—offering up the sacrifice of animals—or break the ordinances of Christ in any other way by going back to the old law of Moses.

Pages 62-63

Now Brethren, seeing they had no High Priests in the church of Christ of old, and none in the church of Christ in these last days until almost two years after its beginning—when the leaders began to drift into error; remembering the fact of the revelation being changed two years after it was given to include High Priests; taking these things into consideration, how is it that any one can say that the office of High Priest should be in the church of Christ to-day? . . .

In no place in the word of God does it say that an Elder is after the order of Melchisedec, or after the order of the Melchisedec Priesthood. An Elder is after the order of Christ. . . . I do not think the word priesthood is mentioned in the New Covenant of the Book of Mormon. . . . This matter of the two orders of priesthood in the Church of Christ, and lineal priesthood of the old law being in the church, all originated in the mind of Sidney Rigdon. He explained these things to Brother Joseph in his way, out of the old Scriptures, and got Brother Joseph to inquire, etc. He would inquire, and as mouthpiece speak out the revelations just as they had it fixed up in their hearts. . . . This is the way the High Priests and the "priesthood" as you have it, was introduced into the Church of Christ almost two years after its beginning. . . .

Page 64

Mormon historian B. H. Roberts makes this statement regarding the historicity of the ordination:

Restoration of the Melchizedek Priesthood.—The promise to confer upon Joseph and Oliver the Melchizedek Priesthood was fulfilled; but as there is no definite account of the event in the history of the Prophet Joseph, or, for matter of that, in any of our annals. . . .

> Joseph Smith, Jr., *History of the Church* 1:40

To further establish the confusion that exists in the Mormon historical records, we add this statement regarding the supposed Biblical support of the Melchizedek Priesthood by an apostle of the Mormon Church, LeGrand Richards:

> We find no direct statement in the Bible to the effect that a presidency of the Church was appointed by the Savior to stand at the head of the Church after his departure.
>
> *A Marvelous Work and A Wonder*, page 140

Apostle Richards was skirting the issue when he made this statement. Not only is there "no direct statement in the Bible . . . that a presidency of the Church was appointed by the Savior . . ." but the Bible refutes this notion. Paul, under the inspiration of the Holy Spirit, stated:

> . . .but because Jesus lives forever, he has a permanent priesthood. Therefore he is able to save completely [or forever] those who come to God through him, because he always lives to intercede for them.
>
> Such a high priest meets our need—one who is holy, blameless, pure, set apart from sinners, exalted above the heavens. . . . For the law appoints as high priests men who are weak; but the oath [Psalm 110:4], which came after the law, appointed the Son, who has been made perfect forever.
>
> Hebrews 7:24-28 NIV

There is considerable confusion regarding the date of the Church's ordination to the Melchizedek Priesthood. B. H. Roberts' research gives us this information:

> On the 3rd of June (1831). . .the authority of the Melchizedek Priesthood was manifested and conferred for the first time upon several of the Elders.
>
> Joseph Smith, Jr., *History of the Church* 1:175-76

But his footnote regarding this statement says that the date is more probably the sixth of June, and that the student should pay particular attention to the fact that this statement does not indicate that this was the first ordination of the Priesthood on anyone in the Mormon Church, but rather that it was the first conferring of the "authority" of the Melchizedek Priesthood on several of the Elders.

The conferring of the Aaronic Priesthood on Joseph Smith and Oliver Cowdery is supposed to have taken place on May 15, 1829 (*History of the Church,* 1:41). This was the ordination to the Aaronic Priesthood, conferred upon Joseph and Oliver by John the Baptist. At this confirmation John the Baptist supposedly promised that Joseph and Oliver would "in due time" have the Melchizedek Priesthood conferred on them by Peter, James, and John. B. H. Roberts stated that there is "no definite account of the event," but he speculates that this ordination "doubtless occurred some time between May 15, 1829, and the expiration of the month of June of that same year" (*History of the Church,* 1:41).

This all seems to be plausible speculation, until we inspect the conflicting data:

> ...when the Elders first received the ordination of the High Priesthood. They met together in June, 1831. . . . While they were there, the manifestation of the power of God being on Joseph, he set apart some of the Elders to the High Priesthood.
>
> *Journal of Discourses* 11:4

This quotation gives no indication of whether Smith included himself in this ordination. But David Whitmer's statement shows that "all [matters of two priesthoods] originated in the mind of Sidney Rigdon," who just *happened* to be one of the Elders ordained to this priesthood in June 1831:

> June 3, 1831. A general conference was called. . . . The Lord made manifest to Joseph that it was necessary that

such of the elders as were considered worthy, should be
ordained to the high priesthood.

. . .these were ordained to the high priesthood, namely:
Lyman Wright, Sidney Rigdon. . . .

> *John Whitmer's History,*
> page 5

David Whitmer also stated:

> . . .seeing they had no High Priests . . . in these last days
> until almost two years after its beginning . . . the revela-
> tion being changed two years after it was given to include
> High Priests. . . .
>
> . . .This is the way the High Priests and the "priest-
> hood" as you have it, was introduced into the Church of
> Christ almost two years after its beginning. . . .
>
> David Whitmer, *Address to All*
> *Believers In Christ,* page 64

It has become clearer that David Whitmer's insistence on
this point may have validity, for the first mention of the
Melchizedek Priesthood is in *Doctrine and Covenants*
68:15, but the following statement is clearly the verdict
upon all this conflicting data:

> [June, 1831]
> . . .About fifty elders met, which was about all the elders
> that then belonged to the church. . . . The Malchisedec
> [sic] priesthood was then for the first time introduced,
> and conferred on several of the elders.
>
> John Corrill, *A Brief*
> *History,* page 18

This evidence is so conclusive that it needs no further comment.

More on the Mormon Muddle

The original "revelation" of Joseph Smith indicated
that there were to be only three High Priests (or members
of the Presidency):

Of the Melchizedek Priesthood, three Presiding High

> Priests . . . form a quorum of the Presidency of the
> Church.
>
> *Doctrine and Covenants*
> 107:22
>
> . . .Christ . . . also appointed three of these Twelve to
> take the keys of presidency. *Peter, James, and John,
> acted as the First Presidency of the Church in their day.* °
>
> . . .at no place has the Lord said that others more than
> the Twelve and a Presidency of three should be called.
>
> Joseph Fielding Smith,
> *Doctrines of Salvation* 3:152-53

But an article appearing in the *Salt Lake Tribune* of
January 19, 1970, shows the "weight" that is given to
Joseph's "revelation":

> In October, 1965, because of the "increasing work load
> on Church leadership and rapid growth of the Church,"
> President McKay appointed two new counselors to the
> First Presidency. They are Joseph Fielding Smith and
> Thorpe B. Isaacson.
>
> During General Conference in April, 1968, Alvin R. Dyer
> also was elevated to the First Presidency, raising the total
> membership to six.

Although Mormonism claims it believes that the Bible is
the Word of God, we shall now see just how little validity it
gives to Biblical revelation in regard to the organization of
the church. First Timothy 3:12 states, regarding the quali-
fications of a deacon in Christ's church:

> Let the deacons be the husbands of one wife, ruling
> their children and their own houses well.

Now let us examine what the Mormon viewpoint of God's
revelation is in this respect, as stated by Joseph Fielding
Smith, who was "elevated to the First Presidency" in April
1968:

> It was the judgment of Paul that a deacon in that day
> should be a married man. That does not apply to our day.

°Emphasis theirs.

Conditions were different in the days of Paul. In that day a minister was not considered qualified to take part in the ministry until he was 30 years of age. Under those conditions deacons, teachers, and priests were mature men. This is not the requirement today. . . .

. . .Young men were ordained and sent out to preach the gospel in the days of the Prophet Joseph Smith. Several young men who had not reached their majority, and who were *unmarried*, went forth to do missionary work with the power of the Melchizedek Priesthood upon them. The Prophet's youngest brother, Don Carlos Smith, was ordained an elder when he was 14 and went out doing missionary work. . . . When he was 19, he was made president of the high priests quorum.°

> Joseph Fielding Smith, *Doctrines of Salvation* 3:109-10

God's Answer

Let us heed the Word of the Lord regarding this kind of confusion:

> For the time will come when men will not put up with sound doctrine. Instead, to suit their own desires, they will gather around them a great number of teachers to say what their itching ears want to hear. They will turn their ears away from the truth and turn aside to myths.
> 2 Timothy 4:3, 4 NIV

Paul, writing to Timothy, also tells us what the results are of listening to "men of depraved minds, who, as far as the faith is concerned, are rejected":

> But they will not get very far because, as in the case of those men [Jannes and Jambres], their folly will be clear to everyone.
> . . .evil men and imposters will go from bad to worse, deceiving and being deceived.
> 2 Timothy 3:9, 13 NIV

° Emphasis theirs.

Let us not abandon the Mormon people to such false prophets; let us, instead, lead them gently away from the morass of conflicting doctrine that is historic Mormon theology and into the glorious light of the simplicity that is in Christ Jesus and His gospel.

Orson Pratt, an early Mormon Apostle, gave this challenge to us, and honest Mormons should admit to its validity today:

> . . .convince us of our errors of doctrine, if we have any, by reason, by logical arguments, or by the word of God, and we will be ever grateful for the information, and you will ever have the pleasing reflection that you have been instruments in the hands of God of redeeming your fellow beings from the darkness which you may see enveloping their minds.
>
> Orson Pratt, *The Seer*, pages 15-16

As we conclude this chapter, we want to include references to some of the contradictions inherent in the Mormon concept of the Priesthood, especially when such concepts are contradictory to the Bible. I am indebted to Hal Hougey's *Latter-day Saints: Where Did You Get Your Authority?*, portions of which are quoted here with permission, and to Otis Gatewood, author of a tract of the same name from which Hougey obtained some of his information.

A. "*Where did you get your authority?*" The Jews asked Jesus and the apostles this question in Matthew 21:23-27 and Acts 4:7-12.
　1. Latter-Day Saints have the same misconception that the Jews had: that authority passes from one to another through some ceremony or ordination. The very fact that the priesthood questioned their authority shows that Jesus and the apostles completely ignored those ceremonies or ordinations. The Jews were wrong, and since the LDS people believe as the Jews did, they are wrong too.
　2. When Jesus was questioned about his authority, He examined the questioners to see if they were competent judges. Therefore, we shall do the

same: We ask, "The authority of Joseph Smith, whence was it? From heaven, or of men?" ·

B. *Was there a total apostasy, making a restoration of authority necessary?*

   1. LDS believe that there was a total apostasy, and therefore a complete loss of authority to baptize, etc. This, they believe, made necessary the restoration of authority (or priesthood) by a heavenly messenger to Joseph Smith.

   2. That there was a general apostasy, we agree. That it was universal, we deny.

      a. Mormons contradict Christ and say the gates of hades did prevail against the church (Matthew 16:18).

      b. We have received a kingdom that cannot be moved or shaken (Hebrews 12:28).

Mormonism claims that the Apostle Paul prophesied a total apostasy when he warned,

> For I know this, that after my departing shall grievous wolves enter in among you, not sparing the flock. Also of your own selves shall men arise, speaking perverse things, to draw away disciples after them (Acts 20:29, 30).

True, false prophets from *outside* the church enter to destroy (Matthew 7:15), and false teachers from within pervert sound doctrine and lead unstable Christians astray. This has been going on for nearly two thousand years, but Paul knew that the church would continue, for he stated,

> Now unto him who is able to do exceeding abundantly above all that we ask or think, according to the power that worketh in us, unto him be glory in the church by Christ Jesus *throughout all ages*, world without end. Amen (Ephesians 3:20, 21).

SIX

MORMONISM'S RACISM

—

The Fraud of The Book of Abraham

One of the standard works of the Mormon Church (acknowledged as divinely inspired and on an equal plane with the Bible, *The Book of Mormon*, and the *Doctrine and Covenants*) is entitled *The Pearl of Great Price*. It will be remembered that Joseph Smith, Jr., maintained that he translated *The Book of Mormon* from "reformed Egyptian hieroglyphics" by use of the Urim and the Thummim, or two stones of remarkable character set in silver bows and attached to a breastplate. When the Prophet gazed through them, they translated the Egyptian characters by the "gift and power of God" into English. Mormon prophets point to *The Pearl of Great Price* as the "standard work" that has forbidden Negroes to attain the priesthood and exaltation to the rank of a god in the Celestial Kingdom. This opens up an important topic—racism. On June 9, 1978, President Spencer W. Kimball—Prophet, Seer, and Revelator to the LDS Church—received a "revelation" allowing "all worthy Mormon men" to be ordained to the Priesthood of the Mormon Church. We will be discussing this subject later on in this chapter.

The alleged translation by Smith known as *The Book of Abraham*, contained in *The Pearl of Great Price*, was claimed to have been written in an Egyptian language by the hand of Abraham when he was in Egypt. Smith was so certain that he had uncovered a document of importance that he wrote a volume on Egyptian grammar (*History of the Church* 2:238), and in 1842 published his translation, called *The Book of Abraham*, in the *Times and Seasons*, a Mormon newspaper. *The Book of Abraham* later became a part of *The Pearl of Great Price* (*History of the Church* 4:524). In the translation of this Egyptian document, Smith was deprived of the presence of the Urim and the Thummim but still maintained that he was guided by the power of God. To this day the Mormon Church has accepted Smith's word and his translation as the Word of God itself.

There is a vast amount of information dealing with the subject of *The Book of Abraham* (see bibliography). In a book entitled *The Message of the Joseph Smith Papyri: An Egyptian Endowment*, Dr. Hugh Nibley, a former Brigham Young University professor and a Mormon apologist who dabbles in Egyptology, attempts to defend Joseph Smith and *The Book of Abraham*. He fails in his defense and succeeds only in distorting the evidence. Other Mormon apologists, such as John Widtsoe and others who preceded Nibley, have likewise defended the authenticity of the document and the prophetic office of Smith. In recent years this task has become increasingly difficult; in fact, the task has become impossible (see Chapter 1). Nibley himself has warned the Mormon Church of the dire consequences that face them as the result of their neglect of scholarship in the area of Egyptology, particularly where *The Book of Abraham* is concerned.

"The papyri scripts given to the Church do not prove *The Book of Abraham* is true," Dr. Hugh Nibley said in an academics Office-sponsored assembly Wednesday night. "LDS scholars are caught flatfooted by this discovery," he went on to say.

According to Dr. Nibley, Mormon scholars should have been doing added research on *The Pearl of Great Price* years ago. Non-Mormon scholars will bring in questions regarding the manuscripts which will be hard to answer because of lack of scholarly knowledge on the subject. . . . Dr. Nibley said worldly discoveries are going to "bury the Church in criticism" if members of the Church don't take it upon themselves to become a people of learning. . . . Mormons ought to know as much or more as others, "but they don't," Dr. Nibley said, quoting Brigham Young.

Daily Universe, Brigham Young
University, December 1, 1967

Dr. Nibley further stated:

. . . a few faded and tattered little scraps of papyrus may serve to remind the Latter-day Saints of how sadly they have neglected serious education. . . . Not only has our image suffered by such tragic neglect, but now in the moment of truth the Mormons have to face the world unprepared, after having been given a hundred years' fair warning.

Brigham Young University
Studies, Winter 1968, pages 171-72

What could call forth such serious statements by a noted Mormon scholar and apologist concerning *The Book of Abraham*? Why should the Mormon Church suddenly become so concerned with this issue? The answers are to be found in the fact that both scholarship and history have caught up with Joseph Smith the "translator," "seer," and "revelator." A scholastic Armageddon is brewing, which Nibley sees only too clearly.

The Book of Abraham was supposedly written by Abraham on papyri approximately four thousand years ago, was secured by Joseph Smith, Jr., in 1835, and was then translated by him. (See *History of the Church* 2:348-49.)

After *The Book of Abraham* was translated, the papyri disappeared, only to be rediscovered in 1967 at the Metropolitan Museum in New York City, presented to the mu-

seum by the Reorganized Church of Jesus Christ, Latter-
day Saints. The Utah Church accepted this document as
authentic on November 27, 1967. It was hailed as a golden
opportunity to confirm Joseph Smith as a genuine prophet
for all the world to recognize.

In *The Improvement Era* for February, 1968, on page
40 it was stated that Dr. Hugh Nibley:

> has been assigned by the Church to direct the investiga-
> tion and research being done on the material.

Dr. Nibley is not an Egyptologist and cannot read
hieratic Egyptian. According to Dee Jay Nelson, an Egyptologist and an acquaintance of Nibley, Nibley is "a
talented amateur" who had only a cram course in Egyptology at the University of Chicago financed by the Church,
but was given the task of confirming the Mormon revelation. Yet the *Deseret News* (December 27, 1967) declared:

> . . . the papyri are in the hands of one of the best quali-
> fied Egyptologists in the world, Hugh Nibley, . . .

Dr. Nibley, while not denying the statement in any official publication of the Church, contacted the Mormon
Egyptologist, Professor Dee Jay Nelson, and stated his
views in a letter to Professor Nelson:

> "I don't consider myself an Egyptologist at all. . . ."

Dr. Nibley, unable to translate the papyri (labeled
22:309), asked Nelson to enter the picture due to his expertise. Nelson, a lifelong Mormon, examined the original
papyri on January 4, 1968, at Brigham Young University.
According to Nelson, he gained access to this because Dr.
Nibley had told N. Eldon Tanner, First Counselor to the
President of the Church, that "it would be a good idea to let
Professor Dee Jay Nelson have copies of the papyri," and
added, "Nelson is best qualified to do the job." Tanner

BRIGHAM YOUNG UNIVERSITY
PROVO, UTAH
84001

ERNEST L. WILKINSON, PRESIDENT

COLLEGE OF RELIGIOUS INSTRUCTION   June 27, 1967

Dear Bro. Nelson,

Brother, you HAVE been around! But I am willing to bet you
that you have reached premature conclusions about the hypocephalus.
The Church has actually been able to procure some jars and other
artifacts from Qumran, and there MAY be some Ms fragments in the
collection: there are complications there that I can't go into. I
don't consider myself an Egyptologist at all, and don't intend to
get involved in the P.G.P. business unless I am forced into it--which
will probably be sooner than that. I actually don't know where the
original PG P Mss are, though I could find out easily enough; so far
my ignorance has served me well. I see no reason in the world why
you should not be taken into the confidence of the Brethren if this
thing ever comes out into the open; in fact, you should be enormously
useful to the Church. I have an colossal collection of notes which has
been building up through the years, and I think there is stuff in it
that would surprise and even conv ince you. As you know, this is a
happy hunting-ground for crackpots, and not being certified in anything
in particular I only rush in where fools fear to tread. I would like
very much to see you (I was in Billings last Thursday!) and hope that
we may collide before too long: this is the sort of thing that has to
be discussed makshufan wa maktuman. *in one place together* As you know, there are parties
in Salt Lake who are howling for a showdown on the P.G.P.; if they
have their way we may have to get together. Well, the nice thing about
discussion is that one never knows where it is going to lead--that is
why the experts are avoiding it as much as I am; what is even more wholesome,
all discussion quickly discloses interesting gaps and defects in the
knowledge of even the total authority. What have we to lose? *Yours Hugh Nibley*

agreed. The importance of the position Nelson held cannot be overestimated—he was the Church's man, designated to translate the newfound papyri of Joseph Smith.

The result of his work was an explosion of scholastic and racial magnitude, and the shock waves are still passing through the Mormon Church. As Dee Jay Nelson put it: "The cracks are beginning to show on that magnificent edifice that is the Mormon Church." The reason for the "cracks" in the foundation of the Mormon Church is the findings of Nelson and the attempts of the Mormon Church to suppress them. According to Nelson, one of the conditions on which he agreed to do the translation (and to which N. Eldon Tanner agreed) was that the Mormon Church would publish his findings. Tanner's convenient loss of memory of the agreement or of ever having heard of Nelson led the professor to Jerald Tanner and the Modern Microfilm Co., who published his translation of the "Joseph Smith Papyri." However, the Church attempts to explain this away, partly through the efforts of Dr. Nibley.

Nelson does not stand alone in his conclusion. Several of the world's foremost Egyptologists have confirmed his translation and findings.[1] The Mormon Church has yet to produce a single qualified Egyptologist who disagrees with those findings. Instead, what the Church has done unofficially is to promote Dr. Nibley's apologetic in an attempt to deny what archaeology, history, and logic have proved untenable.

However, in reply to a letter by John L. Smith, the LDS Church officially denies approval or sanction of Dr. Nibley's writings "concerning the papyri scrolls" (see accompanying photocopy).

---

[1] Klaus Baer, Samuel A. B. Mercer, Richard A. Parker, F. S. Spalding, John A. Wilson..

August 22, 1975

Mr. John L. Smith
Box 47
Marlow, Oklahoma 73055

Dear Mr. Smith:

Answering your letter dated August 19, 1975, the writings of Dr. Hugh Nibley concerning the papyri scrolls have been done entirely on his own responsibility and do not have the official approval and sanction of the Church.

The brethren appreciate your interest and asked me to extend to you their best wishes.

Sincerely yours,

Francis M. Gibbons
Secretary to the First Presidency

The following are reproductions of correspondence from Professor Dee Jay Nelson to the First Presidency of the Mormon Church, the office of the Stake President in Billings, Montana, and to all concerned parties about Professor Nelson's conclusions.

PROF. DEE JAY NELSON
Lecturer
Eryptologist
719 HIGHLAND PARK DRIVE
BILLINGS, MONTANA 57102

Attention: First Presidency
Church of Jesus Christ of Latter Day Saints
Church Office Building
Salt Lake City, Utah

This letter is to inform you that it is our considered desire that my
own name and those of my wife and daughter be removed from the membership rolls of the Latter Day Saint Church.

We:

    Dee Jay Nelson
    Katherine G. Nelson (Mrs. Dee Jay Nelson)
    Kim Cherie Nelson
       do freely, and with full understanding of the implications
of the step, require that our names be removed from all member records
of the L.D.S. Church.

I, Dee Jay Nelson, do herby renounce and relinquish the priesthood
which I now hold.

Following my translation (the first to be published) of the bulk of
the hieratic and hieroglyphic Egyptian texts upon the Metropolitan-
Joseph Smith Papyri fragments three of the most eminent Egyptologists
now living published corroborating translations. These amply prove
the fraudulent nature of the Book of Abraham, in which lies the unjust assertion that negros are unworthy of participation in the highest
privileges of the L.D.S. Church.

We do not wish to be associated with a religious organization which
teaches lies and adheres to policies so blatantly opposed to the
civil and religious rights of some citizens of the United States.

By affixing our signatures to this document we exercise our constitutional rights of religious freedom and separate ourselves from the
Church of Jesus Christ of Latter Day Saints.

                     Dee Jay Nelson

                     Katherine G. Nelson

                     Kim Cherie Nelson

Date: Dec. 8, 1975

PROF. DEE JAY NELSON
Lecturer
Egyptologist
719 HIGHLAND PARK DRIVE
BILLINGS, MONTANA 59102

February 15, 1976

Mr. R. L. Eardley
2124 Lyman Ave.
Billings, Montana 59102

Dear Mr. Eardley,

Your certified letter of February 10, 1976 was received a few days
ago.   We found it offensive, implying by the word "court" that we
were to be judged.   The phrase which you used, "summoned to appear",
might better have been worded, "requested to appear" as we are no
longer under your jurisdiction.

My wife, my daughter and I have already resigned from the L. D. S.
Church by formal written notification addressed to the First Presidency
on December 8, 1975.

The scientific world finds the Book of Abraham an insult to intelligence
Some of the most brilliant and qualified Egyptologists of our time
have labled it fraudulent upon the overwhelming evidence of the recently
discovered Metropolitan-Joseph Smith Papyri.   No truly qualified
Egyptologist has yet supported it.

We do not wish to be associated with a church which teaches lies and
racial bigotry.

Sincerely,

Dee Jay Nelson

DJN/gh

PROF. DEE JAY NELSON
Lecturer
Egyptologist
719 HIGHLAND PARK DRIVE
BILLINGS, MONTANA 59102

AN OPEN LETTER

Dear Elder,

Your letter of November 12th was received. I read it with great interest. It is typical of many I get....pro and con.

I commend you upon your missionary work. Regardless of personal religious convictions this is laudable. The only way for man to truly serve God is to serve his fellow man. In this your efforts will stand you in good stead throughout life.

You presume too much in your letter....a characteristic of those who speak before learning all the facts. The first of sever examples is shown in your question, "Why did you join the Church of Jesus Christ of Latter Day Saints in the first place?" Why should you assume that I joined the Church at all? I was born a Mormon, which is the poorest reason I know for being a member of any church.

Again you say that I am more impressed with wisdom than with religious truth. I fail to see the difference. I am a devoutly religious man. You need not doubt this. In fact, the best effort you have ever made to substantiate Christianity and the divine mission of Christ is insignificant compared to my own. In 1958-59 I walked every foot of ground that Jesus walked in order to learn more about Him. My life was often at considerable risk when it was necessary for me to travel as a Bedouin through Moslem territory forbidden to Christians. Years earlier I was a lay-scholar in what was then Palistine. I later expanded my knowledge as a student of Zakaria Ghoneim, Keeper of Antiquaties at Saqqara Egypt. I read nine ancient Middle and Far Eastern languages so you may assume that I have a good understanding of ancient history as well. This particularly includes Biblical history.

I further take umbrage with the implication that wisdom and Godliness cannot coexist. Surely your letter conveys this idea without intention. I can not believe you that foolish.

Is it inconceivable to you that I could be in possession of better information on Mormon background than you? I suggest that the best way to examine a fish bowl is from the outside. The view from within is distorted at best. The only honest way to evaluate any thesis is to step away from it and take the part of a critic. If it then meets all the measured tests you may comfortably embrace it with all your heart. I suggest for instance, that you closely examine Joseph Smith's character at its source, as I have. Take a good look at his trial of 1826, in which he was convicted of fraud. You will find that the original trial clerk records still exist. Smith was, on this occasion, given full recourse to law and found guilty under fair examination.

In 19 8 the L.D.S. Church First Presidency asked me to translate the newly discovered Joesph Smith Papyri Fragments. They did so with the knowledge that I was the most qualified member of the Church

to do so.   I promised that I would do it without editorializing
and in exchange received a promise that the Church would publish the
manuscript.   All I did - aside from commenting upon the age and
character of the papyrus (200B.C. to 100 A.D.) and explain meanings -
was convert the ancient Egyptian hieratic words to their English
equivalents.   It is not my fault that they did not say what Joesph
Smith claimed they did.   As I read the language with some ease there
is no possibility that I could be mistaken.   They are a remnant
of a much damaged form of ancient pagan funerary text.   One of them
was a copy of the'Per em Heru' (Book of the Dead) and the other a
copy of a'Sha/t en Sensen'(Book of Breathings).   That these were the
same papyri used by Smith can not be honestly denied because some of
the fragments were glued to pieces of heavy paper with hand written
notations on the back linking them to the "Prophet".   They also
display the original counterparts of hieratic characters which had been
copied by Smith (and or) his scribes into three hand written notebooks.
These notebooks are still in existence, owned by the Church.   I have
photo-copies of the pages.

Of particular importance is the original of Facsimile No. 1
(printed in all editions of the Book of Abraham) among the papyri
fragments.   This fact has been freely admitted by the Church.
I wonder at the exclusion, from the Book of Abraham, of the four vertical
lines of hieroglyphic writing which boarder both sides of the original
vignette.   I should think that Joseph Smith, 'being a self-avowed
expert on the Egyptian language', would have thought them vital (in
an otherwise hieratic manuscript).   These four lines are literally
caption data dealing with the individuals shown in the picture.
Smith's explanation insists that this is a picture of Abraham on
an altar of sacrifice.   The original caption states otherwise, telling
that the man on the "funerary bier" is a pagan priest of Osiris named
"Hor".   The same name can be clearly read in two places on printed
copies of the Book of Abraham, Facsimile No. 3.

Despite their promise,the Church fathers refused to publish my
translation so, upon threat of excommunication, I procured private
publication by Modern Microfilm Co., Salt Lake City.   My excommunication was repeatedly ordered and withdrawn over the next several
years.   I remained in the Church only because I thought that a
voice of an elder in the brotherhood would have more impact than
otherwise.   Also I do not like to be threatened.   In December
1975 the order again came so I sent my resignation.   I was commanded
to appear before a local Bishop's court of examination.   In a
telephone conversation with the Stake President I agreed to come
with one proviso.   All I required is that a committee of one or more
persons be sent to examine the massive documentation which I have
collected to prove that the Book of Abraham in the Pearl of Great
Price is untrue.   I asked only one hour of the valuable time of
such a committee.   A letter to the Stake President with the same
proposal was never answered.   I promised a respectful reception to
the committee.   No representative was ever sent so I did not appear.

The proceedures of these excommunication "trials" are illegal
under written regulations of the Church itself, which insists that
it is governed by rules which do not conflict with the constitutional
rights of citizens.   Despite this the "trials" do not offer the
right of defense and rebuttal to the persons being examined.   This
is a clear infringement upon the constitutional privilege.   Several

friends, who dared to question L. D. S. teachings, have been subjected
to gross miscarriages of justice in their excommunicational "trials".
Among these were devoutly Christian men like Dr. John Fitzgerald and
Grant Heward.

I have now published five books and booklets on the Book of Abraham
question. The last of these was in collaboration with John Fitzgerald.

Truth is the positive side of reality, which has a second pole.
You can not assess the value of any belief without first considering
the other viewpoint in an open minded way. No one man is the possessor
of all truth. On the other hand ignorance is not the absence of
knowledge. It is rather, the massive misuse of information.

Let me ask, where is the Egyptologist who will support the Book
of Abraham? My translation was later supported by the published
translations of 3 of the greatest living Egyptian philologists. Since
the turn of this century a dozen of the best Egyptologists have
refuted the Book of Abraham, including Sir W. Flinders Petrie, the
father of modern Egyptology.

Some letters ask how I could dare disagree with Dr. Hugh Nibley,
whom they call the ultimate authority. While I greatly admire
Nibley I can hardly acknowledge him as any kind of an authority on
matters Egyptian. I have honestly refered to him as a talented
amateur. In several of his own publications and lectures he has
refered to himself as "not qualified as an Egyptologist". He is
an honest man which is well demonstrated by the way he invariably
talks in circles about the Book of Abraham without getting to a
definable point.

If the veracity of the Book of Abraham were to be tested in
any court in the land the mountain of evidence would easily overthrow
it. You have said that when you read it your heart burns within
you and that this is your proof of its authenticity. The hard facts
simply do not support that collection of bigoted nonsense called
the Book of Abraham. If it makes your heart burn to read it then
I recommend the Arabian Nights. One is no more outlandish than
the other. Do you doubt that the ancient Egyptian heart burned
any less warmly when he read the Book of the Dead, and how often have
I heard Moslems say the same.

I invite you or anyone else to show me the error of my findings.
Of course, to do so you must closely examine my documentation at the
risk of your own convictions. I have been on both sides of the
issue. Don't question anything until you can say the same.

The Mormon Church is a great humanitarian organization and this
is a good thing. It does, however, teach false history and a
thesis which says that negros are (in some ways) debased humans
by virtue of their race. How does your bosom burn when you swallow
that <u>Christian</u> pill?

Look at <u>all</u> the facts before you are so sure of yourself.

May the grace of God be upon you in all things good and
may you prosper in His word. This I pray, with the hope that
He will forgive me for dipping my pen too deeply in acid.

Nelson's position is unassailable. He now knows that Joseph Smith lied and that the Church of Jesus Christ of Latter-day Saints perpetuates "the fraudulent nature of *The Book of Abraham* . . . ."

Should there be any lingering doubt as to Hugh Nibley's respect for Nelson's scholastic capacities as an Egyptologist, the following quotation from him will clarify his esteem for Nelson.

> . . . a conscientious piece of work for which the Latter-day Saints owe a debt of gratitude to Mr. Dee Jay Nelson.
>
> *Brigham Young University*
> *Studies* 3:245

Considering Dr. Nibley's high regard for Nelson, it is of enormous significance that Dr. Nibley's book does *not* make a single reference to Dee Jay Nelson, his capacities, or the great value of his analyses of the Joseph Smith papyri as related to *The Book of Abraham!*

Book of Abraham—Shadow or Reality?[2]

Dr. Nibley has taken it upon himself to justify Joseph Smith and the divine authority or authenticity of *The Book of Abraham* as contained in *The Pearl of Great Price.* A

---

[2]The author is deeply indebted to the pioneer work of Dee Jay Nelson and the superb critique of Dr. Nibley's arguments published by H. Michael Marquardt in his booklet *The Book of Abraham Papyrus Found,* published by the author in 1975 in Sandy, Utah; to Jerald and Sandra Tanner, *The Mormon Papyri Question* (Salt Lake City: Modern Microfilm Co., 1968); to Rev. Wesley P. Walters, *Joseph Smith Among the Egyptians, The Journal of the Evangelical Theological Society,* 16:1, Winter 1973; to Dr. F. S. Spalding, *Bishop of Utah: Joseph Smith, Jr., as a Translator*; to Dr. Samuel A. B. Mercer, *Joseph Smith as an Interpreter and Translator of Egyptian.* All of these have contributed valuable insights, and their documented research, where utilized, is acknowledged and gratefully appreciated.

thorough refutation of his errors in a field where he has little expertise is surely required.

The following information is not an attack on Dr. Nibley but a critique of both his goals and methods. They appear to follow the old error, "the end justifies the means." The preservation of the reputation of Joseph Smith is imperative to the survival of the Mormon Church. If Joseph was a fraud in his translation of *The Book of Abraham* from hieratic Egyptian, then we can reasonably suspect fraud in his translation of "reformed Egyptian hieroglyphics" in *The Book of Mormon*. That *The Book of Mormon* required almost four thousand alterations from its original publication in 1830 says enough for the integrity of both Joseph Smith and the Mormon Church.

To understand the controversy over the current translations of *The Book of Abraham*, the reader must see the issue in the simplest possible terms so as not to become bogged down in technical terminology too often used by Mormon apologists as a substitute for truth. To do so, we have reproduced here (from *The Pearl of Great Price*) facsimiles from the papyri which Joseph Smith, Jr., claimed comprised *The Book of Abraham*, with the "explanation" of the Egyptian given by him and numbered on the facsimiles. The true translation appears on the right. From the data and the expert opinions about the papyri of *The Book of Abraham*, the position of the Mormon Church is no longer merely shaky; it has been totally destroyed. Dr. Hugh Nibley and his defense of Joseph Smith and *The Book of Abraham* have been dealt with most thoroughly in two excellent reviews.[3]

---

[3]H. Michael Marquardt, *The Book of Abraham Papyrus Found* (Salt Lake City: Modern Microfilm Company, 1975); "An Examination of the Source of Joseph Smith's Book of Abraham," in *Journal of the Evangelical Theological Society*, Vol. 16, no. 1, Winter 1973.

. . . Now here is this illustration which is so important. The picture of, so-called picture, of Abraham lying on an altar about to be sacrificed. Now Egyptologists recognize the pictorial qualities of this illustration as the body upon a funeral bier, being prepared ritualistically or physically for burial. The drawing was broken and I'm convinced it was broken in Joseph Smith's time. Now you'll notice the bird over the head. It says in the explanation accompanying Facsimile #1 . . . that that's . . . the Angel of the Lord. Actually it's the "ba"—the soul of the man who's dead, hovering over him, and it has the head of a human, it does not have the head of a bird. Dr. Klaus Baer has substantiated my diagnosis here and there's enough of it remaining to see the chin, the single stroke indicating the beard, and even possibly the nose, so there's no question that it should be a human head instead of a bird, as in printed representation of the Book of Abraham.

The three objects under the couch, according to Joseph Smith, represent idolatrous gods. I won't argue that point . . . but that doesn't take much figuring. . . .

Now the figure in black should have a jackal head. It is Anubis. Even if he didn't have a jackal head, he'd still be Anubis, because traditionally he's the one that stands over and presides at the separation of the body for embalming. He is always represented as a black figure.

. . . Let's say this is the only piece of evidence in existence. This is enough to throw the whole Book of Abraham out the window . . . three lines of heiroglyphic writing down this side and one on the far side . . . represent caption material describing the scene . . . right here you see the name of the man written in idiogramatic . . . Hor, the ancient Egyptian equivalent of the word we use today, Horus. . . . the name of Hor . . . is written twice on this fragment. It tells of the man named Hor, and so who can claim that that's Abraham when the name is right there?

—Dee Jay Nelson
Egyptologist

A FACSIMILE FROM THE BOOK OF ABRAHAM

No. 1

EXPLANATION OF THE ABOVE CUT

Fig. 1. The Angel of the Lord. 2. Abraham fastened upon an altar. 3. The idolatrous priest of Elkenah attempting to offer up Abraham as a sacrifice. 4. The altar for sacrifice by the idolatrous priests, standing before the gods of Elkenah, Libnah, Mahmackrah, Korash, and Pharaoh. 5. The idolatrous god of Elkenah. 6. The idolatrous god of Libnah. 7. The idolatrous god of Mahmackrah. 8. The idolatrous god of Korash. 9. The idolatrous god of Pharaoh. 10. Abraham in Egypt. 11. Designed to represent the pillars of heaven, as understood by the Egyptians. 12. Raukeeyang, signifying expanse, or the firmament over our heads; but in this case, in relation to this subject, the Egyptians meant it to signify Shaumau, to be high, or the heavens, answering to the Hebrew word, Shaumahyeem.

. . . this is a device that is known to the science of Egyptology as a "hypocephalus." It's an amulet, usually made of pieces of papyrus on which the inscriptions are written, and then attached to layers of plaster or plastered linen, and this amulet is placed under the head of a mummy, and its magical function is to retain body heat in the corpse, so that if the soul wants to come back and reoccupy and reanimate the body it can do so. It represents the "eye of Ra," the sun, the heat-giving sun. It's a picture of it and the various features, the illustrative features in it, are pertinent to the solar religion of Egyptian late periods. These were never found on mummies dated before 660 B.C. It's a late invention and so it cannot possibly have anything to do with Abraham. It was later by 1200 years or so. It's also called an "Ahait" amulet, because the cow that you see on it was a goddess named "Ahait" a form of Hathor, sometimes called The Sister, sometimes called The Wife of the Sun-God Ra. Now the most important inscription on it is the one around the outside. It begins at the top and progresses in a counter-clockwise direction. But when we come around here to a point corresponding to about five o'clock on the circle, we see that suddenly it becomes something that originally I could not recognize at all, and it continues quite alien up till it's about one o'clock and then I see some normal heiroglyphic characters again. Now, Mr. [Grant] Heward, through some remarkable original research, discovered that that was heiratic and that it was copied from the Hor Sen-Sen [Book of Breathings] text.

. . . I have discerned what I have thought was oddities in some of his copied characters in the notebooks, which indicated that he thought that cracks in the papyri were part of the character. I think Grant has done the same thing, so I think the evidence is the whole idea is not one of a man inept in artistic copying, it is in the idea you get as a philologist familiar with these scripts, is that it was copied by a man who didn't know what they were, had no idea what they were.

. . . I've compared it with British Museum Specimen #37909 . . . and one in Leydn, Holland Museum . . . #70 . . . Now the interesting thing about these particular three specimens, is that they read almost word for word the same. This indicates that the Book of Abraham facsimile is a representation of a pagan amulet . . . I believe that's evidence enough from a

A FACSIMILE FROM THE BOOK OF ABRAHAM

No. 2

EXPLANATION OF THE FOREGOING CUT

Fig. 1. Kolob, signifying the first creation, nearest to the celestial, or the residence of God. First in government, the last pertaining to the measurement of time. The measurement according to celestial time, which celestial time signifies one day to a cubit. One day in Kolob is equal to a thousand years according to the measurement of this earth, which is called by the Egyptians Jah-oh-eh.

Fig. 2. Stands next to Kolob, called by the Egyptians Oliblish, which is the next grand governing creation near to the celestial or the place where God resides; holding the key of power also, pertaining to other planets; as revealed from God to Abraham, as he offered sacrifice upon an altar, which he had built unto the Lord.

Fig. 3. Is made to represent God, sitting upon his throne, clothed with power and authority; with a crown of eternal light upon his head; representing also the grand Key-words of the Holy Priesthood, as revealed to Adam in the Garden of Eden, as also to Seth, Noah, Melchizedek, Abraham, and all to whom the Priesthood was revealed.

Fig. 4. Answers to the Hebrew word Raukeeyang, signifying expanse, or the firmament of the heavens; also a numerical figure, in Egyptian signifying one thousand; answering to the measuring of the time of Oliblish, which is equal with Kolob in its revolution and in its measuring of time.

Fig. 5. Is called in Egyptian Enish-go-on-dosh; this is one of the governing planets also, and is said by the Egyptians to be the Sun, and to borrow its light from Kolob through the medium of Kae-e-vanrash, which is the grand Key, or, in other words, the governing power, which governs fifteen other fixed planets or stars, as also Floeese or the Moon, the Earth and the Sun in their annual revolutions. This planet receives its power through the medium of Kli-flos-is-es, or Hah-ko-kau-beam, the stars represented by numbers 22 and 23, receiving light from the revolutions of Kolob.

Fig. 6. Represents this earth in its four quarters.

Fig. 7. Represents God sitting upon his throne, revealing through the heavens the grand Key-words of the Priesthood; as, also, the sign of the Holy Ghost unto Abraham, in the form of a dove.

Fig. 8. Contains writings that cannot be revealed unto the world; but is to be had in the Holy Temple of God.

Fig. 9. Ought not to be revealed at the present time.

Fig. 10. Also.

Fig. 11. Also. If the world can find out these numbers, so let it be. Amen.

Figures 12, 13, 14, 15, 16, 17, 18, 19, and 20, will be given in the own due time of the Lord.

The above translation is given as far as we have any right to give at the present time.

scientific standpoint to prove that the Book of Abraham Facsimile #2 is nothing but a picture of a pagan amulet.

Prof. Dee Jay Nelson
Egyptologist

The prayer at the bottom of the picture is read by Egyptologists as follows: "Osiris Hor, justified," thus making Joseph Smith Papyri I, X, XI and Facsimile No. 3 all related and written for the same deceased person, Hor, a priest of Amon-Ra at Thebes in Egypt.

Fitzgerald, Nelson, Marquardt,
Discrimination: Is It Of God?

. . . The translation is "Osiris Hor, who is true of word (justified), through all eternity." This typical formalized name of the deceased identifies . . . the illustration as having originally been on the papyrus roll from which Facsimile No. 1 was copied (the name Hor is also written on the original of this "Metropolitan Fragment") and that the two unillustrated Sen Sen (Book of Breathings) Fragments were a part of the same roll (Hor is named on them as well). There is no possible way to reconcile Joseph Smith's "explanation" with this translation.

—Dee Jay Nelson, Egyptologist,
A Translation and Study of Facsimile No. 3 in the Book of Abraham, pages 24-25.

Another glaring error in *The Book of Abraham* has been ignored by scribes, historians, and theologians because it too reveals the limitations of Joseph Smith as a translator.

Joseph Smith and the Divine Name

The Book of Abraham 2:6-8 settles forever the spurious nature of the volume.

But I, Abraham, and Lot, my brother's son, prayed unto the Lord, and the Lord appeared unto me, and said unto me: Arise, and take Lot with thee; for I have purposed to take thee away out of Haran, and to make of thee a minister to bear my name in a strange land which I will

A FACSIMILE FROM THE BOOK OF ABRAHAM

No. 3

EXPLANATION OF THE ABOVE CUT

1. Abraham sitting upon Pharaoh's throne, by the politeness of the king, with a crown upon his head, representing the Priesthood, as emblematical of the grand Presidency in Heaven; with the scepter of justice and judgment in his hand.

2. King Pharaoh, whose name is given in the characters above his head.

3. Signifies Abraham in Egypt—referring to Abraham, as given in the ninth number of the *Times and Seasons*. (Also as given in the first facsimile of this book.)

4. Prince of Pharaoh, King of Egypt, as written above the hand.

5. Shulem, one of the king's principal waiters, as represented by the characters above his hand.

6. Olimlah, a slave belonging to the prince.

Abraham is reasoning upon the principles of Astronomy, in the king's court.

give unto thy seed after thee for an everlasting possession, when they hearken to my voice.

For I am the Lord thy God; I dwell in heaven; the earth
is my footstool; I stretch my hand over the sea, and it
obeys my voice; I cause the wind and the fire to be my
chariot; I say to the mountains—Depart hence—and behold, they are taken away by a whirlwind, in an instant,
suddenly.

My name is Jehovah, and I know the end from the beginning; therefore my hand shall be over thee.

The name Jehovah was *not* known to Abraham, so its
usage in *The Book of Abraham* is fraudulent. Second, there
is no name "Jehovah"—it is our improper transliteration of
the Hebrew consonants YHWH, the vowels being inter-
polated from the Hebrew word "Adonai" (Lord). In Exodus
6:3 God states to Moses that His name "Jehovah" (YHWH)
was *not* known to Abraham. Joseph the "translator" did not
know this, and we are presented with one more evidence of
his right to the title of false prophet.

Mormonism: Historically an Anti-Negro Racist Cult

The Mormon Church states in its "Articles of Faith"
that it believes in upholding national laws. This has not
been true in regard to their pursuit of polygamy for 47 years
contrary to law (1843-1890), or in their treatment of the
Negro, whose religious equality they have denied, chiefly
through the usage of what is now recognized in the work of
Nelson as an "insult to intelligence," particularly in the
context of the scientific world. Nelson charged that the
Mormon Church "teaches lies and racial bigotry." Who is
better qualified to know than the man they chose to
translate the papyri of *The Book of Abraham?*

In a personal letter to Dr. John Fitzgerald, (a lifelong
Mormon who was excommunicated from the Church because of his opposition to its racism), Morris K. Udall, a
member of the Congress of the United States, wrote:

. . . My LDS connections haven't been much of an issue as yet, but probably will if my candidacy progresses. The interesting Nelson correspondence you sent simply points up the outdated and very wrong posture of the church on issue of blacks. I admire the Nelsons' courage in dropping their membership. Best regards,
        Mo

On the stationery of the
Congress of the United States,
dated March 17, 1976

Since Nelson's exodus from the Church, members of his local Church have had serious objections to *The Book of Abraham*. A number of them have followed him from Mormonism.

Whenever the Mormon Church has been accused of racism in connection with the Negro, there are cries of protest from Salt Lake City that the Church has always accepted Negroes into its membership, and that they may even attain the Celestial Heaven. What they did *not* state is that when the Negroes reached the Celestial Heaven they would be *servants* there—*not* gods, as white Mormons were privileged to be. Because the Mormon Church was racist, it made virtually no effort to evangelize the Negro with its "restored gospel." Apostle Bruce McConkie, a noted Mormon theologian, made this clear when he stated:

> The gospel message of salvation is not carried affirmatively to them. . . .
>   Bruce R. McConkie, *Mormon Doctrine*, page 527

Arthur Richardson, in the publication *That You May Not Be Deceived*, pages 9 and 10, declares:

> Also, *the gospel is not carried to this segregated black group.* . . . Therefore they were entitled to no better earthly lineage than that of the first earthly murderer, Cain. They were to be the "servant of servants." They were to be segregated. No effort was made to carry the Gospel to them as a people.°

° Emphasis theirs.

On page 13 of the same publication Richardson declares:

> . . . The Church of Jesus Christ of Latter-day Saints has no call to carry the Gospel to the Negro, and it does not do so.

Such statements prompted the *National Observer* Magazine to declare:

> It's hardly a surprise, then, that the Mormon Church has only a few hundred Negroes on its roll. And though Mormon missions seek new members in most parts of the world, its voice is strangely silent in the Negro nations of Africa.
> *National Observer,* June 17, 1963

The *Christian Century,* declared:

> Mormon missionaries are directed not to proselytize negroes and to keep out of transition. Not even Joseph Fielding Smith's invitation to "darkies" is tolerated in the mission program. The membership ranks are being filled with those whose religious commitment is to the maintenance of a racist society and who find Mormon theology a sanctimonious front for their convictions.
> Dr. Glenn Davidson,
> September 29, 1965, page 1183

The Bible is vigorously opposed to racism, particularly in the New Testament. If Mormonism claims to be the restored gospel of Jesus Christ it must explain why the New Testament has been in direct opposition to its stand.

Peter once considered Gentiles "unclean," but then received a direct revelation from God that henceforth "I should not call any man common or unclean" (Acts 10:28). Peter amplified this by stating:

> Of a truth I perceive that God is no respecter of persons, but in every nation he that feareth him, and worketh righteousness, is accepted with him.
> Acts 10:34, 35

If God told Peter not to "call any man common or unclean," and Mormons were unwilling to listen to this testimony, perhaps they should have listened to *The Book of Mormon.* While it declares that the Indians were cursed by God with a dark skin, it makes *no* reference to the Negro, and teaches instead that whatever color a man is, God considers *all* men in the same light:

> Behold, hath the Lord commanded any that they should not partake of his goodness? Behold I say unto you, Nay; but all men are privileged the one like unto the other, and none are forbidden.
>
> 2 Nephi 26:28

> . . . and he doeth nothing save it be plain unto the children of men; and he inviteth them all to come unto him and partake of his goodness; and he denieth none that come unto him, black and white, bond and free, male and female; and he remembereth the heathen; and all are alike unto God, both Jew and Gentile.
>
> 2 Nephi 26:33

Both Joseph Fielding Smith, tenth President of the Mormon Church, and David O. McKay, a former President of the Church, stated that they knew of "no Scriptural basis for denying the Priesthood to Negroes, other than the one verse in the Book of Abraham" [1:26]. President Smith went so far as to say:

> . . . We know of no such statement in any revelation in the *Doctrine and Covenants*, the *Book of Mormon* or the Bible.
>
> *The Improvement Era* 27:565

And President McKay declared:

> . . . however, I believe . . . that the real reason dates back to our pre-existent life.
>
> *Mormonism and the Negro*, Part Two, page 19

It would seem that if the Bible and *The Book of Mormon* are not racist and *The Book of Abraham* is fraudulent, then the Mormon Church had no reason for maintaining its stance. Beyond this, Dr. James Buswell III (of Wheaton

College) in his enlightening volume, *Slavery, Segregation and Scripture*, ruined the appeal of Mormon writers to Ham as the father of the Negro race. This view was extremely popular in the South. It is unfortunate that in some sections of the South the Ham fiction is still pursued.

The divine imperative of the Christian Church is to carry the message of Jesus Christ to the ends of the earth, or, in the words of our Lord:

> Therefore go and make disciples of all nations, baptizing them in the name of the Father and of the Son and of the Holy Spirit, and teaching them to obey everything I have commanded you.
>
> Matthew 28:19, 20 NIV

The New Testament did not discriminate against bringing the gospel to blacks, and Philip was specifically sent by God to proclaim the good news to the Chancellor of the Exchequer of Candace, Queen of the Ethiopians (Acts 8:26-39). The man received Jesus Christ as his Savior, was baptized, and, as the Scripture records, went on his way rejoicing (Acts 8:39).

Mormonism has denigrated the Negro under the guise of the Christian religion. Its consistent racial prejudice has been noticed by many careful students of history. It was not unusual in earlier years to hear or read of Negroes being described by Mormons as "niggers," and in one instance as ". . . rebellious niggers in the slave states . . ." (*Millennial Star* 22:602). In later years diligent Mormon scribes altered that statement to read ". . . rebellious negroes in the slave States . . ." (*History of the Church* 6:158).

The prejudice of the Mormon Church against the Negro continued with such statements as:

> . . .The descendents of Ham, besides a black skin which has ever been a curse that has followed an apostate of the holy priesthood, as well as a black heart, have been servants to both Shem and Japheth, and the abolitionists are trying to make void the curse of God but it will require

more power than man possesses to counteract the de-
crees of eternal wisdom.
Times and Seasons 6:857

I have reproduced a number of quotations from publications of the Mormon Church which reveal their long history of racism, allegedly traceable to *The Book of Abraham*
and Joseph's fraudulent translation of an ancient Egyptian
burial papyri. Judge for yourself the record of Mormonism
and decide whether it could possibly be the restored gospel
of Jesus Christ in the light of its past vitriolic prejudice
against the Negro.

The History of Mormon Racism

1. Negroes in this life are denied the priesthood; under
   no circumstances can they hold this delegation of
   authority from the Almighty. The gospel message of
   salvation is not carried affirmatively to them. . . .

   Negroes are not equal with other races where the receipt of certain spiritual blessings are concerned. . . .

   Bruce R. McConkie,
   Mormon Doctrine, page 527

2. Think of the Negro, cursed as to the Priesthood. . . . This negro, who, in the pre-existence lived the type of life which justified the Lord
   in sending Him to the earth in the lineage of Cain
   with a black skin, and possible being born in darkest
   Africa—if that negro is willing when he hears the
   gospel to accept it, he may have many of the blessings of the gospel. In spite of all he did in the pre-
   existent life, the Lord is willing, if the Negro accepts
   the gospel with real, sincere faith, and is really con-
   verted, to give him the blessings of baptism and the
   gift of the Holy Ghost. If that Negro is faithful all his
   days, he can and will enter the celestial kingdom. He
   will go there as a servant, but he will get celestial
   glory.

   *Race Problems—As They Affect
   the Church*
   Address by Mark E. Petersen at the
   Convention of Teachers of Religion on

the College Level, Brigham Young
University, Provo, Utah
August 27, 1954

3. *From the days of the Prophet Joseph even until now,*
   it has been the doctrine of the Church, never
   questioned by any of the Church leaders, that the
   Negroes are not entitled to the full blessings of the
   Gospel.

Letter from the First Presidency of the
Mormon Church, July 17, 1947,
quoted in
Mormonism and the Negro, by John J.
Steward and William E. Berrett,
Part I, pages 46 and 47

4. We will first inquire into the results of the appro-
bation or displeasure of God upon a people, starting
with the belief that a black skin is a mark of the curse
of heaven placed upon some portions of mankind.
Some, however, will argue that a black skin is not a
curse, nor a white skin a blessing. In fact some have
been so foolish as to believe and say that a black skin
is a blessing, and that the negro is the finest type of a
perfect man that exists on the earth but to us such
teachings are foolishness. We understand that when
God made man in his own image and pronounced
him very good, that he made him white. We have no
record of any of God's favored servants being of a
black race. All his prophets and apostles belonged to
the most handsome race on the face of the
earth—Israel, who still, as represented in the scattered tribe of Judah, bear the impress of their former
beauty. In this race was born His Son Jesus, who, we
are told was very lovely, and "in the express image of
His Father's person," and every angel who ever
brought a message of God's mercy to man was
beautiful to look upon, clad in the purest white and
with a countenance bright as the noonday sun.
Juvenile Instructor 3:157

5. The Negro Mormon can hold no office whatsoever in
a church which offers some office to every one of its
male members at some time in his life. . . . To hold

any church office, a Mormon must be a member of the priesthood.

Wallace Turner,
The Mormon Establishment, Boston,
1966, pages 243-44.

6. At the time the devil was cast out of heaven, there were some spirits that did not know who had authority, whether God or the devil. They consequently did not take a very active part on either side, but rather thought the devil had been abused, and considered he had rather the best claim to the government. These spirits were not considered bad enough to be cast down to hell, and never have bodies; neither were they considered worthy of an honourable body on this earth; but it came to pass that Ham, the son of Noah, saw the nakedness of his father while he lay drunk in his tent . . . and made the wonderful disclosure to his brethren; while Shem and Japeth took a garment, with pity and compassion, laid it upon their shoulders—went backwards and covered their father, and saw not his nakedness. The joy of the first was to expose—that of the second was to cover the unseemliness of their father. The conduct of the former brought the curse of slavery upon him, while that of the latter secured blessings, jurisdiction, power and dominion. Here was the beginning of blessing and cursing in the family of Noah, and here also is the cause of both. Cannan, the son of Ham, received the curse; for Noah wished to place the curse as remote from himself as possible. . . . But those spirits in heaven that rather lent an influence to the devil, thinking he had a little the best right to govern, but did not take a very active part any way were required to come into the world and take bodies in the accursed lineage of Canaan; and hence the Negro of African race.

Speech of Elder Orson Hyde,
delivered before the High Priests'
Quorum in Nauvoo,
April 27, 1845, printed in
Liverpool, page 30

Note the similarity to pagan Greek theology: "He [Pythagoras] taught that 'All mankind lived in some pre-existent state, and that for the sins committed by them in that state, some of their souls were sent into human bodies, and others into brutes, to be punished for, and to be purged from, their former sins.' " (*The Christian Baptist* 1:165).

7. ... Is it not possible to see an act of mercy on the part of God in not having the Negro bear the Priesthood in this world, in view of his living under the curse of a black skin and other Negroid features?
   Mormonism and the Negro,
   Part I, page 50

8. It was the Lord's decision to send those spirits who proved themselves unworthy of the Priesthood in the pre-existence through the lineage of Cain. ... The Priesthood, which is the authority to act in the name of God in performing ordinances of the Gospel, is denied to the Negroes because of their behavior in the pre-mortal existence. ... all those who are descendants of Cain have been restricted concerning the Priesthood because they were unworthy in the pre-existence.

   The curse of no Priesthood for Cain was totally different from the curse of no Priesthood for the Negroes, who are the descendants of Cain. Negroes are kept from holding the Priesthood because of something they did before they came to earth; Cain was damned because of something he did while on the earth.
   The Church and the Negro, pages 107-9

9. In the evening debated with John C. Bennett and others to show that the Indians have greater cause to complain of the treatment of the whites, than the negroes, or sons of Cain.
   Joseph Smith, Jr., *History of the Church* 4:501,
   January 25, 1842

10. Though he was a rebel and an associate of Lucifer in pre-existence, and though he was a liar from the beginning whose name was *Perdition*, *Cain* managed to attain the privilege of mortal birth. Under Adam's tutelage, he began in this life to serve God ... he came out in open rebellion, fought God, worshiped Lucifer, and slew Abel. ...

   As a result of his rebellion, Cain was cursed with a dark skin; he became the father of the Negroes, and

those spirits who are not worthy to receive the priesthood are born through his lineage. He became the
first mortal to be cursed as a son of perdition. As a
result of his mortal birth he is assured of a tangible
body of flesh and bones in eternity, a fact which will
enable him to rule over Satan.

> Bruce R. McConkie, *Mormon
> Doctrine*, 1966 ed., pages 108-9

11. What was that mark? It was a mark of blackness.
    That mark rested upon Cain, and descended upon
    his posterity from that time until the present. To day
    there are millions of the descendants of Cain,
    through the lineage of Ham, in the world, and that
    mark of darkness still rests upon them.

> Wilford Woodruff, *Millennial
> Star* 51:339

12. For behold, the Lord shall curse the land with much
    heat, and the barrenness thereof shall go forth for-
    ever; and there was a blackness came upon all the
    children of Canaan, that they were despised among
    all people.

> *Pearl of Great Price*, Book of
> Moses 7:8 ·

13. Cain slew his brother. Cain might have been killed,
    and that would have put a termination to that line of
    human beings. This was not to be, and the Lord put
    a mark upon him, which is the flat nose and black
    skin.

> Brigham Young, *Journal of
> Discourses* 7:290

14. Frankly, sincerely, and somewhat abruptly, Presi-
    dent Brigham Young has told us that the mark of
    Cain was a "black skin." For the Latter-day Saint no
    further explanation is required. . . . The question as
    to what the mark of Cain was, and is, is thus an-
    swered—a black skin for him and his posterity.

> *The Church and the Negro*,
> 1967, pages 13-14

15. Noah's son Ham married Egyptus, a descendant of
    Cain, thus preserving the negro lineage through the
    flood.

> Bruce R. McConkie,
> *Mormon Doctrine*
> 1966 ed., page 527

16. Now this king of Egypt was a descendant from the loins of Ham, and was a partaker of the blood of the Canaanites by birth.

   From this descent sprang all the Egyptians, and thus the blood of the Canaanites was preserved in the land.

   The land of Egypt being first discovered by a woman, who was the daughter of Ham, and the daughter of Egyptus, which in the Chaldean signifies Egypt, which signifies that which is forbidden.

   When this woman discovered the land it was under water, who afterward settled her sons in it; and thus, from Ham, sprang that race which preserved the curse in the land.

   Now the first government of Egypt was established by Pharaoh, the eldest son of Egyptus, the daughter of Ham, and it was after the manner of the government of Ham, which was patriarchal.

   Pharaoh, being a righteous man . . . seeking earnestly to imitate that order established by the fathers in the first generations, in the days of the first patriarchal reign, even in the reign of Adam, and also of Noah, his father, who blessed him with the blessings of the earth, and with the blessings of wisdom, but cursed him as pertaining to the priesthood.

   Pearl of Great Price, Book of Abraham
   1:21-26

17. We do not believe in the permanency of a race descended from the people so wide apart as the Anglo-Saxon and Negro. In fact we believe it to be a great sin in the eyes of our Heavenly Father for a white person to marry a black one. And further, that it is a proof of the mercy of God that no such race appear able to continue for many generations.

   Juvenile Instructor 3:165

18. Shall I tell you the law of God in regard to the African race? If the white man who belongs to the chosen seed mixes his blood with the seed of Cain, the penalty, under the law of God, is death on the spot. This will always be so.

   Brigham Young, *Journal of Discourses*
   10:110

19. *ANY MAN HAVING ONE DROP OF THE SEED OF CAIN IN HIM CANNOT RECEIVE THE PRIESTHOOD. . . .*°

> Wilford Woodruff, by Mathias F. Cowley, page 351, quoted in *That Ye May Not Be Deceived*, page 8

20. The descendants of Cain were barred from the blessings of the Priesthood. They may be baptized for the remission of their sins, but they cannot hold the Priesthood by divine decree, as pointed out in the Book of Abraham. It would be a serious error for a white person to marry a Negro, for the Lord forbad it.

> Letter from Joseph Fielding Smith, dated May 9, 1966

Those who defend the Mormon Church and its 138 year record of racism should consider the evidence cited, as well as the evidence which space does not permit us to present but which is readily available. In the light of the historic teachings of the gospel of Jesus Christ and the Christian church, we know that the Mormons' "restored gospel" is in reality "another gospel" (Galatians 1:6-9; 2 Corinthians 11:4).

The Muddied Scandal

The Negro issue has snowballed, due to the scandal of *The Book of Abraham* and the evidence of Joseph Smith's conviction as a fortune-teller and "glass-looker." This is a scandal of enormous proportions in the history of religion in the United States.

One incident which recently occurred involved a Mormon High Priest who, disgusted with the racist doctrine of *The Book of Abraham*, ordained a black member of his congregation (Larry Lester, age 22, of Vancouver, Washington) to the Aaronic Priesthood. Mr. Wallace said:

°Emphasis theirs.

"I ordained Lester to force a revision of Mormon doctrine regarding blacks." Wallace chose yesterday, Friday, April 3rd, because the Church opens its annual general conference in Salt Lake City this weekend.

At a news conference preceding the ceremony, Wallace said he is a member of a Vancouver congregation and a High Priest in the Melchizedek Priesthood, which he said involves greater responsibilities than the Aaronic.

Robert Seamons, president of the Church's Portland, Oregon, mission, said Wallace "used the Priesthood in an unrighteous manner and his action will have no validity because the President of the Church has said that blacks are not to hold the Priesthood."

Robert E. McGee, public communications director of Vancouver stake (comparable in size to a Catholic diocese) issued a statement saying the action was null and void. He said:

"Under the established procedures of the Church a person is not ordained to the Priesthood or any office therein until authorization has been given by a presiding officer in the Church and the candidate's name is submitted to the Priesthood membership of the stake of ward for approval."

At the news conference Wallace said he was born into the Mormon Church in Ogden, Utah, and served as a Mormon missionary in England.

He said he had long been bothered by what he calls the Church's bias against blacks and felt the time had come to challenge it. He said the Church's posture on the question is based on the idea that God has not spoken on it.

Honolulu Star Bulletin, April 4, 1976,
page A-4

What Mr. Wallace kindled threatened to turn into a raging inferno. The *Bulletin* again drew attention to the story in an article entitled "Mormons In Stew About Black Priest." It was reported that Jerry Cahill, the Church spokesman in Salt Lake City who released the statement, added,

"I am a High Priest myself and I have no authority to baptize my own children unless they are first interviewed and approved by a Bishop and authorization is granted for the ceremony." He said local Church members as well as the Bishop must approve candidates for baptism before the baptism takes effect.

Cahill said that excommunication proceedings against Wallace or Lester "would be a decision of the Bishop or Stake President." Both are members of the third ward of the Vancouver Stake of the Church.

Wallace said that any move to excommunicate the two would be opposed by more members of their ward.

Ibid., page A-17

Within that same article, however, a very interesting statement appeared:

The Mormon Church said yesterday that Friday's ordination of a black as a Priest is "null and void" because proper procedures were not followed. The Church made no mention of its century-old taboo against blacks.

The Contradictory Teachings

Of many other points that could be raised in this area, none is more interesting than the fact that Joseph Smith, Jr., himself ordained a black man, Elijah Abel, to the Priesthood in direct violation of what "God had said." Further, the descendants of that man were also ordained. Space does not permit us to go into the entire case history, but the reader is urged to consult the publication *Mormons and Negros*, by Jerald and Sandra Tanner, where the entire matter (evidence and quotations) is discussed. (See particularly pages 11-22 under the heading "Negroes in the Priesthood.") Abel was ordained an elder on March 3, 1836, and ordained a member of the Seventy on April 4, 1841, in Nauvoo, Illinois.

The Mormon Church has historically refused (until the "new revelation" of June 9, 1978) to ordain blacks to the Priesthood; however, the case of Elijah Abel remains a historical thorn in Smith's racist religion. When Spencer W. Kimball, current President of the LDS Church, recently received a "revelation" from one of the Mormon gods, this action removed the disagreeable stigma of racial predjudice, but it produced an even greater problem for the prophets of Mormondom and their present-day revelation.

The Mormon Church has already denied the Adam-God revelation of Brigham Young, calling it "false doctrine," (in 1976) and now they must also deny Brigham Young's revelations concerning "when the curse would be lifted" from the black man. They must also deny President Joseph Fielding Smith's present-day revelation concerning the veracity of Brigham Young's revelations on this subject. If the Mormons deny that the revelations were true, they must also deny that their former prophets were inspired by God. But if they admit this, the whole structure of the Church of Jesus Christ of Latter-day Saints (Utah) collapses. Let us listen to Brigham Young as recorded in the writings of Joseph Fielding Smith:

When the Curse Will Be Removed

> On another occasion in a discourse President Brigham Young said:

> Cain conversed with his God every day, and knew all about the plan of creating this earth, for his father told him. But, for the want of humility, and through jealousy, and an anxiety to possess the kingdom, and to have the whole of it under his own control, and not allow any body else the right to say one word, what did he do? He killed his brother. The Lord put a mark on him. . . . When all the other children of Adam have had the privilege of receiving the Priesthood, and of coming into the kingdom of God, and of being redeemed from the four quarters of the earth, and have received their resurrection from the dead, then it will be time enough to remove the curse from Cain and his posterity. He deprived his brother of the privilege of pursuing his journey through life, and of extending his kingdom by multiplying upon the earth; and because he did this, he is the last to share the joys of the kingdom of God.—J. D. 2:142-143.
>
> Joseph Fielding Smith,
> *The Way to Perfection*, page 106

Notice the caption from the book on the above section—"When the Curse Will Be Removed." The time is as follows:

1. When all the other children of Adam have had the privilege of receiving the Priesthood.
2. When all the other children of Adam have been resurrected.

Has every white Mormon male been ordained to the priesthood? According to this "revelation" by President Young, the Mormon Church should only be proselyting the Negro. Also, all the white Mormon Priesthood holders should now have their resurrected bodies of flesh and bone!

Again, President Smith records the words of Young found in a journal by Wilford Woodruff, also a former "Prophet, Seer, and Revelator" to the Mormon people.

> President Woodruff, in his journal, records the words of President Young as follows:

> The Lord said I will not kill Cain, but I will put a mark upon him, and that mark will be seen upon the face of every negro upon the face of the earth; and it is the decree of God that that mark shall remain upon the seed of Cain until the seed of Abel shall be redeemed, and Cain shall not receive the priesthood, until the time of that redemption. Any man having one drop of the seed of Cain in him cannot receive the priesthood; but the day will come when all that race will be redeemed and possess all the blessings which we now have.
>
> *Wilford Woodruff—History*
> *of His Life and Labors*, page 351.

Mormons sometimes attempt to ignore the words of Brigham Young by claiming that he did not always speak as a prophet. To that we heartily agree, but when Brigham acclaimed, "The Lord said" and "it is the decree of God," he was speaking as a Prophet of the Mormon god. What is a requirement for the Priesthood for the black man in the above "revelation"? The mark of the black skin should remain upon the face of every Negro *until* Abel's seed shall be redeemed. When did Abel have children? When were they redeemed? If they have already been redeemed (according to the "new revelation" of June 9, 1978), why does the mark of the black skin for the Negro continue? Let us listen to President Young:

> Cain slew his brother. Cain might have been killed, and that would have put a termination to that line of human beings. This was not to be, and the Lord put a mark upon him, which is the flat nose and black skin. Trace mankind down to after the flood, and then another curse is pronounced upon the same race—that they should be the "servant of servants;" and they will be, until that curse is removed; and the Abolitionists cannot help it, nor in the least alter that decree. How long is that race to endure the dreadful curse that is upon them? That curse will remain upon them, and they never can hold the Priesthood or share in it until all the other descendants of Adam have received the promises and enjoyed the blessings of the Priesthood and the keys thereof. Until the last ones of the residue of Adam's children are brought up to that favourable position, the children of Cain cannot receive the first ordinances of the Priesthood. They were the first that were cursed, and they will be the last from whom the curse will be removed. When the residue of the family of Adam come up and receive their blessings, then the curse will be removed from the seed of Cain, and they will receive blessings in like proportion.
>
> *Journal of Discourses*, 7:290-291
> (October 16, 1859)

Brigham Young's revelation was given during the deplorable days of human slavery in this country, when people who fought this practice were known as "abolitionists." The abolitionists succeeded in abolishing slavery which they knew was *not* a decree of God. There is no denying when the curse would be removed, according to Brigham Young's god: "Until the last ones of the residue of the family of Adam" had received the Priesthood and the blessings they were told will follow. Did President Kimball say that no one *except* black people will now be allowed in the Priesthood? No, so we have one Mormon prophet irreconcilably contradicting another, and both allegedly speaking in the name of God! (See President Kimball's statement given on June 9, 1978, that follows.)

As we have witnessed the expansion of the work of the Lord over the earth, we have been grateful that people of many nations have responded to the message of the re-stored gospel, and have joined the Church in ever-increasing numbers. This, in turn, has inspired us with a desire to extend to every worthy member of the Church all of the privileges and blessings which the gospel affords.

Aware of the promises made by the prophets and presidents of the Church who have preceeded us that at some time, in God's eternal plan, all of our brethren who are worthy may receive the priesthood, and witnessing the faithfulness of those from whom the priesthood has been withheld, we have pleaded long and earnestly in behalf of these, our faithful brethren, spending many hours in the upper room of the temple supplicating the Lord for divine guidance.

He has heard our prayers, and by revelation has con-firmed that the long-promised day has come when every faithful, worthy man in the Church may receive the holy priesthood, with power to exercise its divine authority, and enjoy with his loved ones every blessing that flows therefrom, including the blessings of the temple. Accord-ingly, all worthy male members of the Church may be or-dained to the priesthood without regard for race or color. Priesthood leaders are instructed to follow the policy of carefully interviewing all candidates for ordination to either the Aaronic or Melchizedek Priesthood to insure that they meet the established standards for worthiness.

We declare with soberness that the Lord has now made known his will for the blessing of all his children through-out the earth who will hearken to the voice of his authorized servants, and prepare themselves to receive every blessing of the gospel.

There exists yet another problem in regard to *The Book of Abraham* allegedly denying the Priesthood to the Ne-gro. It *never* mentions that the Negro cannot hold the Priesthood, but it claims that "the curse" was preserved through Ham and Egypt (Abraham 1:21, 22, 24, 26, 27): "From this descent sprang all the Egyptians and thus the blood of the Canaanites was preserved in the land."

Joseph Smith, Jr., claimed to be from the tribe of

Ephraim and many Mormons make the same claim. *The Book of Mormon* informs us that the Nephites and Lamanites, whose father was Lehi, were descendants of Manasseh, whose father was Joseph, who was sold into Egypt. Keeping in mind that the curse which prevented a man from holding either of the Mormon Priesthoods came through *all* the Egyptians, let us listen to what God has revealed about Joseph's wife as recorded by Moses in the Bible:

> And Pharoah called Joseph's name Zaphnathpaaneah; and he gave him to wife Asenath the daughter of Potipherah priest of On. And Joseph went out over all the land of Egypt.
>
> Genesis 41:45

What we want to note in this passage is that Joseph's wife, Asenath, was an Egyptian.

> And unto Joseph were born two sons before the years of famine came, which Asenath the daughter of Potipherah priest of On bare unto him. And Joseph called the name of the firstborn Manasseh: For God, said he, hath made me forget all my toil, and all my father's house. And the name of the second called he Ephraim: For God hath caused me to be fruitful in the land of my affliction.
>
> Genesis 41:50-52

If *all* the Egyptians preserved the curse of Cain and Ham through Egyptus, as *The Book of Abraham* claims, then Joseph Smith, who claimed to be from the tribe of Ephraim (and a great many Mormons also make the same claim, regardless of their nationality) would be ineligible to hold the Mormon Priesthood! *The Book of Mormon* informs us that the Nephites and the Lamanites were descendants of Manasseh, whose father was Joseph, who was sold into Egypt, so they too would have been ineligible to hold the Priesthood!

The New Testament Truth

The New Testament declares that through the gospel

Christ has broken down *all* barriers that separate us from one another as Christians:

> For ye are all the children of God by faith in Christ Jesus. For as many of you as have been baptized into Christ have put on Christ. There is neither Jew nor Greek, there is neither bond nor free, there is neither male nor female; *for ye are all one in Christ Jesus.* And if ye be Christ's, then are ye Abraham's seed, and heirs according to the promise.
>
> Galatians 3:26-29

> Lie not one to another, seeing that ye have put off the old man with his deeds, and have put on the new man, which is renewed in knowledge after the image of him that created him; where there is neither Greek nor Jew, circumcision nor uncirumcision, Barbarian, Scythian, bond nor free, *but Christ is all, and in all.*
>
> Colossians 3:9-11

> And, having made peace through the blood of his cross, by him to reconcile all things unto himself; by him, I say, whether they be things in earth or things in heaven. And you, that were sometime alienated and enemies in your mind by wicked works, *yet now hath he reconciled in the body of his flesh through death,* to present you holy and unblamable and unreprovable in his sight, if ye continue in the faith grounded and settled, and be not moved away from the hope of the gospel, which ye have heard, and which was preached to every creature which is under heaven, whereof I Paul am made a minister.
>
> Colossians 1:20-23

> To whom God would make known what is the riches of the glory of this mystery among the Gentiles, which is Christ in you, the hope of glory; whom we preach, warning every man, and teaching every man in all wisdom, that we may present *every man perfect in Christ Jesus.*
>
> Colossians 1:27, 28

> For in him dwelleth all the fulness of the Godhead bodily. And *ye are complete in him,* who is the head of all principality and power.
>
> Colossians 2:9, 10

Let Mormons consider that the Apostle Paul antedated Joseph Smith, that he alone of all the apostles entered heaven in the spirit (2 Corinthians 12:2-4), yet could still write that *all* the redeemed of the earth are part of God's family in heaven, without racist discrimination. Mormonism is not the New Testament Church with the "restored gospel," but is a careful counterfeit which for 148 years has contradicted the Bible and the Savior which it purports to present.

The Reasoning Behind the New Revelation

The following dialogue with Apostle LeGrand Richards, a close friend and counselor of Mormon President Spencer W. Kimball, is a most important historical document. It shows for the first time why and how the latest Mormon "revelation" admitting Blacks to the Mormon priesthood came about. It cannot be disregarded by any serious student of the Latter-day Saints Church — Mormon or non-Mormon alike — particularly since Apostle Richards gave permission for the interviewer to quote him.

> *Interviewer:* You know, on this revelation of granting the priesthood to the Negro, I have heard all kinds of stories. I have heard that Christ appeared to the Apostles. I have heard that Joseph Smith appeared. And then I heard another story that Spencer Kimball had had a concern about this for some time and that he shared it with the Apostles, and they decided that this was the right time to move in that direction. Now, are any of those stories true?
>
> *Richards:* Well, the last one was pretty true. And I might tell you what provoked it in a way. Down in Brazil there is so much Negro blood in the population that it's hard to get leaders that don't have Negro blood in them. We just built a temple down there and it's going to be dedicated in October. And a lot of those people with Negro blood in them have been raising the money to build that temple. If we don't change, then they can't even use it after it's there.
>
> So Brother Kimball worried about it, and he prayed a lot about it. And he asked each one of us of the Twelve if *we* would pray. And we did, that the Lord would give us the inspiration to know what the Lord wants. And then he invited each one of us in his office individually because,

you know, when you're in a group you can't always say everything that's in your heart. You have to be part of a group, see? So he interviewed each one of us personally to see how we felt about it. And he asked *us* to pray about it.

Then he asked each one of us to hand in all of the references we had for or against that proposal. He was thinking favorably toward giving authority for the priesthood. Then we had a meeting where we meet every week in the temple, and we discussed it as a group. And then we prayed about it in our prayer circle and then we held another prayer circle after the close of that meeting. And he led in the prayer, praying that the Lord would give us the inspiration that we needed to do the things that would be pleasing to Him and for the blessing of His children.

Then, the next Thursday (we meet every Thursday) the Presidency came with this little document written out to make the announcement and see how we felt about it when it was presented in its written form. Well, some of the members of the Twelve suggested that there be a few changes in the announcement. And then, in our meeting, they all voted in favor of it—the Twelve and the Seventy. One member of the Twelve, Mark Petersen, was down in South America; but Brother Benson, our President, had arranged to know where he could be reached by phone. And right while we were in our meeting at the temple Brother Kimball talked to Brother Petersen and read him the article, and he approved of it.

Int: What was the date?

R: The first Thursday, I think, in May.

And then, after we all voted in favor of it, we called another meeting for the next morning, Friday at seven o'clock, of all the others. That included the Seventy Quorum and the Patriarch and the Guiding Bishopric. And it was presented to them and they all had an opportunity to express themselves. Then, there were a few of them that were out guiding in the missions and so the Twelve were appointed to interview each one of them.

I had to interview Brother Rex Reeve. I read him the article and asked him his feelings and he was thrilled because he labors down there in Brazil and he knew what it would mean for those people. And so every member of the General Authority to a man approved it before the announcement was to come out.

Now, we have a letter from our third man up in Ogden. He was a member of the Church and he said: "If the Lord is willing to let me have my wife and children in this life, why wouldn't He be willing to let me have them in the next life?" That makes sense, doesn't it? And then, you know, the Lord gave a revelation to the Prophet Joseph where He said it was "irrevocably decreed in the heavens before the foundations of the earth were laid upon which all blessings are predicated and no blessings can be obtained except by obedience to the laws upon which it's predicated." Now that means if you want to raise wheat, you've got to plant wheat, doesn't it? If you want to raise corn you've got to plant corn. If I plant wheat and get a harvest, and the colored plants wheat and takes good care of it, why isn't he as much entitled to the harvest as I am? And then, couldn't we feel the same with spiritual revelations? If the colored man lives as good as I do and serves the Lord and so forth, why isn't he as much entitled to the blessings as I am? Since we changed the decision, there've been no adverse comments by anyone.

Int: What about intermarriage? Is it okay? Was that in view, too?

R: Well, no, never before this decision was reached. We've always recommended that people live within their own race—Japanese ought to marry Japanese; Chinese ought to marry Chinese; Hawaiians ought to marry Hawaiians; and the colored people ought to marry colored.

Int: And that would still be your position?

R: That is still our position. But they are entitled to their temple blessings—the sealing of their wives to them—all conditioned on their living. Now, if they live right and they're devoted and they're good, clean living, why shouldn't they get the blessings?

Int: Will this become a part of Scripture?

R: Yes, I've already thought in my own mind of suggesting that we add it to the *Pearl of Great Price* just like those last two revelations that we've just added.

Int: Is there a special reason why you added to the *Pearl of Great Price* rather than to *Doctrine and Covenants*? Is it just more convenient to put it in there instead of adding another number or something?

R: I don't know, but we didn't discuss the reasons it should go in which book. But the *Pearl of Great Price* was written and assembled later than the *Doctrine and Covenants* was. (My grandfather was one that organized the *Pearl of Great Price*.) When we discussed it in our meeting we didn't discuss whether it should go in the *Doctrine and Covenants* or the *Pearl of Great Price*; we just discussed how it would be to add those two revelations in the *Pearl of Great Price*.

Int: Now, will this affect your theological thinking about the Negro as being less valued in the previous existence? How does this relate? Have you thought that through?

R: Some time ago the Brethren decided that we should never say that. You don't know just what the reason was. Paul said, "The Lord hath before appointed the bounds of the habitations of all man for to grow upon the face of the earth." And so, if He determined that *before* we were born who knows why—why they were born with black skin and why we aren't and so forth? We'll just have to wait and find out.

Int: Is there still a tendency to feel that people are born with black skin because of some previous existence situation? Or do we consider that black skin is no sign anymore of anything inferior in any sense of the word?

R: Think of it as you will. You know, Paul said, "Now we see in part and we know in part. We see through a glass darkly. When that which is perfect is come, that which is in part shall be done away. Then we will see as we are seen and know as we are known." Now, the Church's attitude for today is just to leave it until we know. The Lord has *never* indicated that that black skin came because of their being less faithful. Now the Indian—we *know* why he was changed, don't we? Because of what *The Book of Mormon* tells us and he gets his dark skin, but he has a promise that through faithfulness that they shall then become a white delightsome people. But we haven't *anything* like that for the colored people.

Int: Now, has this new revelation brought any new insights or new ways of looking at *The Book of Abraham*? Because I think traditionally, he may have thought of the "curse of Cain" coming through Canaanites and on the black-skinned people, and therefore denying the priesthood.

R: Well, we considered that with all the fors and againsts again, and we decided that if they followed that, and if they lived their lives and did the work, that they were entitled to their blessings.

Int: Is the recent revelation in harmony with what the past prophets have taught of when the Negro would receive the Melchizedek priesthood.

R: Well they have held up the thought that they would ultimately get the priesthood, but they never determined a time for it. So Brother Kimball worried a lot about this situation we see down there in Brazil, about a people that are so faithful and devoted. The president of the Relief Society of that stake down there is a colored woman from the stake. They do the work. It seemed like the justice of the Lord would approve of giving them the blessings. It's all conditional on the lives that they live.

Int: Thank you for clarifying that for me, because you know out in the streets there must be at least five to ten different stories about the way this happened.

R: Well, I told you *exactly* what happened.

Int: Right. Well, thank you so much. I appreciate it.

R: And if you quote me, why you'll be telling the truth.

SEVEN

PUBLIC RELATIONS

—

Mormonism's Masquerade

As our analysis of the Mormon Church is revealing, Mormonism is a vast religioeconomic and political empire. It lays a great deal of stress upon its public image, and goes out of its way to maintain good public relations wherever possible. However, the Mormons have not yet convinced even the liberal National Council of Churches or the World Council of Churches that they are a Christian denomination. As liberal as some elements of these organizations are, they are not devoid of the capacity to differentiate between a polytheistic cult and a Christian sect.

The Mormon Tabernacle Choir is an excellent public relations device for the Church. The Church is also promoted by its members in the public eye (like, for example, Donnie and Marie Osmond and the Osmond Family). As mentioned in Chapter 1, each year the Mormon Church Conference is broadcast throughout the United States. The well-known King and Marriott families also actively promote the Church.

The Mormon cultural center in Hawaii, innocently called the Polynesian Cultural Center, testifies to the ingenuity of the LDS Church. Hundreds of thousands of people are exposed each year to Mormonism under the guise of a tour and lecture on Polynesian culture! Around the world, the Mormon Church has invested billions of dollars in business enterprises. All of these are, in one way or another, utilized to enhance the public image of the Mormon Church.

Mormonism is apparently determined to win approval as uniquely Christian. For them this means that they are, to the exclusion of all other groups, the Church of Jesus Christ, the sole voice of God on earth today. Brigham Young clearly believed the idea that the Mormon Church was God's only organization and Joseph Smith its greatest spokesman:

> Every intelligent person under the heavens that does not, when informed, acknowledge that Joseph Smith, jun., is a Prophet of God, is in darkness, and is opposed to us and to Jesus and his kingdom on the earth. What do you suppose I think of them? They cannot conceive their own degradation. If they could, they would turn away from their wickedness. I know them, but they do not know me. We live in an atmosphere they do not approach; they have not ability to see the path we walk in. Would I treat them as badly as they would treat us? No. They would murder us in a moment, if they had the power, unless we would renounce our religion. But they are trifling with their own existence, when they measure arms with the Almighty. All the day long we have extended to our enemies the hand of mercy and charity. We would offer to them life and salvation. What would they offer to us? Death and damnation, if they had the power; but they have not the power, and never will have.
>
> Brigham Young, *Journal of Discourses* 8:223

The Vulnerable Image

In 1975 I challenged that image by suing the corporation of the Presidency of the Church of Jesus Christ of

Latter-day Saints, Bruce A. Johnson (president of a local quorum of Mormon elders in his church), the Santa Ana Institute of Religion in Santa Ana, California, the Anaheim Mission in Anaheim, California, and various bishops and individuals in the Mormon Church for defaming, libeling, and slandering me publicly. It is the counter-claim of the Mormon Church that I have misrepresented what Brigham Young and Joseph Smith said and what Mormonism teaches, even though the material which I have quoted repeatedly in lectures (spanning over 25 years) are more than 90 percent from LDS sources. This case will come to trial in Orange County, California, assuming the success of our petition to the California Court of Appeals. The challenge was made to establish the truth. However, my appeal was rejected and the case never came to full court. While the testimony already heard is invaluable, one can only wonder what else would have been revealed had the case not been refused on technical grounds. Utilizing the principle of the Apostle Paul, "I appeal to Caesar" (Acts 25:11), I attempted to have the Mormon Church once and for all legally confirm or deny its own prophets and their teachings.

I am not in the business of attacking other people's religions, but I am responsible for both proclaiming and defending the gospel of Jesus Christ against those who attack it. The Mormon Church, from Joseph Smith to the present-day leaders, has in its theological pronouncements mounted precisely such an attack, and silence in the face of such attacks surely constitutes the sin of omission.

My suit against the Mormon Church was not for the intent of personal gain. All recovered funds (aside from expenses) would have been used exclusively for the continued ministry of the gospel among Mormons and other cultists. It is perfectly true that Christians are not permitted to sue other Christians in courts of law (1 Corinthians 6:1-8), but the Mormon Church had never been classified as Christian by the Christian Church. It is in the interest of both the

Christian church and sincere but misled Mormons that I undertook this difficult action.

Mormonism asserts not only that all non-Mormons are "Gentiles" but that all professing Christian churches are apostate from the true Christian religion. They claim it was restored to earth by their prophet, Joseph Smith. It was Smith who affirmed that God told him that "sects . . . were all wrong," that all the creeds of Christendom "were an abomination" in God's sight, and that those who professed the Christian religion, regardless of denomination, were "all corrupt" (*Pearl of Great Price*, Joseph Smith, 2:1-25). It is the Mormon Church which attacks Christianity, and it is therefore the responsibility of every Christian minister and every disciple of Jesus Christ to defend by all lawful means "the faith once for all delivered to the saints" (Jude 3).

What Is A Christian?

Samuel W. Taylor, a Mormon author, wrote in answer to the question, "Are Mormons Christian?" the following reply:

> Yes, indeed—but neither Protestant nor Catholic. Mormons believe that there was a breaking away of the other churches from true Christianity and that their religion is the restored Gospel.[1]

It is evident that Mormonism strives to masquerade as *the* Christian church, complete with an exclusive message, infallible prophets, restored priesthoods, and higher revelations.

The Mormon Church's public relations approach has been most successful in recent years. As far back as 1940, Hollywood produced a stirring motion picture entitled

---

[1]*The American Weekly*, April 3, 1955.

"Brigham Young." This was actually a historical travesty, glorifying Smith's polygamous successor and carefully omitting his unsavory past and open immorality. A new motion picture entitled "Brigham" was released in 1978, dealing with the same subject matter as the 1940 film.

The Mormons have been aided in their propaganda by two seldom-considered factors: 1) the concept that people who "live good lives" and establish a religion that "lasts" and multiplies must be Christian, and 2) the lethargy of the Christian church in failing to recognize the goals of the Mormon Church and in failing to implement steps to unmask, combat, and effectively evangelize them.

A very clear-cut example of the first point is found in S. W. Taylor's article previously referred to. To the question "Was Joseph Smith a fraud?" Mr. Taylor answered:

> Mormons answer this by pointing to the fruits of Mormonism. Could a fraud, they ask, have established a Church that would thrive under almost a century of unrelenting attack?

The answer to Mr. Taylor's question is, of course, a most emphatic *yes*. Turn to the history of cultic pied pipers, and you will see that many of them have thrived under persecution. Charles Russell and Joseph Rutherford of Jehovah's Witnesses, Mary Baker Eddy of Christian Science, Charles and Myrtle Fillmore of the Unity School of Christianity, "St. Germain" Ballard of The Mighty I Am Movement, Madam Blavatsky of Theosophy, the late Father Divine (who graphically demonstrated that he was not God by dying!), and currently such pseudo-Christian entrepreneurs as Reverend Ike, L. Ron Hubbard of Scientology, Sun Myung Moon of the Unification Church, Moses David Berg (pornographic false prophet of the Family of Love cult), and Herbert Armstrong have all suffered opposition and still thrived. Religions founded by others have also endured great persecutions, are apparently growing, and are spiritual enemies of historic Christianity. If the Mormons regard attacks and endurance as a test of spiritual validity or reliability, they would have to accept other cults—and this they are unwilling to do!

The New Testament painstakingly warns Christians not to be deceived by a "form of godliness" (2 Timothy 3:5) but are instead to "test the spirits" (1 John 4:1) by God's Word to see if the teachings conform to sound doctrine. Mormonism's teachings do *not* pass this test.

False prophets often duplicate miracles through Satan (Exodus 7:11, 22) and live lives that appear "good" but which in reality are devoid of the faith that saves (Ephesians 2:8, 9). The Lord Jesus Christ taught that "the work of God" is to "believe on him whom he [God] hath sent" (John 6:29). This He said in answer to those who wanted to know how to do the "good" works of His Father. The Mormon Church may appear Christian by human standards of judgment, and its religion is apparently productive of "good works." However, underneath its pseudo-Christianity lies the denial of "the only Lord God and our Lord Jesus Christ" (Jude 4). It is a subtle substitution of "another gospel" allegedly delivered by "an angel from heaven" as Paul predicted Satan would do (Galatians 1:8, 9).

There are good-hearted people who claim that Mormonism "just couldn't be such a bad religion. After all," they say, "it quotes the Bible and speaks of faith in Jesus Christ, along with other Christian doctrines. How can you be so sure, then, that it is false and even at times devilish?"

Recently I was vigorously criticized by a Christian businessman who said that all the Mormons he knew were Christians. When I produced evidence to show the semantic maze which the Mormon Church utilizes to convey just such an impression, he was shocked and visibly shaken. He had been taken in by them, because they redefined their terms and practiced some Christian principles.

The Nature of a Counterfeit

We must understand the nature of a counterfeit, and

the elaborate preparations necessary to fashion an effective counterfeit.

Dr. Donald Grey Barnhouse, noted Bible teacher and late editor of *Eternity* Magazine, wisely pointed out that if someone wishes to counterfeit a ten-dollar bill, a definite form must be followed. The careful counterfeiter does not make the bill triangular or circular, nor does he print it in purple and yellow ink with Donald Duck's picture on it. Instead, he faithfully reproduces the size, shape, and details of the bill, complete with Alexander Hamilton's portrait, knowing that if he is to "pass" it successfully it must resemble the genuine in every particular.

This analogy holds true where pseudo-Christian sects, such as Mormonism, are concerned. Satan, the great counterfeiter, must construct counterfeits of Christianity as near to the original as conceivable in order to deceive the unwary soul. He makes them appear genuine and appeals to the unenlightened while at the same time he cunningly undercuts the true gospel. Mormonism is a doubly dangerous counterfeit because it boldly claims to be Christian and is very deceptive in its approach to prospective converts. Frequently it misleads many, especially young converts to Christianity. At a series of my lectures, an example of this was forcibly brought to my attention. A young housewife approached me and told me of how she had come to know Christ at a Billy Graham crusade. She went on to tell of how she drifted into contact with the Mormon Church through the activities of its zealous missionaries. It was only after being baptized into the church and participating as a member for over a year that she finally came to see what they *meant* by what they *said*. She then lost no time in leaving the Mormon church and today is a member of a Christian congregation. This incident and many others show that Mormonism can deceive even true Christians, but—God be thanked—not forever. The Lord Jesus said,

> My sheep hear my voice, and I know them, and they follow me; and I give unto them eternal life, and they

shall never perish, neither shall any man pluck them out of my hand. My Father, which gave them me, is greater than all, and no man is able to pluck them out of my Father's hand. I and my Father are one.

John 10:27-30

Our Lord also reminds us that He is the "Good Shepherd," and that His sheep will respond to Him: "Another's voice they will not hear" (John 10:1-11).

Misrepresentation

To perpetuate its masquerade, the Mormon Church is not above resorting to misrepresentation. A clear example is found in Mormon answers to a set of questions that *Look* Magazine originally published in its famous series of articles on various religions (now in book form, *Religions in America*, by Leo Rosten, Simon and Schuster, publishers, 1963). I have quoted the following material from it. To simplify the reader's following of Mormonism through its maze of shifty language, I have stated certain of the questions as they appear in Rosten's book and given Mormonism's answer, followed by my own documentation entitled "The Evidence," which shows the Mormon Church's actual position according to its own literature and sources.

Question: Do Mormons believe in the Holy Trinity?
Answer: Yes. The Latter-day Saint accepts the Godhead as three literal, distinct personalities: God the Father; His Son, Jesus the Christ (who is one with the Father in purpose and in thought, but separate from Him in physical fact); and the Holy Ghost, a Personage of spirit (Acts 7:55, etc.). . . .

Page 189

The Evidence: The Mormon Church (see Chapter 3) has never accepted the historic Christian doctrine of the Holy Trinity. Mr. Evans, who answered the question for the Mormons, was well aware of this. The question as it was asked of many spokesmen for the various religions included in the survey was referring directly to the historic Christian

doctrine of the Trinity as defined at Nicea in A.D. 325[2] and
as held historically by all orthodox bodies. Mr. Evans would
also have known this from the answers given by those
whose articles preceded his own. It is interesting to observe
that Milton G. Henschel, who wrote on the views of Jehovah's Witnesses (dedicated antitrinitarians), knew exactly
what was meant when Rosten spoke of the Holy Trinity (see
pages 95-102 of Rosten). I cannot, therefore, accept the possibility that Mr. Evans misunderstood the question. This
alternative removed, it is apparent that Evans could have
deliberately avoided giving his church's true position on the
Trinity because he knew it was not accepted by the truly
Christian churches in the world.

The key to the Mormon doctrine of the Trinity is found
in the words, "but separate from Him in physical fact," as
previously quoted from Evans. Smith, whose words rule all
Mormons, once described the Trinity in the following
terms:

> The Father has a body of flesh and bones as tangible as
> man's; the Son also; but the Holy Ghost has not a body of
> flesh and bones but is a personage of Spirit. . . .
> *Doctrine and Covenants* 130:22

> Many men say there is one God; the Father, the Son and
> the Holy Ghost are only one God! I say that is a strange
> God anyhow. . . . All are to be crammed into one
> God. . . .
> *History of the Church* 6:476

To dismiss any further doubt, I cite Brigham Young:

> Gods exist, and we had better strive to be prepared to be
> one with them.
> *Journal of Discourses* 7:238

(See also the documentation quoted in Chapter 3.)

---

[2]Briefly, the doctrine states essentially that "within the nature of
the one eternal God there are three persons: the Father, the
Son, and the Holy Ghost."

It is evident for all to see that the Mormon church is polytheistic and antitrinitarian, but masquerades under Christian terminology in an attempt to appear as an "angel of light." Evans' answer when questioned on the Trinity was indicative of the scholastic dishonesty and twisted semantics which seem to be standard practices in the Church's ever-expanding attempt to masquerade as Christian. For the Christian, God is spirit (John 4:24) and Jesus Christ is His manifestation in the flesh, truly "the image of the invisible God" (Colossians 1:15), not a hybrid monstrosity as historic Mormon theology interprets him. While Christ is the "express image" of the Father, that reference is to the *character* and *nature* of the Father (Hebrews 1:3, Greek). Mormon apologists are fond of using this text to prove "that since Christ had a physical form and was the Father's image, the Father must have a physical form." The Greek contradicts any such idea by the use of the terms "character" and "substance."

Question: Do Mormons believe in the Virgin Birth?
Answer: Yes. The Latter-day Saint accepts the miraculous conception of Jesus, the Christ.

Page 189

The Evidence: In this example of Mormon public relations, Mormonism deliberately evaded the issue of the Virgin Birth of Jesus Christ. It has done this because it dare not present before the Christian public or even the nominally Christian congregations of our day the true concept of the "Virgin Birth" as revealed by Joseph Smith and Brigham Young. No informed person, upon learning what these "inspired revelations" say, could fail to comprehend the redefinition of terminology and term-switching involved in this deception. Notice Evans' answer that the Latter-day Saint accepts the "miraculous conception" of the Lord Jesus. The Mormon Church appeared to give verbal confirmation of the Biblical doctrine of the Virgin Birth of our Lord by utilizing the term "miraculous."

However, that Mormonism denies the Biblical account of the Virgin Birth of Jesus Christ (Luke 1:26-35) no thorough student of the movement can ever deny (see Chapter 4 of this book). Evans, in his response to the question, should have stated the historic position of his chief prophets on the subject. However, knowing that Christians everywhere would openly attack such a perverted and unscriptural view, projected under the guise of Christianity,[3] Evans verbally assented to what he evidently knew was not the position of his founding prophets on the Virgin Birth of Christ. This historic position has never been repudiated by the Mormon Church. The "miraculous conception" of historic Mormon theology, derived from the "revelations" of Smith and Young, teaches that Adam, who had become a god by resurrection, progression, and exaltation, fathered Jesus Christ through sexual relations with Mary. It does not teach that Jesus Christ was conceived by the Holy Spirit.[4] As a result, its whole concept is a pagan caricature reminiscent of ancient mythology rather than of the Biblical birth of our Savior. This is completely foreign to the Bible, on which Mormonism professes to stand.

I leave to the judgment of the reader this further evidence of deception, a deception which began with Smith

---

[3] Though many debates have raged over the nature of the Virgin Birth of Christ, the orthodox position has always been based upon literal acceptance of the accounts of Matthew and Luke, and even the dissenters repudiate the Mormon concept, even if they do not hold the orthodox position.

[4] Many people who claim to be Mormons vigorously deny some of the revelations of Brigham Young today, and when I have said that "the only miraculous conception or Virgin Birth that Mormon theology admits to is an act of sexual relations," I am relying on the revelations of Joseph Smith and Brigham Young, as well as on the writings of Joseph Fielding Smith and present Apostle Bruce R. McConkie. When Mormons who reject the virgin birth (as interpreted by Mormon prophets) discover what the Church really teaches on the subject, they either accept it reluctantly or else leave the Church.

and which is still continued by the Mormon Church today. Mormonism has apparently succeeded in deceiving some of the public into believing that it is Christian, and thus they classify it with the leading Protestant denominations, all of whom consider the Mormons a non-Christian sect or cult!

On the Virgin Birth, Young declared:

> . . .When the Virgin Mary conceived the child Jesus, the Father had begotten him in his own likeness. He was *not* begotten by the Holy Ghost. And who is the Father? He is the first of the human family; and when he took a tabernacle, it was begotten by *his Father* in heaven, after the same manner as the tabernacles of Cain, Abel, and the rest of the sons and daughters of Adam and Eve. . . . Jesus, our elder brother, was begotten in the flesh by the same character that was in the garden of Eden, and who is our Father in Heaven. Now, let all who may hear these doctrines, pause before they make light of them, or treat them with indifference, for they will prove their salvation or damnation.
>
> *Journal of Discourses* 1:50-51

Let us further analyze Evans' answers to see if more Mormon semantics are discernible.

> Question: What do Mormons believe about the Bible?
> Answer: The Bible is basic to Mormon belief. The King James Version is officially used, and is believed to be "the word of God as far as it is translated correctly" (8th Article of Faith).
>
> Page 189

The Evidence: The Mormon church does *not* accept the Bible as uniquely the Word of God, as Evans so casually states it, but adds to the Scriptures three other books: *The Book of Mormon, Doctrine and Covenants,* and *The Pearl of Great Price*. These "inspired" writings are declared to be of equal authority with the Bible, and the four are considered to be, as a whole, the Word of God, despite the fact that the three latter works not only contradict the Bible in numerous places, but each other as well![5]

Downgrading the Bible

The old Mormon dodge regarding the "correct" translation of the Bible is also utilized by the disciples of Prophet Smith, who use it as one of their loopholes of escape whenever the Scriptures puncture one of their peculiar teachings, as is often the case! Mormonism claims that all "offending" Scripture is "incorrectly translated." This is done on the authority of Smith, who declared:

> Ignorant translators, careless transcribers, or designing and corrupt priests have committed many errors.
> *Teachings of the Prophet Joseph Smith*, page 327

Apostle Orson Pratt wrote:

> If it be admitted that the apostles and evangelists did write the books of the New Testament, that does not prove of itself that they were divinely inspired at the time thy [sic] wrote. . . . Add all this imperfection to the uncertainty of the translation, and who, in his right mind, could, for one moment, suppose the Bible in its present form to be a perfect guide? Who knows that even one verse of the whole Bible has escaped pollution, so as to convey the same sense now that it did in the original?
> *Divine Authenticity of the Book of Mormon*, pages 45 and 47

Christians should remember that whenever Mormonism talks about the Bible being "correctly translated," it is in reality saying that it does not teach that the Bible is the ab-

---

[5]Contrast *Book of Mormon*, Alma 34:36, with *Doctrine and Covenants* 130:3. Contrast *Pearl of Great Price*, Abraham 4:1, with *Book of Mormon*, 2 Nephi 31:21. Contrast *Doctrine and Covenants* 20:28 with *Pearl of Great Price*, Abraham 4:18. Contrast *Pearl of Great Price*, Abraham 4:3, with *Pearl of Great Price*, Moses 2:3.

solute authority, or the oldest revelation, to be relied upon with absolute certainty. And yet, not one Mormon missionary in a thousand could "correctly translate" any portion of the Old or New Testament, because the missionaries are not trained in the original languages of Scripture. What we are really facing is a clever denial of the sole authority of Scripture and a higher devotion to Mormonism's extrabiblical authority.

Joseph Smith began a revision of the Bible under "divine inspiration" known as the *Inspired Version*.[6] A sample of how "Prophet" Smith went about "revising" God's Word is found in Smith's alleged translations of John 1:18 and 1 John 4:22. In his attempt to improve upon the Holy Spirit and his seeming desire to presume instruction from God Himself, Smith wrote:

"INSPIRED" VERSION	KING JAMES VERSION
And no man hath seen God at any time, except he hath borne record of the Son; for except it is through him no man can be saved.	No man hath seen God at any time; the only begotten Son, which is in the bosom of the Father, he hath declared him.
John 1:19 [18]	John 1:18
No man has seen God at any time, except them who believe. If we love one another, God dwelleth in us, and his love is perfected in us.	No man hath seen God at any time. If we love one another, God dwelleth in us, and his love is perfected in us.
1 John 4:12	1 John 4:12

---

[6]"The revision of the *Bible* which was done by Joseph Smith at the command of the Lord was not a complete revision of the *Bible*. There are many parts of the *Bible* in which the Prophet did not change the meaning where it is incorrect. *He revised as far as the Lord permitted him at the time*, and it was his intention to do more, but because of persecution this was not accomplished. However, all that he did is very helpful for the major errors have been corrected" (Joseph Fielding Smith, *Doctrines of Salvation*, Vol. 3:191).

Any simple comparison of the New Testament Greek of these verses quickly reveals that Smith inserted the two phrases "except he hath borne record of the Son," and "except them who believe" in an amateurish attempt to support his manufactured revelation of God as a physical being rather than spirit, as the Bible teaches. LeGrand Richards, an Apostle of the Mormon Church, reveals that for Mormons the Bible alone is *not* the Word of God.[7] In fact, it cannot logically be God's Word at all where the Mormon Church is concerned. The Church often contradicts the Bible openly, supplementing it at will with its other three works and, wherever it suits the Church, ignoring it as "incorrectly translated."

Considering these facts, then, it is clear that once more Evans had neglected to tell the whole story for what appears to be the obvious reason that a half-truth is safer than a full deception. The Mormon Church has historically clung to half-truths, from Smith and Young down to Evans and its now-presiding president.

The Best Foot Is Not Enough

In the final analysis of Mormonism, we should not forget that it always puts its best foot forward. The quintessence of Mormon public relations was evidenced when then-Secretary of Agriculture, Ezra Taft Benson, a Mormon Apostle, appeared with his family on a national television program, "Person to Person," narrated by the late Edward R. Murrow. Throughout the entire broadcast, Benson exemplified the down-to-earth religious family man typical of the Mormon heritage, and was an effective advertisement for his religion. More recently, the Barbara Walters interview of Donny and Marie Osmond on the ABC network exuded the same sweet odor of "wholesomeness" that the

---

[7]LeGrand Richards, *A Marvelous Work and a Wonder* (1950 edition) pages 18 and 19.

Mormon Church has carefully cultivated and personified in these two young entertainers.

To sum up our analysis of the Mormon masquerade in public relations, it is clear that underneath the veneer of pseudo-Christian vocabulary and testimony, Benson, George Romney, and all Mormons in the Church, of high or low position, adhere tenaciously to the dogmas of Joseph Smith and Brigham Young. It is to the advantage of all sincere seekers for truth that they carefully examine the unvarnished doctrines of the Mormon Church, and not be deceived by appearances, apparent good lives, and forms of godliness which our Lord cautioned us to beware of when He said:

> Judge not according to the *appearance*, but judge righteous judgment.
>
> John 7:24
>
> Many will say to me in that day, Lord, Lord, have we not prophesied in thy name? and in thy name have cast out devils? and in thy name done many wonderful works? And then will I profess unto them, I never knew you; depart from me, ye that work iniquity.
>
> Matthew 7:22, 23

As we examine Mormonism, not as it projects its image for public consumption, but as it really is, let us not forget that Satan himself masquerades as an angel of light (2 Corinthians 11:14). His influence is frequently visible in what is clearly a Madison Avenue public relations approach on the part of the Mormon Church to evade, if at all possible, the real issues underlying some of its beliefs.

EIGHT

THE OCCULTIC SIDE OF MORMONISM

Mormon theology, as we have seen from the beginning of this analytical study, is riddled with contradictions that are internal and external, historical, theological, and scientific. What is *not* generally known about the Mormon Church, however, is its occultic background. It is a tale that has seldom been told or even discussed in analyses of the Mormon kingdom.

The Weird World of Occultism

When the subject of occultism is mentioned, immediately one conjures up the image of spiritist mediums holding hands around a table, listening for mysterious rappings or materializations, and trumpets indicating the presence of "departed loved ones." If one asked the average Mormon whether he believed in seances, he would vigorously oppose such spiritism. But what most Mormons do not recognize is the fact that Joseph Smith was an occultist, and that Mormonism had occultic origins.

So that there will be no linguistic difficulty in our discussion of this subject, we must understand from a Biblical and historical perspective precisely what we mean when we talk about occultic phenomena. The word "occult" itself comes from the Latin *occultus*, which refers classically to hidden, secret, or mysterious things—various things which God has specifically forbidden those who believe in Him to practice or to attempt to investigate.

Such practices as ouija boards, fortune-telling, tarot cards, seances, palm reading, water witching, witchcraft, Satan worship, astrology, gazing in crystal balls, or so-called peep- or peek-stones (in order to locate lost objects or learn something about someone's past or the future) come under divine prohibition. It is only necessary to read Deuteronomy 18:9-14 in a good modern translation of the Scriptures to learn that God considered such practices by the occupants of the land of Canaan "abominations" worthy of capital punishment:

> When you enter the land which the Lord your God gives you, you shall not learn to imitate the detestable things of those nations.
>
> There shall not be found among you anyone who makes his son or his daughter pass through the fire, one who uses divination, one who practices witchcraft, or one who interprets omens, or a sorcerer, or one who casts a spell, or a medium, or a spiritist, or one who calls up the dead.
>
> For whoever does these things is detestable to the Lord; and because of these detestable things the Lord your God will drive them out before you.
>
> You shall be blameless before the Lord your God.
>
> For those nations, which you shall dispossess, listen to those who practice witchcraft and to diviners, but as for you, the Lord your God has not allowed you to do so.
>
> Deuteronomy 18:9-14 NASB

We see before us an index of occultic practices. If one further examines Isaiah 47 and the Book of Daniel, where astrology and other such practices are condemned by God in the strongest terms, there is little doubt that the Lord did not change His mind and was still diametrically opposed to all occultism. The divine edict, "I am the Lord, I change not" (Malachi 3:6), extends also to the New Testament revelation. In Acts 19:19 those who heard the word of the Lord and believed it brought all the tools of the occult in their possession to the feet of the Apostles, and there burned them because such practices were accursed.

The practice of witchcraft is condemned in the Old and the New Testaments (Deuteronomy 18:9-14; Exodus 22:18; Galatians 5:20; 1 Samuel 28; Leviticus 19:31). God recognized what men had failed to recognize—that knowledge of the future is in *His* hand, and to attempt to obtain from the hand of demons what has been denied to them by the will of the Divine is an experiment fraught with perils and dangers undreamed of by the human soul.

The Dimension of Darkness

The Bible is a dimensional Book in the sense that a dimension is a realm of reality, sometimes imperceptible but nonetheless genuine.

We live in a dimension subject to our five senses, and because of this we tend to make the mistake of believing that anything beyond the realm of those senses simply isn't there. To accept such reasoning would be a fatal mistake from a Biblical perspective.

The second dimension is that of heaven, or the throne of God Himself. That realm is more real than our senses can perceive, and a dimension which was bridged when God chose to become man in the Person of Jesus Christ. Because of Him we now have access into a dimension of infinite power, indescribable love, and cosmic justice.

The third dimension is that which the Bible describes as hell, or the alienation of the spiritual nature of man from fellowship with his Creator. It is described variously in the Bible as "outer darkness" (Matthew 8:12; 22:13; 25:30), "fire" (Matthew 5:22; 13:42; 18:8, 9; 25:41; Mark 9:22-49), "suffering" (Jude 7), consciousness of separation from God and fear of others suffering the same (Luke 16), "prison" (1 Peter 3:19), and (metaphorically) a vast lake of molten sulphur, from which there is no deliverance (Revelation 19:20; 20:10, 14, 15; 21:8). Perhaps this dimension is best described in terms of the condition of its occupants, who are described as "wandering stars, to whom is reserved the blackness of darkness forever" (Jude 13). Biblical theology teaches us that Jesus Christ came into the world to deliver men from this, because hell had been prepared originally not for man but for Satan and his followers. They go there by divine decree, while man is the only creation that chooses it freely. No one is competent to pronounce on the chemical composition of the fires of hell, but one thing is absolutely certain: if it required the death of the most perfect Being who ever lived to deliver mankind from it, then at all costs God's warning against it should be heeded!

The last dimension which the Bible mentions is that which belongs to the "prince of the power of the air, the spirit that now worketh in the children of disobedience" (Ephesians 2:2). This dimension is portrayed for us in Ephesians 6, where we are warned that it is the domain of forces of incalculable wickedness presided over by the one whom the Bible designates as "the prince of this world . . . the god of this world" (John 14:30; 2 Corinthians 4:4). It is against this domain of darkness that the Christian is in mortal combat, and not against mere flesh and blood. This dimension is the unopened door with its handle on our side in the dimension of earth. It is with the tools of the occult that men open this door through which proceeds power of awesome evil. No force on earth can overpower Satan except Jesus, who is head of all principalities and powers, and the church, which is His body (Colossians 1:15-20; Ephesians 6:12).

The Christian is urged to put on the full armor of God (Ephesians 6:11) to do warfare in the spiritual dimension, confident that if he resists the Devil he will flee from him (James 4:7).

The world of the occult is to be avoided by believers in Christ because they are the temples of the Holy Spirit (1 Corinthians 6:19), and "greater is he that is in you than he that is in the world" (1 John 4:4), a reference to Satan and all his hosts, whether spiritual or corporeal. Christ has risen from the dead and is triumphant over all the forces arrayed against Him, because it was impossible "that death should hold him" who alone is designated in Scripture "Prince of Life" (Acts 3:15). The Great High Priest of the Christian church rebuked Satan on earth (Luke 4) and defeated him on the cross to redeem the sons of men. The King of eternity disdained occultic practices, for they originate with Satan, and those who practice them are indeed fools who rush in where the angels fear to tread (Jude 9). Unlike the believer who cannot be demonized (controlled or possessed by Satanic powers), those who do not have the Spirit of God can become controlled by Satan's spiritual forces (demons), a horror almost too vile to contemplate.

The Holy Spirit and the Occult

In the Book of Acts, the Apostles Paul and Barnabas had been sent forth by the Holy Spirit (Acts 13:2, 3), and, passing through the city of Paphos, they encountered a sorcerer (occultist), a false prophet who called himself Bar-Jesus or "Son of Jesus":

> They traveled through the whole island until they came to Paphos. There they met a Jewish sorcerer and false prophet named Bar-Jesus, who was an attendant of the proconsul, Sergius Paulus. The proconsul, an intelligent man, sent for Barnabas and Saul because he wanted to hear the word of God. But Elymas the sorcerer (for that is what his name means) opposed them and tried to turn the proconsul from the faith. Then Saul, who was also called Paul, filled with the Holy Spirit, looked straight at Elymas and said, "You are a child of the devil and an enemy of everything that is right! You are full of all kinds of deceit and trickery. Will you never stop perverting the

right ways of the Lord? Now the hand of the Lord is against you. You are going to be blind, and for a time you will be unable to see the light of the sun."

Immediately mist and darkness came over him, and he groped about, seeking someone to lead him by the hand. When the proconsul saw what had happened, he believed, for he was amazed at the teaching about the Lord.

Acts 13:6-12 NIV

A number of interesting things emerge from this encounter to reveal the unchanging attitude of God toward all forms of occultic practices and those who are involved in them. The word "sorcerer" (Greek *magos*) means a magician or one employed in occultic practices. Bar-Jesus' primary goal was to divert Sergius Paulus, governor of the island, from the Christian faith. When Paul addressed Bar-Jesus it should be noted that Paul was filled with the Holy Spirit, and so it was really the Holy Spirit who spoke in condemnation of the occultist and occultic practices in general. The words of the Spirit are definitive, potent, and judgmental. He accused the occultist of fraud and of being filled up with all deceit, and termed him a son of Satan and an enemy of all that is right. He accused him of perverting the path or the way of the Lord, which is termed right in contrast to his wrong. Then followed swift judgment (blindness). As a result of that judgment by the Holy Spirit, salvation came to Sergius Paulus because he saw the power of the Lord and was convinced of the truth of the teaching of Paul and Barnabas.

Let us note precisely what the occult's practitioners, knowingly or unknowingly, really are:

1. They are in league with Satan and possess certain supernatural powers.
2. They are false prophets.
3. They seek to influence people politically and ecclesiastically, particularly those in positions of power (verses 6, 7).
4. They attempt to prevent those who are seeking to

hear the Word of God from learning it by opposing those who preach it (verse 8).

5. They deliberately attempt to divert prospective converts from the faith (verse 8) as their ultimate goal.

In contrast to this, the judgment of the Holy Spirit is explicit:

1. He calls such attempts and practices "full of all kinds of deceit and trickery" (verse 10).

2. He designates occultism and the occult as having its origin with the Devil ("child of the Devil"—verse 10).

3. He unmasks the occultists' tactics and declares them to be enemies of all that is righteous; He calls them perverters of the ways of the Lord, which are designated as "right" (verse 10).

If this were not sufficient, the Spirit then struck the occultist, or the medium, blind and used this judgment to convince Sergius Paulus, the seeker after truth, that the gospel of Jesus Christ is the truth, and that the way of occultism leads to destruction.

This attitude of God has not altered toward occultism and occultic practices. Neither has His attitude altered toward those who teach such practices and those who persist in pursuing them for their own ends. Occultism promises power. If you can tell someone something about himself that only he knows, and can predict something that does indeed occur, you have secured power over him through fear.

The occult promises love, but it is not the divine love of Scripture (*agape*). Rather, it is psychosexual love (*eros*), which explains why many of those who are in the world of the occult are immoral, recognizing only a standard of authority established by their own reasoning. The occult offers some degree of certainty in a world of uncertainty. Moving outside the realm of established religion, it promises things which the church does not deal in, but forbids. The occult also offers a sense of belonging—so desperately needed by people who reject God's love in Jesus Christ and instead accept substitutes rather than regeneration in the image of God through faith in the Lord Jesus Christ. The occult also offers pseudoknowledge of the future and supposed control over the lives of others. At its heart it is egocentric; the occultist seeks first his own ends and then the ends of others and their goals.

As one Christian theologian has put it, occultism provides no exit from the actual realities of life and the problem of sin, but is merely a Satanic diversion which frequently masks itself in Christian terminology. That is why we frequently see spiritist churches deny the Trinity, the deity of Christ, His atonement on the cross for our sins, and His bodily resurrection—yet still use Christian terminology, quote the Bible, and sing hymns (altered to fit their theological system). They have the *form* of Christian unity, as did the sorcerer in the Book of Acts, but they are devoid of the saving, historic gospel. It should come as no surprise to us that Satan, who has created "another Jesus . . . another spirit . . . and another gospel" (2 Corinthians 11:4), should introduce under the guise of Christianity practices which seem to follow a Biblical pattern but culminate in eternal spiritual death.

This fact we discover when we study the origins of Mormonism, which utilized in its founders and their successors occultic practices, particularly that practice most vigorously condemned by God—mediumship, or attempted communication with departed spirits.

Mormon Theology and the Occult

In our study of Joseph Smith and his "revelations," and of the early history and development of the Mormon religion, we noted that Smith was involved in the occult practice of "glass-looking," or "peepstone-gazing," and that he claimed to have revelations from God the Father, His Son Jesus Christ, Nephi, the angel Moroni, John the Baptist, Peter, James, and John. Smith claimed to have supernatural powers, and there is evidence that he exercised the power to heal when the Mormons were plagued by disease in Nauvoo. Joseph passed through the people, laying hands on them and praying for them, and a great many of them were restored. The early Mormons also claimed the gifts of the Holy Spirit as recorded in 1 Corinthians chapter 12, and they particularly emphasized the capacity to speak in tongues, prophesy, discern spirits, interpret tongues, and work miracles.

The Mormon Church today maintains the perpetuity of spiritual gifts (carefully redefined) while at the same time denying God the Holy Spirit and the identity of the historic Jesus of Nazareth. This immediately raises the question of counterfeit gifts. How is it possible to manifest gifts from the Holy Spirit when one rejects the Holy Spirit, and to utilize the name of Jesus Christ when one considers Him the brother of Lucifer, who became the Devil? In early Mormonism there were probably Christians who were misled and drawn into the movement by the dynamic leadership of Smith and Young. They could have had gifts from the Holy Spirit derived from their past experience as true Christians. But as the church extended and expanded its influence and doctrines, many of these people dropped away, recognizing the polytheism and polygamy of Smith and Young as proof that this was not the historic gospel. What then arose in the Mormon Church was a Satanic counterfeit of the gifts of the Holy Spirit brought about by "the other Jesus, a different spirit, and the other gospel" (2 Corinthians 11:3, 4).

We are told in 2 Thessalonians 2 that Satan will counterfeit miracles through the great antichrist, who is but an agent of his power. If antichrist, who is but an *agent* of Satan, can perform miracles and imitate the gifts of the Holy Spirit, then *Satan himself* can duplicate the gifts of the Holy Spirit, just as the magicians, mediums, sorcerers, and priests of the demon-gods of Egypt duplicated some of the miracles of Moses (see Exodus 7:1ff). This could explain the existence of so-called spiritual gifts within the Mormon Church today.

It is also possible that some Mormons know Jesus Christ as their Savior but are unaware of the early teachings of Joseph Smith, Brigham Young, and the leaders of the church. God may honor their faith and bestow upon them gifts, standing ever ready to reveal to them the false doctrines of the Church if they will only seek in his Word corroboration of the historic Christian message. But occultism in Mormon theology is undeniable, connected not with *believers* who were deceived either in the beginning of the Church or today, but instead connected with the practices of the early leaders of the Church and some of the teachings which grew out of occultic manifestations. To understand this, it is necessary to go back into Mormon history and compare these things with the Word of God.

Penetration of the Occult in Mormonism

In *Between Christ and Satan*, Dr. Kurt Koch, one of the world's leading authorities on occultic phenomena, makes the following statement:

> There are in existence occult text books on the subject of mirror mantic and mirror magic. The mirror magician with the help of a magic mirror, may attempt to heal or to persecute through magic, to treat people at a distance or to use love and defence magic, and so on. Mirror mantic is often directed at discovering things unknown to the inquirer, in uncovering crimes or diagnosing difficult diseases, and it can embrace any physical event which happens in the world. Mirrors are not the only occult tools used in this field, but crystal balls, rock crystal and other reflecting objects all play a part. Some even use water as a reflecting surface.
>
> Historically, mirror mantic or crystal gazing can be traced back over hundreds of years.
>
> Page 42

W. J. Fielding, in *Strange Superstitions and Magical Practices*, declares:

> Among primitive peoples there is a widespread belief in

the magical efficacy of quartz crystals—one of the most common of all luminous stones. These mineralogical specimens are frequently the main prop of the magician. They are used for this purpose by the Aborigines of Australia, Polynesia and North America, among others.

Page 53

In 1833 Willard Chase, a native of Manchester, Ontario County, New York, swore an affidavit about Joseph Smith, Jr., and his use of a particular "stone" for purposes we have discussed in Chapter 2. It underscores Smith's preoccupation with the supernatural as it is connected with occultic tools:

I became acquainted with the Smith family, known as the authors of the Mormon Bible, in the year 1820. At that time, they were engaged in the money digging business, which they followed until the latter part of the season of 1827. In the year 1822, I was engaged in digging a well. I employed Alvin and Joseph Smith to assist me; the latter of whom is now known as the Mormon prophet. After digging about twenty feet below the surface of the earth, we discovered a singularly appearing stone, which excited my curiosity. I brought it to the top of the well, and as we were examining it, Joseph put it in to his hat, and then his face into the top of his hat. It has been said by Smith, that *he* brought the stone from the well; but this is false. There was no one in the well but myself. The next morning he came to me, and wished to obtain the stone, alleging that he could see in it; but I told him I did not wish to part with it on account of its being a curiosity, but would lend it. After obtaining the stone, he began to publish abroad what wonders he could discover by looking in it, and made so much disturbance among the credulous part of community, that I ordered the stone to be returned to me again. He had it in his possession about two years.—I believe, some time in 1825, Hiram Smith (brother of Joseph Smith) came to me, and wished to borrow the same stone. . . . I told him it was of no particular worth to me, but merely wished to keep it as a curiosity, and if he would pledge me his word of honor, that I should have it when called for, he might take it; which he did and took the stone. I thought I could rely on his word at this time, as he had made a profession of religion. But in this I was disappointed, for he disregarded both his word and honor.

In the fall of 1826, a friend called upon me and wished to
see that stone, about which so much had been said; and I
told him if he would go with me to Smith's, (a distance of
about half a mile) he might see it. But to my sur-
prize, [sic] on going to Smith's, and asking him for the
stone, he said, "you cannot have it;" I told him it belonged to me, repeated to him the promise he made me,
at the time of obtaining the stone: upon which he faced
me with a malignant look and said, "I don't care who in
the Devil it belongs to, *you* shall not have it." . . .

In April, 1830, I again asked Hiram for the stone which
he had borrowed of me; he told me I should not have it,
for Joseph made use of it in translating his Bible, I remind-
ed him of his promise, and that he had pledged his
honor to return it; but he gave me the lie, saying the
stone was not mine nor never was. Harris at the same
time flew in a rage, took me by the collar and said I was a
liar, and he could prove it by twelve witnesses. After I
had extricated myself from him, Hiram, in a rage shook
his fist at me, and abused me in a most scandalous manner. . . . Although they left this part of the country
without paying their just debts, yet their creditors were
glad to have them do so, rather than to have them stay,
disturbing the neighborhood.

Signed, WILLARD CHASE.

On the 11th December, 1833, the said Willard Chase appeared before me, and made oath that the foregoing
statement to which he has subscribed his name, is true,
according to his best recollection and belief.

FRED'K SMITH,
*Justice of the Peace
of Wayne County.*
(From E. D. Howe, *Mormonism,*
pages 240-42, 247-48)

David Whitmer declares that Joseph Smith, Jr., translated *The Book of Mormon* by the use of a "seer" stone:

I will now give you a description of the manner in which
the Book of Mormon was translated. Joseph Smith would
put the seer stone into a hat, and put his face in the hat,
drawing it closely around his face to exclude the light;
and in the darkness the spiritual light would shine. A
piece of something resembling parchment would appear, and on that appeared the writing. One character at

a time would appear, and under it was the interpretation in English. Brother Joseph would read off the English to Oliver Cowdery, who was his principal scribe, and when it was written down and repeated to Brother Joseph to see if it was correct, then it would disappear, and another character with the interpretation would appear. Thus the Book of Mormon was translated by the gift and power of God, and not by any power of man.

David Whitmer, *An Address to all Believers in Christ*, 1887, page 12

If any doubt lingers about the occultic sources in early Mormonism, it is only necessary to consult *The Book of Mormon* itself, where the Lord is represented as authorizing:

. . . a stone, which shall shine forth in darkness unto light, that I may discover unto my people who serve me, that I may discover unto them the works of their brethren, yea, their secret works, their works of darkness, and their wickedness and abominations.

And now, my son, these interpreters were prepared that the word of God might be fulfilled, which he spake, saying:

I will bring forth out of darkness unto light all their secret works and their abominations; and except they repent I will destroy them from off the face of the earth; and I will bring to light all their secrets and abominations, unto every nation that shall hereafter possess the land.

Book of Mormon, Alma 37:23-25

The book of Mosiah, chapter 8, verses 13-18, also declares:

Now Ammon said unto him: I can assuredly tell thee, O king, of a man that can translate the records; for he has wherewith that he can look, and translate all records that are of ancient date; and it is a gift from God. And the things are called interpreters, and no man can look in them except he be commanded, lest he should look for that he ought not and he should perish. And whosoever is commanded to look in them, the same is called seer.

And behold, the king of the people who are in the land of

Zarahemla is the man that is commanded to do these things, and who has this high gift from God.

And the king said that a seer is greater than a prophet.

And Ammon said that a seer is a revelator and a prophet also; and a gift which is greater can no man have, except he should possess the power of God, which no man can; yet a man may have great power given him from God.

But a seer can know of things which are past, and also of things which are to come, and by them shall all things be revealed, or, rather, shall secret things be made manifest, and hidden things shall come to light, and things which are not known shall be made known by them, and also things shall be made known by them which otherwise could not be known.

Thus God has provided a means that man, through faith, might work mighty miracles; therefore he becometh a great benefit to his fellow beings.

Joseph was carefully laying the groundwork for his own role as "interpreter" and "seer," so that he could become (in the eyes of the Mormons) "a great benefit to his fellow beings" (Mosiah 8:18). Joseph did not stop there. In Ether 3:22-25, 28 Smith again returned to the theme of the "stones," which appear to be the seal of the seer and the indication of divine authority!

And behold, when ye shall come unto me, ye shall write them and shall seal them up, that no one can interpret them; for ye shall write them in a language that they cannot be read.

And behold, these two stones will I give unto thee, and ye shall seal them up also with the things which ye shall write.

For behold, the language which ye shall write I have confounded; wherefore I will cause in my own due time that these stones shall magnify to the eyes of men these things which ye shall write.

And when the Lord had said these words, he showed unto the brother of Jared all the inhabitants of the earth which had been, and also all that would be; and he withheld them not from his sight, even unto the ends of the earth. . . .

And it came to pass that the Lord commanded him that

he should seal up the two stones which he had received,
and show them not, until the Lord should show them
unto the children of men.

Ether 3:22-25, 28

Mormonism contained from its very beginnings a
relationship and recognition of occultic practices, and nowhere was this more clearly demonstrated than in the
writings of Charles W. Penrose, a leading Mormon
theologian. He wrote on the subject of "results of work
done for the dead" in his informative little book *Mormon
Doctrine*, published by the Mormon Church in 1888
through "the Juvenile Instructor's office, Salt Lake City,
Utah." Penrose, in the introduction to the volume, stated:

> There is no subject of popular comment on which there is
> so little general information as that called "Mor-
> monism." This little work is designed to explain in a sim-
> ple way, leading features of "Mormon" doctrine.

Mr. Penrose then went on (pages 40-41) to point out:

> The living are thus authorized, under prescribed condi-
> tions, to act for the dead, and the fathers in the spirit
> world look to the children in the flesh to perform for
> them the works which they were unable to attend to
> while in the body. . . . This glorious doctrine bears the
> key to the sphere within the vail. *It regulates the com-
> munion of the living with the dead. It saves those who re-
> ceive it from improper and deceptive spirit communi-
> cations.°* Tidings to the living from their friends who have
> passed away do not come in disorder and confusion, nor
> by the will of men or women, whether corrupt or pure.
> Order is maintained in all the works and ways of God.
> *Knowledge that is needful concerning the spiritual
> sphere will come through an appointed channel and in
> the appointed place. The temple where the ordinances
> can be administered for the dead, is the place to hear
> from the dead. The Priesthood in the flesh, when it is
> necessary, will receive communications from the Priest-
> hood behind the vail. Most holy conversations on all
> things pertaining to the redemption of the race, belong
> in the places prepared in the temples.°*

°Emphasis the author's.

These are strange words indeed for a disciple of the "restored" gospel, because they are declaring that communication with departed loved ones is within the power of the Mormon priesthood and is to be exercised *within* the Temple, where such practices obviously went on, or else Mr. Penrose would not have alluded to such a reality. What the Mormons were being told was, in effect, "don't go to spiritistic mediums, ouija boards, or other unauthorized sources of communication from the spirit world, because you run the risk of encountering evil spirits." Rather, they were told, in effect, "if you want to communicate with your relatives, seek counsel of the Priesthood and go to the right place for such spirit communications" (i.e., the Temples of the Mormon Church!).

This is not an isolated case, because President Wilford Woodruff of the Mormon Church declared that he had interviews with Heber C. Kimball, Brigham Young, and Joseph Smith *after* their deaths. He further maintained that Smith particularly communicated many important things to him.

> Joseph Smith continued visiting myself and others up to a certain time, and then it stopped.
>
> > *Deseret Weekly News* 53:112;
> > Temples of the Most High, 10th
> > Edition, 1896, page 345

President Woodruff also stated:

> I have had many interviews with Brother Joseph until the last 15 or 20 years of my life; I have not seen him for that length of time.
>
> > *Journal of Discourses* 21:317-18,
> > October 10, 1880; see also
> > *Journal of Discourses* 19:229

Other manifestations of occultic phenomena also occur within the structure of Mormonism, one of which is known as "astral projection" or the supposed leaving of the body and the travel of the soul into another dimension. Heber C. Kimball said during his remarks at the funeral of President Jedediah M. Grant, December 4, 1856 (recorded in the *Journal of Discourses* 4:135-36):

> I went to see him [Jedediah M. Grant] one day last week, and he reached out his hand and shook hands with me. . . . He said to me, brother Heber, I have been into the spirit world two nights in succession, and, of all the dreads that ever came across me, the worst was to have to again return to my body, though I had to do it. But O, says he, the order and government that were there! When in the spirit world, I saw the order of righteous men and women. . . .
>
> He would mention one item after another and say, "Why, it is just as brother Brigham says it is; it is just as he has told us many a time. . . ."
>
> After mentioning the things that he had seen, he spoke of how much he disliked to return and resume his body, after having seen the beauty and glory of the spirit world, where the righteous spirits are gathered together.

In an article entitled "Raised From the Dead," by LeRoi C. Snow (*Improvement Era*, 32:972-80, October 1929), a similar instance of soul travel is recorded in the experience of Ella Jensen, who entered the spirit world, met many friends and relatives (after leaving her body), and was called back by the President of the Church because her work on earth was not yet completed. She later married and rose to become President of the Young Ladies' Mutual Improvement Association in Brigham City. The experience to which she alluded took place on March 3, 1891, when she was twenty years of age.

Solomon F. Kimball, also writing in the *Improvement Era*, stated that the spirit of his father, Heber, told him that he felt "the history spirit," which

> came upon me [Solomon] again stronger than ever. . . . Soon after I had commenced work it seemed to me at times as though I was in the very presence of my father. I could plainly feel his spirit working with me. It became so strong that I could not rest until we had called the representative members of the family together and laid this subject before them. At that meeting a committee of

five was chosen, and we decided to employ Bishop Orson F. Whitney to write the history over again. . . . The day that the history was to be bound and placed upon the market, one of the most wonderful events of my life took place. As I was giving the prisoners their breakfast, imagine my joy and satisfaction when I heard the voice of my father's spirit saying to me that he had something more to add to the history, and would give it to me as a reward for my faithfulness in helping to bring that work forth. As soon as I could get the prisoners to work I took a pencil and tab and father's spirit told me what to write. Under his dictation I wrote for about twenty minutes. I scribbled as fast as I could and a minute or two before I had finished several prisoners who were doing janitor work came into the room and father's spirit left. I undertook to complete the unfinished part was unable to do so. Then I began to feel uneasy, fearing that Bishop Whitney would reject the communication. I went into the old council chamber and prayed to the Lord to prepare his mind to believe it. When he came to work that morning I told him that I had just received word from father and he had given me something more to go into the history. I handed him the communication. He read it over carefully and said, "That is splendid." He completed the unfinished part and corrected my mistakes. We decided to say nothing about it and it went into the history in that form. . . .

Pages 583-85

This is known in the history of occultism as "automatic writing," in which a spirit takes control of an individual and communicates in writing through him.

As described above, the spirit terminated the communication at an interruption. I do not doubt that what Mr. Kimball reported occurred, although not under the direction of his father's spirit, but of quite a different spirit—one who has a very long record of deceiving the sons of men.

Seances are forbidden by God because spiritism is an attempt to communicate contrary to God's will; yet the Mormons practiced such things through their Priesthood in the Temple. Astral projection, or soul travel, is common in such occultic groups as Eckankar, Rosicrucianism, Spiritism, Theosophy, and a number of Eastern religious sects. It is never associated with historic Christianity or Judaism. The only seance ever conducted in the Bible was interrupted by God personally and visited with death and destruction upon Israel and her apostate king (1 Samuel 28; cf. 1 Chronicles 10:13).

In *Spirit World Experiences* (published by Pioneer Press, Dougway, Utah) numerous instances of Mormon occultic manifestations are catalogued, including Heber Kimball's remarks at the funeral of President Grant. The book is interesting reading for anyone who wants to analyze the deadly parallels between occultic practices and their manifestation within the structure of the Mormon religion.

Brigham Young himself once dealt with the subject of demonic forces, or "evil spirits," and their various activities:

> You know that we sometimes need a prompter; if any one of you is called by the government of the United States to go to Germany, Italy, or any foreign nation, as an Ambassador, if you did not understand the language somebody would have to interpret for you. Well, these evil spirits are ready to prompt you. Do they prompt us? Yes, and I could put my hands on a dozen of them while I have been on this stand; they are here on the stand. Could we do without the devils? No, we could not get along without them. They are here, and they suggest this, that, and the other.
>
> *Journal of Discourses* 3:369,
> June 22, 1856

Can this indeed be a prophet of the restoration of Christianity informing the church in the name of God that we cannot get along without devils when the Scriptures plainly declare that they are the enemies of our souls and that we are to resist all Satanic forces (James 4:7)?

In the theology of the Mormon Church angels are supposedly the departed dead (*Doctrine and Covenants* 129:1). They visit the earth and communicate information to their former loved ones. As we have seen from statements made by President Wilford Woodruff, he had a number of occultic encounters and apparently spoke freely about them:

I will here make a remark concerning my own feelings. After the death of Joseph Smith I saw and conversed wlth [sic] him many times in my dreams in the night season. On one occasion he and his brother Hyrum met me when on the sea going on a mission to England. . . . the prophet talked freely to me about the mission I was then going to perform. And he also talked to me with regard to the mission of the Twelve Apostles in the flesh, and he laid before me the work they had to perform; and he also spoke of the reward they would receive after death. . . . I have had many interviews with Brother Joseph until the last 15 or 20 years of my life. . . . But during my travels in the southern country last winter I had many interviews with President Young, and with Heber C. Kimball, and Geo. A. Smith, and Jedediah M. Grant, and many others who are dead. They attended our conference, they attended our meetings. And on one occasion, I saw Brother Brigham and Brother Heber ride in carriage ahead of the carriage in which I rode when I was on my way to attend conference; and they were dressed in the most priestly robes. When we arrived at our destination I asked Prest. Young if he would preach to us. He said, "No, I have finished my testimony in the flesh I shall not talk to this people any more. But (said he) I have come to see you; I have come to watch over you, and to see what the people are doing. Then (said he) I want you to teach the people—and I want you to follow this counsel yourself—that they must labor and so live as to obtain the Holy Spirit, for without this you cannot build up the kingdom; without the spirit of God you are in danger of walking in the dark, and in danger of failing to accomplish your calling as apostles and as elders in the church and kingdom of God. And, said he, Brother Joseph taught me this principle."

Journal of Discourses 21:317-18,
October 10, 1880

The demon impersonating Brigham Young lied when it stated that the Mormons "must labor and so live as to obtain the Holy Spirit," because the New Testament flatly declares that the Holy Spirit is a gift of God, and that God gives His Holy Spirit to those who obey Him (Acts 1:4). If the Holy Spirit is a gift, one does not labor and strive to obtain Him. He regenerates the believer (2 Corinthians 5) and is bestowed by the Lord Jesus Christ in the manifestation of

His spiritual gifts. One does not labor for a gift because, as Paul states, if one does, it is really not a gift at all but something which is due because of human effort (Romans 4:1-5).

President Wilford Woodruff expanded upon his occultic encounters when he wrote:

> Joseph Smith visited me a great deal after his death and taught me many important principles. . . . Among other things, he told me to get the Spirit of God, that all of us needed it. He also told me what the Twelve Apostles would be called to go through on the earth before the coming of the Son of Man and what the reward of their labors would be, but all of that was taken from me for some reason. . . . Joseph Smith continued visiting myself and others up to a certain time and then it stopped. The last time I saw him was in Heaven. In a night vision I saw him at the door of the Temple in Heaven. He came and spoke to me. He said he could not stop to talk with me because he was in a hurry. The next man I met was Father Smith. He could not talk with me because he was in a hurry. I met a half dozen brothers who had held high positions on earth and none of them could stop and talk with me because they were in a hurry. I was very much astonished. By and by I saw the Prophet again and I got the privilege to ask him a question. Now, said I, I want to know why you are in a hurry. I have been in a hurry all of my life but I expected my hurry would be over when I got into the kingdom of Heaven, if I ever did. Joseph said, "I will tell you Brother Woodruff. Every dispensation that has had the priesthood on the earth has gone to the Celestial Kingdom and has had a certain amount of work to do to prepare to go to the earth with the Saviour when He goes to reign on the earth. This dispensation has had ample time to do His work. We have not. We are the last dispensation and so much work has to be done and we need to be in a hurry in order to accomplish it." Of course, that was satisfactory with me, but it was new doctrine to me.
>
> *Deseret Weekly News* 53:642-43,
> No. 21, November 7, 1896

Parley P. Pratt, author of *The Key to the Science of Theology*, a standard Mormon publication on theological issues, stated:

> Many spirits of the departed, who are unhappy, linger in lonely wretchedness about the earth, and in the air, and especially about their ancient homesteads, and the places rendered dear to them by the memory of former scenes.
>
> *The Key to the Science of Theology*, page 117

Brigham Young, successor to Joseph Smith, stated:

> There is evil in the world, and there is also good. Was there ever a counterfeit without a true coin? No. Is there communication from God? Yes. From holy angels? Yes; and we have been proclaiming these facts during nearly thirty years. Are there any communications from evil spirits? Yes; and the Devil is making the people believe very strongly in revelations from the spirit world. This is called spiritualism, and it is said that thousands of spirits declare that "Mormonism" is true; but what do that class of spirits know more than mortals? Perhaps a little more in some particulars than is known here, but it is only a little more. They are subject in the spirit world to the same powers they were subject to here.
>
> *Journal of Discourses* 7:240, September 1, 1859

It can be seen from this that while Brigham Young opposed spiritualism and traced it to the Devil, he boasted that even the demons proclaim that Mormonism is true. Who could exercise any confidence in the agents of him who is called by Jesus Christ "a liar" and "a murderer from the beginning [who] abode not in the truth" (John 8:44)?

Parley Pratt, in company with other Mormon theologians, did not hesitate to state:

> The fact of spiritual communications being established, by which the living hear from the dead—being no longer a question of controversy with the well-informed, we drop that point, and call attention to the means of discriminating or judging between the lawful and the unlawful mediums or channels of communication—between the holy and the impure, the truths and falsehoods, thus communicated. . . .
>
> By what means, then, can a people seek unto their God, for such an important blessing as to hear from the dead? And how shall we discriminate between those who seek

to Him, and those who seek the same by unlawful means? . . . None, then, can be lawful mediums, who are unbelievers in Jesus Christ, or in modern revelations; or who remain in their sins; or who act in their own name, instead of the name appointed.

And moreover, the Lord has appointed a Holy Priesthood on the earth, and in the heavens, and also in the world of spirits; which Priesthood is after the order or similitude of His Son; and has committed to this Priesthood the keys of holy and divine revelation, and of correspondence, or communication between angels, spirits, and men, and between all the holy departments, principalities, and powers of His government in all worlds.

Journal of Discourses 2:45-46,
April 6, 1853

Pratt and Penrose are in complete agreement—the Mormon priesthood holds the keys of communication between angels, spirits, and men; this authority, according to Penrose, was exercised in the Temple. The Bible knows nothing of lawful mediums, and Jesus Christ is never called a medium, but an "intercessor between God and man." It should be observed that He is the *only* intercessor, according to the Apostle Paul, who is a far greater authority on the subject of mediation than Smith, Young, Pratt, Kimball, Woodruff, Grant, or any other member of Mormondom's hierarchy.

President Joseph F. Smith also followed in the footsteps of his predecessors when he stated:

We are told by the Prophet Joseph Smith, that "there are no angels who minister to this earth but those who do belong or have belonged to it." Hence . . . they are not strangers, but from the ranks of our kindred, friends, and fellow-beings and fellow-servants. . . . our fathers and mothers, brothers, sisters and friends who have passed away from this earth, having been faithful, and worthy to enjoy these rights and privileges, may have a mission given them to visit their relatives and friends upon the earth again, bringing from the divine Presence messages of love, of warning, or reproof and instruction, to those whom they had learned to love in the flesh.

Joseph F. Smith, *Gospel
Doctrine*, pages 435-36

The Verdict of the Evidence

The entire record of Holy Scripture is adamant in its condemnation of any form of occultism. In fact, it was God who decreed the capital nature of spiritistic offenses by commanding the execution of mediums (witches) in Exodus 22:18. In Leviticus He declared:

> Regard not them that have familiar spirits, neither seek after wizards [high-ranking male mediums], to be defiled by them: I am the Lord your God. . . . The soul that turneth after such as have familiar spirits, and after wizards, to go whoring after them, I will even set my face against that soul, and will cut him off from among his people. . . . A man or woman that hath a familiar spirit or that is a wizard shall surely be put to death: they shall stone them with stones; their blood shall be upon them.
>
> Leviticus 19:31; 20:6, 27

All attempts at necromancy (communication with the dead) are forbidden by Hebrew law and by Christianity, witchcraft itself being listed as one of the "works of the flesh." God makes it very clear that those who "practice such things shall not inherit the kingdom of God" (Galatians 5:19-21 lit. trans.).

In concluding this section, one other important occultic practice of Mormonism should not be neglected. Joseph Smith wrote:

> And inasmuch as mine enemies come against you . . . ye shall curse them; And whomsoever ye curse, I will curse, and ye shall avenge me of mine enemies.
>
> *Doctrine and Covenants* 103:24-25

Smith was joined in this totally unchristian concept by Heber Kimball, First Counselor to Brigham Young, who stated:

> . . . There are men and women in this congregation of that stamp. I wish I had some stones; I want to pelt your cursed heads. . . . There is a poor curse who has written the bigger part of those lies . . . and I curse him, in the name of Israel's God, and by the Priesthood and

authority of Jesus Christ; and the disease that is in him shall sap and dry up the fountain of life and eat him up. . . . That is the curse of that man; it shall be so, and all Israel shall say, Amen.

Journal of Discourses 5:32;
see also *Mormonism—Shadow or Reality*, page 114

Mr. Kimball's statement and curse were directed at the President of the United States, and the record shows that the Mormon congregation joined him with an "Amen!"

The verdict of the New Testament on this kind of reasoning is in direct contradiction to occultic curses. In fact, our Lord taught:

But I say unto you, Love your enemies, bless them that curse you, do good to them that hate you and pray for them who despitefully use you, and persecute you.

Matthew 5:44

The Apostle Paul reinforced this by saying, "Bless them which persecute you; bless, and curse not" (Romans 12:14).

We can agree with Brigham Young in at least one detail in the area of the occult—Satan does counterfeit the things of God (2 Corinthians 11:14). Even the spiritual gifts which the Mormon Church manifests, drawn from the "other Jesus, the other spirit, and the other gospel" bear the stamp of the cloven hoof and the smell of sulphur.

The sixteenth chapter of the Gospel of Luke, in which Jesus Christ discusses the state of the wicked dead, reminds us that there is a great gulf fixed between those in the paradise of God, symbolized by Abraham's bosom, and those who are bound in chains of darkness in what the Bible describes as hell. There is also a great gulf or chasm between the dimension of earth and heaven, which is bridged only by God the Holy Spirit, the Comforter of the church (John 14), and the abiding presence of the Lord Jesus, who never leaves nor forsakes those who are His Temple. There is not one shred of Biblical evidence that our departed loved ones appear on earth to communicate messages to us, but there are Biblical statements which indicate that demonic impersonators attempt this very illusion for the purpose of deceiving, if possible, the elect.

Many sincere Mormons today are unaware of the occultic influences in the early days of Mormonism, and of the occultic practices and beliefs of its founding prophets and leaders. But the verdict is in, having been delivered by the Holy Scriptures and testified to by the Spirit of God and the Christian church. God has chosen to communicate through His Word (Hebrews 1:1; John 20:31), through the church, which is His body (1 Corinthians 14:29-31), and through the Person of His Spirit (Acts 13:1-3). Jude 3 reminds us that the faith has been once for all delivered to the saints. The pseudorevelations and occultic teachings of Joseph Smith, Brigham Young, and their successors cannot alter or impeach the divine record. God has exalted His Word above every name (Psalm 138:2), and "while the grass withers and the flower fades, the Word of the Lord endures forever, and it is this Word which through the gospel we preach to you" (1 Peter 1:24, 25 lit. trans.).

Christians can understand the occultic roots of Mormonism. They can understand the counterfeit gifts and fruits of the alien force which pulsates through the Mormon Church, as well as the nature of the false prophets who have uttered unspeakable blasphemies in the name of the very God who forbids the practices they maintain He endorses! As Scripture reminds us, the role of the false prophet is to lead us "away from the Lord your God." Let us remember the great threat of the occult, that dimension of darkness against which God warns us, and against which we are to stand clothed in the full armor of Deity. We are not warring against Mormons (flesh and blood) but against the spiritual rulers of the darkness of this age, against the wickedness enthroned in the heavenlies (Ephesians 6:11-18).

NINE

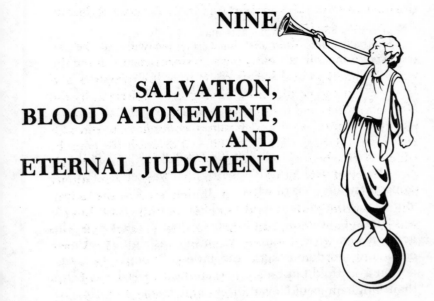

SALVATION, BLOOD ATONEMENT, AND ETERNAL JUDGMENT

The Mormon Church constantly emphasizes its concept of salvation and of judgment.[1] One thing crucial to understanding the Mormon message is knowing the Mormon meaning of the terms "salvation and exaltation," and how each is attained.

In the theological structure of Mormonism, salvation is different from exaltation, the former being the deliverance of the individual from sin and everlasting punishment, and the latter being progression to eventual godhood or deity.

Salvation in Mormonism is realized by faith, repentance, baptism for the remission of sins, good works, and obedience to the laws and ordinances of the gospel as taught by the Church of Jesus Christ of Latter-day Saints. There is no room for salvation by grace alone, through faith in Jesus Christ. To quote Brigham Young:

---

[1] I am indebted to Sandra Tanner of Modern Microfilm in Salt Lake City for the chart included in this chapter, which explains many of the topics I refer to.

Some of our old traditions teach us that a man guilty of
atrocious and murderous acts may savingly repent when
on the scaffold; and upon his execution will hear the
expression, "Bless God! he has gone to heaven, to be
crowned in glory, through the all-redeeming merits of
Christ the Lord." This is all nonsense. Such a character
never will see heaven.

Brigham Young
Discourses of Brigham Young,
by John A. Widtsoe, page 157;
also *Journal of Discourses* 8:61

The "lion of the Lord" (as Brigham was referred to) was
apparently unaware of what was taught in the history of the
Bible, and therefore taught in violation of its record of the
salvation of the thief on the cross (Luke 23:39-43). In this
account a man who quite obviously was "guilty of atrocious and murderous acts" did indeed "savingly repent,"
not on a scaffold but on a cross. He heard words far better
than Brigham could ever utter, and from the only One
capable of speaking with such authority: "Truly, truly I tell
you, today you shall be with me in paradise." Brigham
Young stated in a sermon that *Lucifer* would be the one
"that will say to the thief on the cross, to the murderer on
the gallows, and to him who has killed his father, mother,
brothers, and sisters and little ones, 'Now, if you will say, I
repent and believe on the Lord Jesus Christ, or on the
Savior of the world, you shall be saved'" (*Journal of
Discourses*, 13:282). Brigham Young was a legalist who,
when asked whether the water of baptism by itself could
wash sin away, stated:

No; but keeping the commandments of God will cleanse
away the stain of sin.

Discourse of Brigham Young page 159;
Journal of Discourses 2:4

James Talmage (whose *Articles of Faith* are sent out
with the recommendation and stamp of approval of the
Mormon Church concerning their accurate representation
of the Mormon faith) has no use for the great Pauline doctrine of "justification by faith." He refers to it as the "sec-

tarian dogma of justification by faith alone," which he says has "exercised an influence for evil since the early days of Christianity" (*Articles of Faith*, 1909 edition, page 120).

Mormonism and Human Sacrifice

Listed below are a number of authoritative quotations from classic Mormon theology on the subjects of blood atonement,[2] salvation, and the Mormon concept of "justice."

> If you want to know what to do with a thief that you may find stealing, *I say kill him on the spot*, and never suffer him to commit another iniquity. . . . if I caught a man stealing on my premises I should be very apt to send him *straight home*,° and that is what I wish every man to do, to put a stop to that abominable practice in the midst of this people.
>
> I know this appears hard, and throws a cold chill over our revered traditions received by early education. I had a great many such feelings to contend with myself, and was as much of a sectarian in my notions as any other man, and as mild, perhaps, in my natural disposition, but I have trained myself to measure things by the line of justice, to estimate them by the rule of equity and truth, and not by the false tradition of the fathers, or the sympathies of the natural mind. If you will cause all those whom you know to be thieves, to be placed in a line before the mouth of one of our largest cannon, well loaded with chain shot, I will prove by my works whether I can mete out justice to such persons, or not. I would consider it just as much my duty to do that, as to baptize a man for the remission of his sins. That is a short discourse on thieves, I acknowledge, but I tell you the truth as it is in my heart.
>
> Brigham Young, *Journal of Discourses* 1:108-9

---

[2]This doctrine was defined by Brigham Young, and his statements are self-explanatory. Essentially, it involved executing individuals and spilling their blood so it would atone for the sins they had committed. He maintained that Christ's blood could not accomplish this.

°Emphasis theirs.

President Young then spoke against thieving. . . .said he, I should be perfectly willing to see thieves have their throats cut; some of you may say, if that is your feelings Brigham, we'll lay you aside sometime, well, do it if you can; I would rather die by the hands of the meanest of all men, false brethren, than to live among thieves.

History of the Church 7:597

. . . Let me suppose a case. Suppose you found your brother in bed with your wife, and put a javelin through both of them, you would be justified, and *they would atone for their sins,* ° and be received into the kingdom of God. I would at once do so in such a case; and under such circumstances, *I have no wife whom I love so well that I would not put a javelin through her heart, and I would do it with clean hands.* ° . . .

There is not a man or woman, who violates the covenants made with their God, that will not be required to pay the debt. *The blood of Christ will never wipe that out, your own blood must atone for it;* ° and the judgments of the Almighty will come, sooner or later, and *every man and woman will have to atone for breaking their covenants.* °

Brigham Young,
Journal of Discourses 3:247

. . . Now take a person in this congregation who has knowledge with regard to being saved in the kingdom of our God and our Father, and being exalted, one who knows and understands the principles of eternal life . . . and suppose that he is overtaken in a gross fault, that he has committed a sin that he knows will deprive him of that exaltation which he desires, and that he cannot attain to it without the shedding of his blood, and also knows that by having his blood shed he will atone for that sin, and be saved and exalted with the Gods, is there a man or woman in this house but what would say, "shed my blood that I may be saved and exalted with the Gods?"

All mankind love themselves, and let these principles be known by an individual, and *he would be glad to have his blood shed.* ° . . .

I could refer you to plenty of instances where men have been righteously slain, in order to atone for their

---

° Emphasis ours.

sins. . . . This is loving our neighbor as ourselves; if he needs help, help him; and if he wants salvation and it is necessary to spill his blood on the earth in order that he may be saved, spill it.

Brigham Young,
Journal of Discourses 4:219, 220

There are sins that men commit for which they cannot receive forgiveness in this world, or in that which is to come, and if they had their eyes open to see their true condition, *they would be perfectly willing to have their blood spilt upon the ground, that the smoke thereof might ascend to heaven as an offering for their sins; and the smoking incense would atone for their sins,*° whereas, if such is not the case, they will stick to them and remain upon them in the spirit world.

I know, *when you hear my brethren telling about cutting people off from the earth, that you consider it is strong doctrine; but it is to save them, not to destroy them.*° . . .

. . . And furthermore, I know that there are transgressors, who, if they knew themselves, and the only condition upon which they can obtain forgiveness, would beg of their brethren to shed their blood, that the smoke thereof might ascend to God as an offering to appease the wrath that is kindled against them, and that the law might have its course. I will say further; I have had men come to me and offer their lives to atone for their sins.

It is true that the blood of the Son of God was shed for sins through the fall and those committed by men, yet men can commit sins which it can never remit.° As it was in ancient days, so it is in our day; and though the principles are taught publicly from this stand, still the people do not understand them; yet the law is precisely the same. There are sins that can be atoned for by an offering upon an altar, as in ancient days; and there are sins that the blood of a lamb, of a calf, or of turtle doves, cannot remit, but they must be atoned for by the blood of the man. That is the reason why men talk to you as they do from this stand; they understand the doctrine and throw out a few words about it. You have been taught that doctrine, but you do not understand it.

Brigham Young,
Journal of Discourses 4:53-54

°Emphasis ours.

I say, that there are men and women that I would advise to go to the President immediately, and ask him to appoint a committee to attend to their case; and then let a place be selected, and let that committee shed their blood.°

We have those amongst us that are full of all manner of abominations, those who need to have their blood shed, for water will not do, their sins are of too deep a dye.

You may think that I am not teaching you Bible doctrine, but what says the apostle Paul? I would ask how many covenant breakers there are in this city and in this kingdom. *I believe that there are a great many; and if they are covenant breakers we need a place designated, where we can shed their blood.°* . . .

. . . I go in for letting the sword of the Almighty be unsheathed, not only in word, but in deed. . . .

You can scarcely find a place in this city that is not full of filth and abominations. . . .

Brethren and sisters, we want you to repent and forsake your sins. *And you who have committed sins that cannot be forgiven through baptism, let your blood be shed, and let the smoke ascend, that the incense thereof may come up before God as an atonement for your sins,°* and that the sinners in Zion may be afraid.

Pres. J. M. Grant,
Journal of Discourses 4:49-51

. . . for if men turn traitors to God and His servants, their blood will surely be shed, or else they will be damned, and that too according to their covenants.

Pres. Heber C. Kimball,
Journal of Discourses 4:375

These are my views, and the Lord knows that I believe in the principles of sanctification; and when I am guilty of seducing any man's wife, or any woman in God's world, I say, sever my head from my body. These have ever been my feelings from the days of my youth. This is my character, and the character of President Brigham Young. It was the character of Joseph Smith and of Jesus Christ;

°Emphasis ours.

and that is the character of the Apostles of Jesus, and that must be sustained by this people.

> Pres. Heber C. Kimball,
> *Journal of Discourses* 7:20

I feel the Lord designs the thing should move along and no blood be shed, because I do not consider God is so anxious that we should be blood-thirsty men as some may be. God designs we should be pure men, holding the oracles of God in holy and pure vessels; but when it is necessary that blood should be shed, we should be as ready to do that as to eat an apple. . . . and if men and women will not live their religion, but take a course to pervert the hearts of the righteous, we will "lay judgment to the line and righteousness to the plummet," and we will let you know that the earth can swallow you up, as it did Korah with his host; and *as brother Taylor says, you may dig your graves, and we will slay you, and you may crawl into them.* °

> Pres. Heber C. Kimball,
> *Journal of Discourses* 6:34-35

It is believed in the world that our females are all common women . . . but they are not unclean, for we wipe all unclean ones from our midst: *we not only wipe them from our streets, but we wipe them out of existence.* ° And if the world want to practise uncleanness, and bring their prostitutes here, if they do not repent and forsake such sins, we will wipe the evil out. We will not have them in this valley, unless they repent; for, so help me God, while I live, I will lend my hand to wipe such persons out; and I know this people will.

> Pres. Heber C. Kimball,
> *Journal of Discourses* 7:19

. . . Judas lost that saving principle, and they took him and killed him. It is said in the Bible that his bowels gushed out; but they actually kicked him until his bowels came out.

"I will suffer my bowels to be taken out before I will forfeit the covenant I have made with Him and my brethren." Do you understand me? Judas was like salt that had lost its saving principles—good for nothing but to be cast out and trodden under foot of men. . . . It is so

---

° Emphasis ours.

with you, ye Elders of Israel, when you forfeit your convenants.

... I know the day is right at hand when men will forfeit their Priesthood and turn against us and against the covenants they have made, and *they will be destroyed as Judas was.*°

Pres. Heber C. Kimball,
Journal of Discourses 6:125-26

... It is not so much polygamy that they are opposed to, but they hate this people because they strive to be pure, and will not believe in whoredom and adultery, *but declare death to the man who is found guilty of those crimes.*°

Brigham Young,
Journal of Discourses 7:146

... The principle, the only one that beats and throbs through the heart of the entire inhabitants of this Territory, is simply this: *The man who seduces his neighbor's wife must die, and her nearest relative must kill him!*†

George A. Smith,
Journal of Discourses 1:97

In debate, George A. Smith said imprisonment was better than hanging.

I replied, I was opposed to hanging, even if a man kill another, *I will shoot him, or cut off his head, spill his blood on the ground, and let the smoke thereof ascend up to God;*° and if ever I have the privilege of making a law on that subject, I will have it so.

Joseph Smith,
History of the Church 5:296

... They know, that if they have any connections out of the marriage covenant, *they not only forfeit their lives by the law of God,*° but they forfeit their salvation also.

Apostle Orson Pratt,
The Seer, page 42

Mormon Salvation

Leaving the subject of blood atonement, we turn to the

° Emphasis ours.
† Emphasis theirs.

subject of salvation in Mormon theology. Below are quotes defining and substantiating what the Mormon position on salvation is. From these quotes, it is abundantly clear that the salvation in Mormonism is nothing like the salvation revealed by God in the Bible.

> *Unconditional or general salvation*, that which comes by grace alone without obedience to gospel law, consists in the mere fact of being resurrected. In this sense salvation is synonymous with immortality. . . . But this is not the salvation of righteousness, the salvation which the Saints seek. . . . *Conditional or individual salvation*, that which comes by grace coupled with gospel obedience, consists in receiving an inheritance in the celestial kingdom of God. . . . *Salvation*, in its true and full meaning, is synonymous with *exaltation* or *eternal life* and consists in getting an inheritance in the highest of the three heavens within the celestial kingdom. With few exceptions this is the salvation of which the scriptures speak. . . . This full salvation is obtained in and through the continuation of the family unit in eternity, and those who obtain it are gods.*
>
> Bruce R. McConkie,
> *Mormon Doctrine*, (1966 edition),
> pages 669-70

> . . . the mere fact of resurrection is called *salvation by grace alone*. . . . Salvation in the celestial kingdom of God, however, is not salvation by grace alone. Rather it is *salvation by grace coupled with obedience* to the laws and ordinances of the gospel.*
>
> Bruce R. McConkie,
> *Mormon Doctrine*, (1966 edition),
> page 671

Salvation is two-fold: *General*—that which comes to all men irrespective of belief (in this life) in Christ—and, *Individual*—that which man merits through his own acts through life and by obedience to the laws and ordinances of the gospel.

> Joseph Fielding Smith,
> *Doctrines of Salvation* 1:134

---

*Emphasis theirs.

Full salvation is attained by virtue of knowledge, truth, righteousness, and all true principles. Many conditions must exist in order to make such salvation available to men. Without the atonement, the gospel, the priesthood, and the sealing power, there would be no salvation. Without continuous revelation, the ministering of angels, the working of miracles, the prevalence of gifts of the spirit, there would be no salvation. . . . There is no salvation outside the Church of Jesus Christ of Latter-day Saints.

> Bruce R. McConkie,
> *Mormon Doctrine*, (1966 edition),
> page 670

The Mormon Church does not accept the historic Christian doctrine of redemption. There is a strong emphasis instead upon works in Mormonism as a means of attaining "full" salvation. Paul contradicts this:

> But to him that worketh not, but believeth on him that justifieth the ungodly, his faith is counted for righteousness.
>
> Romans 4:5

The Apostle goes on to affirm that God has blessed the man to whom the Lord will not impute (or put to the account of) sin (Romans 4:7, 8). Elsewhere he is adamant in declaring that, if salvation comes by works, then Christ has died for nothing (Galatians 2:21).

In the revelation that God gave Paul, the law is shown to bring us to Christ only by convicting us of the guilt of our sins, but it is faith in Jesus Christ through grace that is the means of man's complete salvation (Romans 3:20-28). There is no doubt in the mind of Paul that if a man works for something he has earned it, and it is a debt to be repaid. But in the case of redemption through the Lord Jesus Christ, it is the "employer" who paid the debt, by the sacrifice of Himself (Hebrews 9:26b). Man is the recipient of a gift which he cannot earn or merit in any way. He therefore has no opportunity or right to boast of his eternal salvation.

Utilizing the past tense in the Greek of Ephesians, Paul says,

> For it is by grace we have been saved [or, you have been saved] through faith, and that not by yourselves; it is the gift of God, not of works, lest any man should boast.
>
> Ephesians 2:8-10 lit. trans.

He is quick to add, however, that we are God's creations, created in Christ Jesus to perform good works which *God* has ordained that we should walk in.

Mormonism emphasizes many "works," but when Jesus Christ was asked what the ultimate work was, He said, "This is the work of God, that ye believe on him whom he [God] hath sent" (John 6:29). Mormons frequently quote James (chapters 1 and 2) and maintain that "faith without works is dead" or, in other words, salvation is by works. This is not accurate. It is true that James 2:17 and 26b declare that faith without works is dead, but we must ask the nature of the word "faith" here and the nature of the term "dead." James tells us that if you have the kind of faith that can sit by while your brother has needs and you have the means to meet them, then you do not possess saving faith (2:15-17). He tells us that profession about God will not save us, any more than it can save the demons (2:19). He makes the important point that our works justify us before men (who can see our faith and its true nature only in our works), whereas God can see the nature of our faith which *produces* the works. We are therefore justified before God on the basis of faith (Romans 4:1-8) and before men on the basis of our works (James 2:18).

It is significant that James and Paul both cite Abraham as their illustration. God knew that Abraham had faith enough to kill Isaac, because Abraham knew that God was able to raise Isaac from the dead (Hebrews 11:19). Men could not see this faith; therefore, it was necessary for their sakes for Abraham to take Isaac to Mount Moriah and to raise the knife over his breast so that men might say, "Look, Abraham is a man of faith." By the act of raising the knife,

Abraham's work demonstrated the existence of his faith. The faith that acquits a man before God in company with the work that justifies him before men is a living faith.

It is a tragedy that Mormonism has confounded the doctrine of justification by faith with that of works, and settled for the chaos which is the Mormon doctrine of salvation and exaltation. The interested reader should study the following Scriptures which demonstrate that salvation, full and complete, is by grace only, through faith, and that true salvation produces works which testify to the world of the existence of the person's faith. See Ephesians 2:8-10; Philippians 2:12, 13; Acts 16:31; John 3:16; Titus 2:11; 1 Peter 1:3-9; Acts 4:12; Romans 6:23; Romans 5:1, 2, 21; Romans 4:16, 17; Romans 3:20-28; Romans 1:17; Romans 9:30-33; and Hebrews 7:18, 19.

Mormonism and Universal Salvation

Since the days of Hosea Ballou (the great Universalist preacher of New England), the United States has increasingly become a mecca for the theology of Universalism. This is the theory that at the final consummation of the ages God will punish in a *remedial* way the souls of men who have rejected Jesus Christ as Lord and Savior, reconciling them to Himself after a proper period of chastisement. This is a "Protestant purgatory" and finds no support in the Bible. Outside the Universalist Church in the United States (which has only a small membership and which merged with the Unitarian Church) there are also splinter groups of universalists, such as the Scripture Studies Concern, located in Corona, California. In addition, there are numerous cults which have borrowed the doctrine of universalism and added it to their own theological systems.

The largest cult embracing universalism in the United States today is the Mormon Church. We shall examine some of the basic texts used by some Mormons and universalists in their attempts to "prove" that the Bible teaches that God intends to save everyone. Some universalists have even gone so far as to say that God intends to save the Devil and his demons!

Listed below are quotations from unimpeachable Mormon sources that teach Mormon adherence to a very real type of universal salvation. However, *The Book of Mormon* does *not* teach universalism and, in fact, condemns it.

> I see no faults in the Church, and therefore let me be resurrected with the Saints, whether I ascend to heaven or descend to hell, or go to any other place. And if we go to hell, we will turn the devils out of doors and make a heaven of it.
>
> Joseph Smith,
> *History of the Church* 5:517

> I doubt whether it can be found, from the revelations that are given and the facts as they exist, that there is a female in all the regions of hell. . . .
>
> I assuredly believe that all brother Hyde has said in regard to the restoration of the Saints to their inheritances, &c., will come to pass. . . .
>
> Brigham Young,
> *Journal of Discourses* 8:222

> It is the duty of men in this life to repent. *Every man who hears the gospel message is under obligation to receive it.* If he fails, then in the spirit world he will be called upon to receive it, but he will be *denied* the fulness that will come to those who in their faithfulness have been just and true, whether it be in this life or in the spirit world.
>
> Joseph Fielding Smith,
> *Doctrines of Salvation* 2:183

> OFFER OF SALVATION MADE EITHER NOW OR IN SPIRIT WORLD . . . .
>
> If they die without that opportunity in this life, it will reach them in the world of spirits. The gospel will there be declared to them, and if they are willing to accept, it is counted unto them just the same as if they had embraced it in mortality. In this way justice is meted out to

every man; all are placed on an equality before the bar of God.

> Joseph Fielding Smith,
> *Doctrines of Salvation* 2:182

. . . It is decreed that the unrighteous shall have to spend their time during this thousand years in the prison house prepared for them where they can repent and cleanse themselves through the things which they shall suffer.°

> Joseph Fielding Smith
> *Doctrines of Salvation* 3:60

. . . That is loving the wicked, to send them there to hell to be burnt out until they are purified. . . . and then their spirits may be saved in the day of God Almighty.

> Heber C. Kimball,
> *Journal of Discourses* 4:223

You have often heard me speak about my kindred. . . . Will they be saved? Yes, they will, but they will be saved as I have told you many of this people will; they will first go to hell and remain there until the corruption with which they impregnated is burnt out; and the day will yet come when they will come to me and acknowledge me as their savior, and I will redeem them and bring them forth from hell to where I live and make them my servants; and they will be quite willing to enter into my service.

> Heber C. Kimball,
> *Journal of Discourses* 3:109

Those who reject the gospel, but who live honorable lives, shall also be heirs of salvation, but not in the celestial kingdom. The Lord has prepared a place for them in the terrestrial kingdom.

Those who live lives of wickedness may also be heirs of salvation, that is, they too shall be redeemed from death and from hell *eventually.*

> Joseph Fielding Smith,
> *Doctrines of Salvation* 2:133

We, Joseph and Sidney, being in the Spirit on the sixteenth of February, in the year of our Lord, one thousand eight hundred and thirty two, and through the power of

---

°Emphasis theirs

the Spirit, our eyes were opened, and our understandings were enlightened, so as to see and understand the things of God; even things which were from the biginning [sic] before the world was, which was ordained of the Father, through his only begotten Son, who was in the bosom of the Father, even from the beginning, of whom we bear record . . . whom we saw and with whom we conversed in the Heavenly Vision. . . . And we saw a vision of the eternal sufferings of those with whom he maketh war and overcometh, for thus came the voice of the Lord unto us. . . .

. . . they are they who are the sons of perdition . . . for they are vessels of wrath doomed to suffer the wrath of God, with the devil and his angels, throughout eternity. . . . this is the end of the vision of the eternal sufferings of the ungodly!

Evening and Morning Star,
Vol. 1, No. 2, July 1832, page 2

. . . Every possession and object of affection will be taken from those who forsake the truth, and their identity and existence will eventually cease.

Brigham Young,
Journal of Discourses 4:31-32

I believe in annihilation in one degree. Men will sin so that they will be damned spiritually and temporally. There will be a dissolution of the natural body and of the spirit, and they will go back into their native element, the same as the chemist can go to work and dissolve a five-dollar gold piece, and throw it into a liquid. Does not that show there can be a dissolution of the natural body and of the spirit? This is what is called the second death.

Heber C. Kimball,
Journal of Discourses 5:95

. . . He had not the power of endless life in him, and he will be decomposed, and the particles which compose his body and spirit will return to their native element. . . . What can you make of this but decomposition, the returning of the organized particles to their native element, after suffering the wrath of God until the time appointed. . . . When the elements in an organized form do not fill the end of their creation, they are thrown back again, like brother Kimball's old pottery were, to be ground up, and made over again.

Brigham Young,
Journal of Discourses 1:275

... The rebellious will be thrown back into their native element, there to remain myriads of years before their dust will again be revived, before they will be re-organized. Some might argue that this principle would lead to the re-organization of Satan, and all the devils. I say nothing about this, only what the Lord says—that when he comes, "he will destroy *death*, and him that has the power of it." It cannot be annihilated; you cannot annihilate matter.

Brigham Young,
Journal of Discourses 1:118

Misapplied Texts

Consequently, just as the result of one trespass was condemnation for all men, so also the result of one act of righteousness was justification that brings life for all men. For just as through the disobedience of the one man the many were made sinners, so also through the obedience of the one man the many will be made righteous.

Romans 5:18, 19 NIV

This first text utilized by some LDS theologians, when properly understood in its context, does not teach that salvation is ultimately to be possessed by all men. The Bible teaches that, although salvation is offered freely to all men, there are many who just will not accept it! These are the persons of whom Jesus spoke when He said, "Depart from me, ye cursed, into everlasting fire, prepared for the devil and his angels" (Matthew 25:41).

Paul also teaches in Romans 5 that sin entered the world through one man, Adam. Through this sin the judgment of God came upon all men to eternal death, but in the fullness of time God sent forth His Son, made under the Law, to ransom those who had become transgressors. Nowhere does the Scripture say that every man will either now or at some future time accept this gift. Christ Himself stated:

O Jerusalem, Jerusalem, you who kill the prophets and stone those sent to you, how often I have longed to

gather your children together, as a hen gathers her chicks
under her wings, but you were not willing.
Matthew 23:37 NIV

As the judgment came to all men to condemnation for
sin, the justification of life to all men was supplied only on
the condition of acceptance of the Lord Jesus Christ as
Savior. Justification itself is the result of faith—conclusive
proof indeed that believing the Word of God is the basis for
justification before God. So we see that Mormonism's argument on the basis of the word "all" melts into nothingness
when the context is clearly understood. The word "all" does
not in every instance mean "every." In some instances it is
definitely a restrictive term (for a detailed study of this subject the reader is referred to A. H. Strong's *Systematic
Theology*, pages 1047-56).

For God was pleased to have all his fullness dwell in him,
and through him to reconcile to himself all things,
whether things on earth or things in heaven, by making
peace through his blood, shed on the cross.
Colossians 1:19, 20 NIV

In this text, many universalists claim that God will
unquestionably reconcile all things to Himself. But the
usage of the word "all" is again governed by the context
and is definitely not used as a universal, all-inclusive word
(see John 12:19 for a clear example). It is true that Christ
died to provide a sacrifice through His blood for all men
and that His sacrifice is sufficient for the sins of all men. But
the Scripture tells us that it is only in operation for those
who accept it. This is particularly true in the light of John
3:16, 36, where it is stated that God loved the world and
sent His Son to be its Savior. Therefore, those who accept
this sacrifice have everlasting life while those who do not
believe "continue to abide under the wrath of God" (lit.
trans.). We are never to forget that there are two classes of
people in Scripture: the sheep and the goats (Matthew
25:32, 33). The sheep are destined for eternal life and the
bliss of Christ's eternal presence. The goats, on the other

hand, are sentenced to eternal punishment in company with the Devil and his angels.

When universalists attempt to teach that the reconciliation provided for all through Calvary will be realized by all, they are reading into the Scripture what they desperately want the Scripture to teach. No qualified exegetical scholar has ever been able to defend universalism from the standpoint of the original languages of Scripture. Some men from the LDS Church have tried, but they have repeatedly met with failure and theological disaster.

Paul never taught that the reconciliation provided by God the Father would eventually be accepted by all men. He taught that the grace of God *provided* redemption, so that *potentially* all men might be saved *if* they repented and accepted the gospel. Scripture tells us that it is not that man *cannot* believe, but that they *will* not.

> This is a trustworthy saying that deserves full acceptance (and for this we labor and strive), that we have put our hope in the living God, who is the Savior of all men, and especially of those who believe.
> 1 Timothy 4:9, 10 NIV

To argue that this text teaches that God intends to save all men is grammatical folly. It is very true that God's *desire* is that all men should be saved (Ezekiel 33:11; 2 Peter 3:9). He could not be a loving God unless His desire was that His creations be delivered from the fruit of their own wickedness, but the text does not say that all men *will* be saved. It teaches that God in the measureless depths of His eternal love had made *provision* for their salvation, a provision which some of them will *never* accept.

First Timothy 2:4 is also used in connection with this text, although it gives no ground for supposing that God has decreed that all shall be saved. This simply is not true! If our universal-salvation friends would study the second half of 1 Timothy 4:10, they would find that Paul qualifies his use of the term "all" by stating "especially those that believe." We see that while God is the Savior of all men in the *potential* sense of the word, He is *actually* the Savior only of those who believe and accept the historic Jesus Christ as Lord and Savior.

The statement of Christ to Nicodemus in John 3:3 is as true today as when He uttered it almost two thousand years ago: "Except a man be born again, he cannot see the kingdom of God." All the LDS arguments in the world cannot change the fact that if a man rejects the sacrificial blood of Jesus Christ (apart from which there is no remission for sin—Hebrews 9:22) then he certainly cannot be cleansed by "fire," as the Mormons teach. This method of cleansing affirms that God will punish for many "eons" of time the unrepentant souls of men until they see the evil of their rejection of Christ and accept Him. This is "meriting" salvation the Mormon way. It is, in effect, "salvation by suffering."

The Bible clearly teaches that it is only the blood of Jesus Christ, God's Son, that cleanses us from all sin—not the suffering of the soul.

> When he has done this, then the Son himself will be made subject to him who put everything under him, so that God may be all in all.
> 1 Corinthians 15:28 NIV

The argument is that because God will eventually become all in all, the "all" must refer to everything in creation which possess a spiritual nature (i.e., lost men). However, the context is neglected. The Apostle states clearly that only the *redeemed* are to be transformed into the likeness of Christ after their resurrection to immortality. Nowhere is there a suggestion that the "all" refers to anyone but those raised in the image of Christ—i.e., the regenerated and redeemed souls of believers.

Some writers couple this text with verse 22 of the same chapter ("For as in Adam all die, so in Christ all will be made alive"). This is an attempt to establish the tenet that as spiritual death came to Adam through sin and so passed upon all men, so God in Christ intends to make *all* men spiritually "alive." That this position is Biblically untenable can be seen by a study of this passage in the original Greek. The context is clearly one of resurrection—physical resurrection for judgment. To capture the sense of the Greek properly it should be rendered, "As in Adam all die, so in Christ all shall be raised to life, or resurrected." This we know to be true, because there will be a resurrection of the just and of the unjust (Acts 24:15).

The preceding brief examination of universalist "texts" demonstrates the danger of building doctrines such as universalism upon isolated words with little or no consideration of context or the related background of the language both grammatically and exegetically.

Mormonism manifests another misleading trait. In a supposed emphasis upon exegesis from the original languages of Scripture, individuals who are hardly qualified to read technical exegetical books continually pose as scholars of the original languages! For instance, they say that the meaning of the Greek noun *aion* (eon) cannot possibly mean "without end." This argument is recognized by qualified Greek scholars as an evasion of the fact that the Greek language teaches eternal punishment for sin.

If *aion* or *aionion* refers only to "ages," then Romans 16:26 teaches beyond a question that Almighty God Himself has an end in time! A comparison of the usage of the word *aionion* in the Greek New Testament would show that in numerous contexts the word indisputably means "everlasting" or "forever."

As Dr. Strong has pointed out in a devastating chapter on everlasting punishment (see his *Systematic Theology*, pages 104ff.), the term *aionion* or *aionas* appears in the same context in Matthew's Gospel referring to the condition of the saved as does Christ's reference to the damned: "These shall go away into everlasting punishment, but the righteous into life eternal" (Matthew 25:46). If we would limit the duration of the punishment of the damned, then we must limit the eternal habitation of the saved! Even Mormon universalists are unwilling to do this!

There are, of course, contexts in the New Testament in which the words *aionion* or *aionas* could not possibly refer to eternal things. However, the context clearly determines their meaning. For Mormonism to claim on the basis of a Greek form that the Bible does not teach everlasting retribution when the majority of scholars—classical and New Testament—have taught the opposite is an evidence of their lack of scholastic resources.

Because Mormon theology cannot conceive of eternally punishing the infinite sin of rejecting His Son, they have sought to conform Scripture to their own extrabiblical revelations and "prophecies," which neither scholarship nor common sense can allow. Since they cannot conceive of God so punishing the unregenerate soul, they have set up their own standard of how God must act, based upon what they believe is justice. The juggling of the Greek terms for "everlasting" and "eternal" is one more evidence of the limitations of their resources.

Dr. Francis Pieper, the great Lutheran scholar and author of *Christian Dogmatics* (volume III, pages 544-45), states the historic Christian view when he says:

> Holy Scripture teaches the truth of an eternal damnation so clearly and emphatically that one cannot deny it without at the same time rejecting the authority of Scripture. Scripture parallels the eternal salvation of the believers and the eternal damnation of the unbelievers. Whoever therefore denies the one must, to be consistent, deny the other. Matt. 25:46: "These shall go away into everlasting punishment . . . , but the righteous into life eternal . . . ." We find the same juxtaposition and antithesis in other passages of Scripture, e.g., John 3:36, etc. This parallelism proves that the term "eternity" in the sense of limited duration as sometimes used in Holy Writ (Ex. 12:14, 24; 21:6; etc.), is inapplicable here. We must take the predicate "eternal" in its proper, or strict, sense, a sense of *sine fine*, in all Scripture texts which use it to describe the duration of the penalties of the wicked in yonder life (II Thess. 1:9: "everlasting destruction";

Matt. 18:8: "everlasting fire"; Mark 3:29: "eternal damnation"). . . .

The objections raised in all ages to the endlessness of the infernal punishment are understandable; for the thought of a never-ending agony of rational beings, fully realizing their distressing plight, is so appalling that it exceeds comprehension. . . . But all objections are based on the false principle that it is proper and reasonable to make our human sentiments and judgments the measure of God's essence and activity. This is the case in particular with those who contend that an everlasting punishment of a part of mankind does not agree with the unity of God's world plan ("dualism"), or that it is compatible neither with divine love nor with divine justice, who accordingly want to substitute for eternal damnation eventual salvation by gradual improvement in the next life, or an immediate or later annihilation of the wicked. Against such views we must maintain the general principle that God's essence, attributes, and actions exceed our comprehension, that we can therefore not know *a priori*, but only from God's revelation in His Word, what agrees, or conflicts, with God's essence and attributes.

The *nature (forma)* of eternal damnation consists in eternal banishment from the sight of God, or, in other words, in being forever excluded from communion with God. . . . To illustrate the terrible agony setting in with this banishment from the sight of God, the dogmaticians point to the agony of a fish removed from its element. But there is this difference: the fish which is removed from its element soon dies, whereas the man who is banished from communion with God must by God's judgment live on, "is guilty of eternal judgment . . . ," Mark 3:29.

We ought to fix in our minds these three facts: (1) the grammar of the New Testament teaches that there will be everlasting bliss for those who accept Jesus Christ as Lord and Savior (John 5:24; 6:47; etc.); (2) this same grammar teaches, with the same words, and many times in the same context, that there will be everlasting punishment for those who willfully reject Jesus Christ as Lord and Savior (John 3:36; Matthew 25:32, 33; Revelation 20:10; etc.); (3) salvation from sin has been provided for all men through the blood of the Cross (1 John 2:2), and whoever will may come, according to the will of God. But God has declared in His Word that many will not accept His provision of redemption and will in fact "trample underfoot the blood of Jesus." These are the persons described in Scripture "whose end is destruction, whose god is their belly" (Philippians 3:19); "raging waves of the sea, foaming out their own shame; wandering stars, to whom is reserved the blackness of darkness forever" (Jude 13).

If we keep these three points before us, recognizing that the Scriptures teach these truths (whether or not we can understand the character of God this side of eternity), we will protect ourselves from the error of Mormon universalism. This is the error which has plagued the Christian church since the days of Origen. His form of theology has laid the groundwork for many heresies, since it has the tendency to lead the unwary further into fields of doctrinal deviation.

Let us heed the Apostle Paul and faithfully "put on the whole armor of God, that ye may be able to stand against the wiles of the devil" (Ephesians 6:11).

Universal Salvation, Joseph Smith, and The Book of Mormon

The following information will establish beyond doubt that Joseph Smith's "revelations from God" irreconcilably contradict the "revelations from God" contained in *The Book of Mormon* concerning universal salvation.

> Now, repentance could not come unto men except there were a punishment, which also was eternal as the life of the soul should be, affixed opposite to the plan of happiness, which was as eternal also as the life of the soul.
>
> Alma 42:16 (all quotes are from portions of *The Book of Mormon*, current edition)
>
> Therefore if that man repenteth not, and remaineth and dieth an enemy to God, the demands of divine justice do awaken his immortal soul to a lively sense of his own

guilt, which doth cause him to shrink from the presence of the Lord, and doth fill his breast with guilt, and pain, and anguish, which is like an unquenchable fire, whose flame ascendeth up forever and ever. And now I say unto you, that mercy hath no claim on that man; therefore his final doom is to endure a never-ending torment.

Mosiah 2:38-39

For behold, this life is the time for men to prepare to meet God; yea behold the day of this life is the day for men to perform their labors. And now, as I said unto you before, as ye have had so many witnesses, therefore, I beseech of you that ye do not procrastinate the day or your repentance until the end; for after this day of life, which is given us to prepare for eternity, behold, if we do not improve our time while in this life, then cometh the night of darkness wherein there can be no labor performed. Ye cannot say, when ye are brought to that awful crisis, that I will repent, that I will return to my God. Nay, ye cannot say this; for that same spirit which doth possess your bodies at the time that ye go out of this life, that same spirit will have power to possess your body in the eternal world. For behold, if ye have procrastinated the day of your repentance even until death, behold, ye have become subjected to the spirit of the devil, and he doth seal you his; therefore, the Spirit of the Lord hath withdrawn from you, and hath no place in you, and the devil hath all power over you; and this is the final state of the wicked.

Alma 34:32-35

And behold, others he flattereth away, and telleth them there is no hell; and he saith unto them: I am no devil, for there is none—and thus he whispereth in their ears, until he grasps them with his awful chains, from whence there is no deliverance.

2 Nephi 28:22

And there is a place prepared, yea, even that awful hell of which I have spoken, and the devil is the foundation of it; wherefore the final state of the souls of men is to dwell in the kingdom of God, or to be cast out because of that justice of which I have spoken.

1 Nephi 15:35

. . . nevertheless there was a space granted unto man in which he might repent; therefore this life became a probationary state; a time to prepare to meet God; a time to prepare for that endless state which has been spoken of by us, which is after the resurrection of the dead.

Alma 12:24b

Therefore, O my son, whosoever will come may come and partake of the waters of life freely; and whosoever will not come the same is not compelled to come; but in the last day it shall be restored unto him according to his deeds. If he has desired to do evil, and has not repented in his days, behold, evil shall be done unto him, according to the restoration of God.

Alma 42:27-28

And my soul was rent with anguish, because of the slain of my people, and I cried: O ye fair ones, how could ye have departed from the ways of the Lord! O ye fair ones, how could ye have rejected that Jesus, who stood with open arms to receive you! Behold, if ye had not done this, ye would not have fallen. But behold, ye are fallen, and I mourn your loss. O ye fair sons and daughters, ye fathers and mothers, ye husbands and wives, ye fair ones, how is it that ye could have fallen! But behold, ye are gone, and my sorrows cannot bring your return. And the day soon cometh that your mortal must put on immortality, and these bodies which are now moldering in corruption must soon become incorruptible bodies; and then ye must stand before the judgment seat of Christ to be judged according to your works; and if it so be that ye are righteous, then are ye blessed with your fathers who have gone before you. O that ye had repented before this great destruction had come upon you. But behold, ye are gone, and the Father, yea, the Eternal Father of heaven, knoweth your state; and he doeth with you according to his justice and mercy.

Mormon 6:16-22

Wherefore, if ye have sought to do wickedly in the days of your probation, then ye are found unclean before the judgment-seat of God; and no unclean thing can dwell with God; wherefore, ye must be cast off forever.

1 Nephi 10:21

. . . and thus we see that the devil will not support his children at the last day, but doth speedily drag them down to hell.

Alma 30:60b

The Mormon Plan of Eternal Progression

The chart (opposite) indicates the whole Mormon scheme from preexistence to exaltation, and we are indebted to Sandra Tanner, a former Mormon and top researcher in the field, for her reproduction of it. The reader will note that in Mormon theology the soul preexists, that spirit children are born of God and a wife, and that they are born on earth according to merit. As we have pointed out, the Negro has not merited a white form and is considered cursed and inferior; therefore, as you progress in reading the chart, it becomes obvious that the Negro could not attain to the exaltation of the Celestial Kingdom, until the "revelation" of June 9, 1978.

In Mormon theology, as the chart also indicates, death brings about a state of Paradise, and those in Paradise go to Hell to preach or teach to the ones caught in the spirit prison of Hell. The first resurrection takes place and the Millennial Kingdom (which is literally interpreted) also occurs, and at the end of that period comes the second resurrection, which is of the unjust. Judgment occurs, and then there is the second death for the "sons of perdition," or Satan and all his demons. Then there is the Telestial Kingdom, a level for those who inhabited the world and pursued wickedness. The Terrestrial Kingdom is the home of those who have obeyed God and have attempted to the best of their ability to be honorable but did not accept the teachings of Joseph Smith and Brigham Young and Mormonism. Finally, there is the Celestial Kingdom. The second and third levels of this kingdom are for Mormons who have not been married in the Temple, while the top or first level is actual godhood or exaltation to a deified position.

Since the Bible does not teach according to this chart, its theology refutes this "revelation" of the Mormon prophets. Again and again we are drawn inexorably to the conclusion

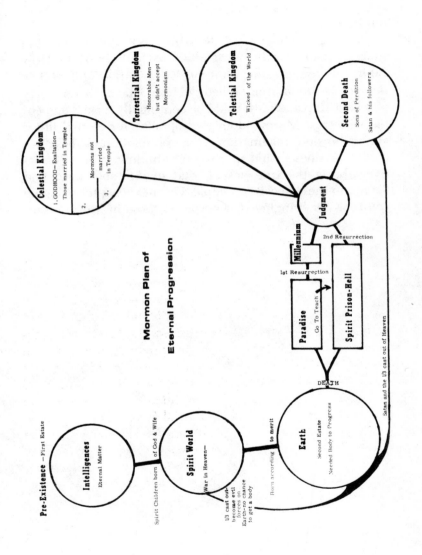

Mormon Plan of

Eternal Progression

Pre-Existence — First Estate

Intelligences
Eternal Matter

Spirit Children born of God & Wife

Spirit World
— War in Heaven —

1/3 cast out—
become evil
forces on
Earth—no chance
to get a body

Born according to merit

Earth
Second Estate
Needed Body to Progress

DEATH

Paradise
Go To Teach

Spirit Prison-Hell

Satan and the 1/3 cast out of Heaven

1st Resurrection

Millennium

2nd Resurrection

Judgment

Celestial Kingdom
1. GODHOOD—Exaltation—
Those married in Temple
2.
3. Mormons not married in Temple

Terrestrial Kingdom
Honorable Men—
but didn't accept
Mormonism

Telestial Kingdom
Wicked of the World

Second Death
Sons of Perdition
Satan & his followers

that Mormonism is completely devoid of any Biblical basis and is truly "another gospel" (Galatians 1:6-9; 2 Corinthians 11:4).

Mormon salvation, judgment, and everlasting life (universalism)[3] has been examined in the light of the Holy Bible and found sadly wanting. Even in the light of *The Book of Mormon*, it has failed the test. That such a travesty of scholarship and faith could be continually foisted on people who trust Mormondom's "prophets" for eternal life is almost beyond imagination. Our examination of these ungodly doctrines should spur us on to finding a way to effectively bring the true gospel, that of our only Lord and Savior, to these deceived people. Our next chapter will give you tools for bringing that gospel to those in Mormonism.

---

[3]See Appendix F for an examination and refutation of the Mormon doctrine of preexistence.

TEN

HELPFUL HINTS ON REFUTING AND EVANGELIZING MORMONS

More and more Christian and non-Christian homes are being subjected to the visitations of personable, intelligent, and zealous disciples of Mormonism, and for the Christian church this poses no small problem. The early Christians fearlessly campaigned in the market places, synagogues, jails, and private dwellings of the world in which they lived. There was no hesitation, and their efforts were characterized by conviction, dedication, and zeal. We are told in Scripture that they had a reputation for "turning the world upside down" (Acts 17:6).

Now, however, it seems that the church has fallen behind in her evangelistic efforts. Too often we have allowed people to go on without hearing the gospel because we're afraid to hurt their feelings or to "judge them" by saying they are not following the truth. Jesus said, "I am the way and the truth and the life. No one comes to the Father except through me." If a person has the wrong Jesus, he cannot have fellowship with God. The Word of

God demands that we present the gospel positively to all who have not embraced it.

Jude 3 instructs us "to contend for the faith that God has once for all entrusted to the saints" (NIV). In 1 Peter 3:15, 16 we find, "But in your hearts acknowledge Christ as the holy Lord. Always be prepared to give an answer to everyone who asks you to give the reason for the hope that you have. But do this with gentleness and respect, keeping a clear conscience" (NIV). Can any true Christian honestly say that he is acting in love by letting someone go to hell without hurt feelings, instead of risking his feelings to show him how to go to heaven?

We also must evangelize the members of the Mormon Church. They have historically attacked the true church and have claimed that it is wrong, so we must be on the defensive as well as the offensive. Jesus' claim to the truth is challenged when Mormonism claims that its contrary "gospel" is the *only* truth and that all others are an abomination.

Joseph Smith himself raised the initial challenge when he had his first vision in 1820, as recorded in *The Pearl of Great Price* (Joseph Smith 2:18, 19). He was told that he "must join none of them [the churches] for they were all wrong; and the Personage who addressed me said that all their creeds were an abomination in his sight; that those professors were all corrupt; that they draw near to me with their lips, but their hearts are far from me, they teach for doctrines the commandments of men, having a form of godliness, but they deny the power thereof." This attitude toward historic Christianity is consistently held by the Mormon Church. In *Journal of Discourses* 8:223, we find:

> Every intelligent person under the heavens that does not, when informed, acknowledge that Joseph Smith jun., is a Prophet of God, is in darkness and is opposed to us and to Jesus and his kingdom on the earth.

The third president of the Mormon church, John Taylor, reiterated:

What does the Christian world know about God?
Nothing; . . . Why, so far as the things of God are con-
cerned, they are the veriest fools; they know neither
God nor the things of God.

Journal of Discourses 13:225

Our job is clear: we must earnestly "contend for the
faith," and we must vindicate our right to proclaim the
gospel preached by Jesus and His disciples to all who will
listen. The Mormons have raised the challenge by disputing
our position. The Bible has seconded it by giving us the responsibility to "give an answer."

Understanding the Missionary

In order to deal effectively with Mormon missionaries, it
is essential to understand their *background, training,* and
position in the Mormon Church.

Although the missionaries are called "elders" and are
addressed as "Elder So-and-So," they are usually anything
but "elder." Since they are isolated from their families and
friends and have to live extremely austere lives during their
missions, the Mormon Church cultivates single young Mormons between the ages of 19 and 25. Thus, nine times out
of ten the Mormon missionary you present the gospel to will
be no more than nineteen or twenty years old. Even at such
a tender age, they are revered by the congregations they
serve, since they have freely given two years of their lives to
the service of their god and the "everlasting gospel."
Perhaps the only ones who receive more admiration than
the missionaries are those who are in the armed forces. After the early years the LDS Church became very patriotic,
and an almost disproportionate number of Mormons serve
in the armed forces.

The training background of the usual Mormon missionary is slight. If he was brought up in the LDS Church, he attended Sunday school classes in which the principles of the
church are expounded, but very little doctrine. Before his
mission training he may also have attended "seminary"

and/or the local LDS Institute of Religion, where he could earn credits in doctrine and theology. After this brief exposure to his Mormon heritage he is sent for his mission training. First there are three days of formal training in Salt Lake City, and then (for missionaries to English-speaking areas) brief training in Provo, Utah. (Missionaries to foreign countries study the new language for several months.)°
With this bit of preparation the missionary is ready to begin his two-year commitment.

He is often sent more than a thousand miles from home, and contact between him and his friends and family is severely limited. He shares an apartment, usually with one or more other missionaries. He is not allowed to drive a car except in unusual circumstances, but must travel almost everywhere he goes by bicycle. For two years he is totally dependent on his own savings, his family, or church members for financial support. He is not allowed free social intercourse with members of the opposite sex, although it has been said that many missionaries get married within a week to ten days after returning from their missions.

The pressure placed on him by the Church is immense. His only friends are Mormons, his only occupation is with the Church, his small amount of free time is with Mormons, and he has been convinced that he is doing God's service by spending these two years of sacrifice among the "Gentiles." Since much of his conviction is based on emotion, his partner or friends who see that he might be wavering can use emotional tactics to try to convince him to stay. He knows that if he leaves the Church he will lose his family, his friends, and his faith.

It is only if and when he gains the sure knowledge that he will gain everlasting life and membership in a new family—the family of God, the *true* church of Jesus

---

°The Mormons have now closed the Salt Lake City Missionary Home, and all incoming missionaries are now being sent directly to Provo, Utah, for approximately five weeks of training.

Christ—that he becomes willing to leave behind all that he has known.

The missions undertaken by young Mormon males are twofold in purpose. The primary concern of the Mormon Church is to proselytize what they call the Gentile world (all who are not members of the Church of Jesus Christ, Latter-day Saints). Secondly, the Mormon Church knows that the missionary's own personal commitment will be strengthened by his sacrifice for the Church. The missionary's duties include aiding the regional "stakes" in making calls to interested Gentiles, calling on all of the visitors to the temple visitor's centers, and providing personal contact and information to those members who have fallen in their participation in the Church. Since they are looked on as authorities and are continually reinforcing their own "testimonies" by presenting the same material over and over again to prospective members, they are accomplishing both goals of the Church at the same time.

Define Your Terms

Mormonism thrives on the use of Biblical terminology. It is possible for a Mormon missionary to visit the home of the average Christian several times, and, by careful avoidance of areas of theological conflict, appear to be in essential agreement with the foundational truths of Christianity. This is possible because the Mormon missionaries are taught to avoid careful definition of terms when approaching the "Gentiles." The Christian must be on his guard in order to detect this subterfuge.

Several years ago I visited a Christian school that prepared missionaries for the field. The instructor in the course on non-Christian religions and cults had encouraged his students to invite cultists to the campus with the aim of exposing them to the methodology of various groups. That day the Mormons were on campus.

Two Mormon missionaries spoke for some 25 minutes

concerning their views of God. I could discern from the faces of the students that what they were hearing conflicted with what they had been taught in their classes concerning Mormonism's doctrine of God. The two missionaries were careful to use the terms "God," "Jesus Christ," "the Lord," "Heavenly Father," and numerous other theological synonyms for the Deity, but not once did they discuss their true view of God.

When the opportunity presented itself, I pointed out to the two missionaries that there was definitely an area of conflict involved, and that the problem was one of communication and terminology. They reluctantly agreed, and I reviewed the various terms they used to describe God. At the conclusion the older of the two missionaries said, "But, Mr. Martin, we too accept the doctrine of God as taught in the Scriptures. We too believe in God, the God who made the heavens and the earth." I asked them, "But which God are you talking about—Jesus, known as Jehovah in your theology, or Elohim, the Father of spirits and the Creator of Adam-god?" There was a moment of frustrating silence, and then one missionary said: "I see you are well-read in our theology."

I answered that I was familiar with their views and kept pressing him on the point of definition until he (with great reluctance) admitted that instead of believing in just *one* God, the Creator of the heavens and the earth (as he had originally stated), he actually believed in many gods, in the preexistence of the human soul, that the gods were polygamists, and finally that he himself aspired to godhood. The shocked expressions of the students and obvious embarrassment of the missionaries were evident; forthwith a host of theistic arguments descended upon the two "elders," whom I left vigorously protesting their belief in the prophetic office of Joseph Smith and attempting to escape the now-aroused audience of students.

Once the veneer of Biblical terminology is removed from many Mormon doctrines, it is possible to find out what Mormonism really teaches. Interested Christians might well think over the problem of terminology, and train themselves to define exhaustively the terms of any discussion, which is one of the surest ways to cut through the maze of Mormon semantics.

If a Mormon says "God," "Jesus Christ," "atonement," "salvation," etc., we must recognize that these terms are not defined in the context of historic Christianity. When the Christian says "God," he is talking about God triune—Father, Son, and Holy Spirit—three Persons, one Nature, coeternal. When we are talking about Jesus Christ we are talking about God the Son, the second Person of the Holy Trinity, of one essence or nature with the Father. We are not talking about one of many gods, but the eternal God Himself, all that He on this earth can ever mean to man. Colossians 2:9 states, "For in Christ all the fullness of the Deity lives in bodily form" (NIV).

When we are talking about the atonement, we mean that Christ died *once* for all of our sins (Romans 3:24-31), and that His blood shed for us is sufficient for *all* our needs (Hebrews 10:10; 9:22). The Christian believes that salvation is a free gift from the one and only God, made possible by the shedding of His own blood (Acts 20:28). This salvation cleanses us from all sin and makes us completely blameless and righteous in His sight. There is nothing we can do to improve on it or to earn it (Ephesians 1:4-7; 2:8, 9).

The Mormon concept of salvation is very different. To the Mormons, salvation in the sense of resurrection is conferred upon all human beings. However, salvation in the sense of exaltation or freedom from sin and guilt is obtainable only by our own works and efforts (see Chapter 9).

What the Mormons mean by theological terms and what the Bible and the true church mean by them are entirely different. The importance of destroying the "terminology block" cannot be overemphasized. No matter how good your presentation is and no matter how much you have researched and studied, so that you can present the gospel in an orthodox manner, if you cannot communicate, you are wasting your time. Don't even start talking to a Mormon without first defining your terms (see Appendix F).

Eliminate Misconceptions

The second important preliminary to witnessing to the Mormon missionary is to know what he thinks of Christianity. We have seen that he believes that he has the only truth, that he is bringing the message of the everlasting gospel to an apostate world. But—what does he think of historical Christianity, in distinction from the present-day Christian and non-Christian cults and religions of the world?

The Mormon Church has a shallow concept of the meaning of "church" in New Testament theology. In Mormon thinking, the church is composed of Latter-day Saints (all non-Latter-day Saints are characterized as Gentiles). This "church" is characterized by temples, secret ceremonies, celestial marriage, and baptism for the dead, and is presided over by a well-developed hierarchy headed by the First President of the Church, his counselors, a Quorum of Twelve Apostles, other Councils, and priests. The oracles of this "church" are the writings of Joseph Smith and Brigham Young, as well as *The Book of Mormon, Doctrine and Covenants, The Pearl of Great Price,* and, of course, the Bible, which is interpreted in the light of the foregoing books and present-day revelations by the prophets of Mormondom.

After showing the "strength" of their restoration concept and insisting that Christendom is split and divided, "all factions constantly warring among themselves," the Mormons point with pride to their monolithic structure and its evident growth and economic success in a relatively short period of time. Unless the Christian is on his guard, he will be led to believe that there is no unity outside Mormonism, a tremendous fallacy in view of the fact that the true church or "body" of Jesus Christ is not composed of bricks, mortar, priests, hierarchies, or missionary endeavors. The true Church is a mystical organism composed of Christians *in every denomination* who have been quickened by God the Holy Spirit and who confess the fundamental truths of the Christian gospel while living effective lives for Christ. The eleventh and twelfth chapters of 1 Corinthians are particularly helpful here in refuting the Mormon idea of "church."

The basis for the Mormon concept of future life is the lack of a belief in hell or eternal punishment or separation from God. The Mormon has been taught that there is no such thing as "damnation," but that it is "dam-nation" (meaning exclusion from eternal sexual relations that produce Spirit-children). In other words, one is not condemned for refusing to serve God; his progress toward final exaltation is merely stopped or "dammed up." The good Mormon may reach exaltation to godhood in the next life. The non-Mormon will probably only reach the Terrestrial or second heaven while the antagonist to Mormonism (or the murderer) will reach only the Telestial or first heaven.

To the Mormon the average Christian is simply ignorant. He does not mean any harm, and if he can be reached with the gospel of the restoration and if the Holy Spirit will give him a "sure testimony," then he will come to God's true church, the Church of Jesus Christ, Latter-day Saints. In the Mormon view, the Christian who actively evangelizes the Mormons is not ignorant. He has been deceived and is trying to propagate the same deception that caught him. Even he will not be condemned, because he has been deceived. He must have been deceived—anyone who sees the Mormon truth must know that it is the truth and follow it. This evangelistic Christian must settle for the lowest existence in the next life, that of the Telestial heaven.

Every true Christian who would be successful in witnessing to Mormons must overcome the Mormon's preconceived attitude that the Christian has been deceived.

Prophets, Revelation, and Priesthood—The "Authority" Argument

Most important is Mormonism's conviction that no persons on earth have the authority from God that the members of the Mormon Church have. How can they listen to a Christian when that Christian has no prophet, no continuing revelation, and no priesthood? This is the first lesson presented by the missionaries to prospective members and is the foundation of their attitude toward the non-Mormon world. Without prophets, present-day revelation, and priesthood, one cannot have authority.

If it were true that one had to have the Mormon type of prophet, the Mormon type of revelation, and the Mormon type of priesthood in order to have authority, then they would be right in saying that historic Christianity has no authority. But is this the case?

Absolutely not. Every regenerate Christian has Christ's authority to proclaim the gospel to everyone on the earth. We do have a priesthood. To refute the Mormon concept of priesthood, the interested Christian need only point out that the Levitical-Aaronic priesthood, as in the words of the writer of Hebrews, has been "changed" (Hebrews 7:12) and that the Melchizedek priesthood (Hebrews 7:11-17) is an office held only by the Lord Jesus Christ, our great High Priest. The Greek of Hebrews 7:24 utterly devastates the Mormon claim to the restoration of the Melchizedek priesthood by stating that, as far as this exalted office is concerned, only Jesus Christ possesses it, for "this man, because he continues forever, has an untransferable priesthood," i.e., literally a priesthood that does not pass to another. Sometimes when confronted with this the Mormon will refer to Revelation 1:6: "And hath made us kings and priests unto God and his Father," a fact amplified by the Apostle Peter, who declared of *all* Christians:

> But you are a chosen people, a royal priesthood, a holy nation, a people belonging to God, that you may declare

the praises of him who called you out of darkness into his wonderful light.

1 Peter 2:9 NIV

From this point the Christian can conclude with an exposition of John 1:12 and establish that he actually has a priesthood far superior to the Mormon priesthood. John 1:12 elucidates Jesus' great gift to those who would believe on Him to the saving of their souls (cf. Hebrews 10:39). John said of Jesus,

Yet to all who received him, to those who believed in his name, he gave the right to become children of God.

John 1:12 NIV

The word translated "power" in the King James Version of this verse is the Greek word *exousia,* which means not power but authority. Authority entails the legal right to something. As Christians we have the right to proclaim what Jesus commanded us to proclaim in Matthew 28:19, what Paul defined in 1 Corinthians 15:1-3 and Galatians 1:8-10, and what Jesus promised that the Holy Spirit would teach us in John 14:25, 26. When we go out, we proclaim the gospel to the ends of the earth. We do it in the authority of Jesus Christ and with the might of God, which is working in the hearts and minds and souls of men. We do not know precisely how this operates, and we cannot describe the mechanism, but we do know that whenever we proclaim Christ with His authority, there is the might of God, and that extends itself to the souls of men and to the conversion of those who accept it. We have a far superior authority to the Mormon authority, for the church has Christ's promise that the "gates of Hades will not overcome it" (Matthew 16:18ff NIV). This would *not* be so if the Mormon claim were true: that the gospel disappeared after the first century and needed Joseph Smith, Jr., to "restore" it.

The Mormon authority is grounded upon what Joseph Smith said, passed on to him through the Aaronic and Melchizedek "priesthoods," and all Mormon authority rests there.

But the Christian church has the real authority. We derive our authority from Jesus Christ Himself, not from John the Baptist, or Peter, or James, or John. Christ is the Son of God with power by resurrection from among the dead (Romans 1:3, 4), and it is He who grants us authority. Since Mormonism claims to have restored the original Church with all the same offices, etc., the question to ask is, "Where does the Bible state that any of the apostles held either the Aaronic or Melchizedek Priesthood? Since you believe that *The Book of Mormon* is an account of "Jesus the Christ" appearing upon this continent and establishing His church, where does it say He restored the Aaronic Priesthood and gave the Melchizedek Priesthood to his disciples?" (See Chapter 5 of this book for a full discussion and refutation of the authority of Mormonism's priesthood.)

The second Mormon objection to our possession of authority is that we do not have a "prophet." They say that Joseph Smith was the first in the long line of "restoration prophets." They say that the Bible has always had prophets, and that if Christendom does not have a prophet today, this is not Biblical. They imply (using Amos 3:7 out of context) that we cannot possibly speak of God without God communicating to us through a prophet. However, does the Bible say this?

There is nothing in the Bible that says that revelation or prophecy has ceased in Christ's church. First Corinthians 14 clearly teaches that God still works supernaturally through His people for their edification and the saving of men's souls. Romans 11:29, speaking primarily of the gift of salvation, unequivocally states that "God's gifts and his call are irrevocable" (NIV). First Corinthians 13:8-12 and John 14:16 promise us that until we are with Jesus we will have the Comforter bestowing on the body of Christ those gifts that are needful to further His work.

So that we need have no confusion, God has also promised us that He will never change (Malachi 3:6) and that we can know what comes from Him, for, "Every good and perfect gift is from above, coming down from the Father of the heavenly lights, who does not change like shifting shadows" (James 1:17 NIV). This is how we test all "revelations" and all "prophets." Deuteronomy 13 teaches that any prophet who teaches other gods (such as Mormonism's polytheism) is *not* a prophet from God. In other chapters we have shown that the Mormon prophets both teach a false concept of God and predict things that never happen (see Appendix G). Christians, on the other hand, continue to look to God, for He never fails and His Word is dependable.

Finally, Biblical prophecy and revelation is better and more complete than any other "prophecy" or "revelation," for it has stood the test of time. Not only do we have the God of all ages as our Teacher, but He has spoken to us in a unique way that no other religion can equal. Even the Old Testament believers, although in every way as much believers and as much followers of Christ as we are (Galatians 3:8, 9), did not have the extent of knowledge that we possess. In Hebrews 1:1-3 NIV we see the marvelous extent of the communication that we have with God:

> In the past God spoke to our forefathers through the prophets at many times and in various ways, but in these last days he has spoken to us by his Son, whom he appointed heir of all things, and through whom he made the universe. The Son is the radiance of God's glory and the exact representation of his being, sustaining all things by his powerful word. After he had provided purification for sins, he sat down at the right hand of the Majesty in heaven.

Jesus Christ is the greatest Priest, the greatest Prophet, and the greatest Revelation—He is God's indescribable, unutterable gift to mankind.

Present to the Mormon missionary your credentials as a follower of Jesus Christ. Present *your* priesthood: sanctified in Christ. Present *your* Prophet: the Biblical Jesus, the Word of God made flesh (John 1:1, 14). Present *your* revelation: occupied entirely with the knowledge of Jesus Christ. As Christians, we have a greater authority, based on a greater Priest, a greater Prophet, and a dependable revelation. We have the true authority of the living God; the

Mormon missionary does not. We must assert our authority and bring the good news of God's victory over sin by the shedding of His own blood (Acts 20:28) to all who are lost in their sins—both Mormon and non-Mormon. This is the reason for our authority, that we might go into all the world preaching the gospel.

Mormon Discussion Tactics

A third area of Mormon missionary training should be discussed before one enters into the "battle" with the forces of darkness that would keep members of Mormonism from knowing the truth as it is in Jesus. This area concerns the mechanics of the discussion tactics taught to the missionaries. In contrast to the missionary methods of most of the non-Christian cults, the Mormon Church has a well-developed, systematic approach both in the preparation of its missionaries and in the subsequent presentaton of the Mormon "gospel."

The Mormons have a great respect for education, but, in common with other non-Christian cultists, the average Mormon does not generally have an answer for biblical questions. Whenever his limited stock of pat answers is exhausted, he promises to return with an answer, although the answer is just another "pat" one that he hadn't learned before. This delay, of course, enables the Mormon to solicit more information from his superiors and take up where he left off.

The first tactic is what I call the "passing the authority" method. Unless the average Christian is aware of what the missionaries are doing, this can be a very effective method for keeping him occupied while the missionaries steadily infiltrate the conversation with their doctrines. The Christian never has an opportunity to witness effectively, since he is kept busy defending his position.

According to accepted Mormon procedure, if a "saint" in the company of one or more of his brother missionaries gets into difficulty in the course of conversation with Christians, he will "pass the authority," i.e., the authority of his priestly office to one of his cohorts, and that "saint" or "elder," as he is called, will either make a salient contribution or change the subject. The "passing of the authority" can be stopped right in its tracks by an informed Christian. One can refuse to talk to either of the other two "elders" and insist that the first elder, retaining the authority, answer him. When thus confronted the elder will "bear his testimony" as the only way out. Then the other elders will take up the discussion. The Mormons believe that one may "lose his authority" in a debate with a Gentile, so they will either pass their authority or remain silent. If you refuse to allow them to pass their authority and they become silent, then you may preach the gospel uninterrupted.

However, in an area where Christians are well-prepared and are actively witnessing and looking for the Mormon missionary, those "Elders" are advised by their superiors to "avoid contention," to bear their "testimony" (as to the truthfulness of Joseph Smith, *The Book of Mormon*, the Mormon Church, and the present-day prophet of the Mormon Church), and then leave as rapidly as possible should opposition to the "restored gospel" arise. They zip up their "standard works" and on your doorstep shake the dust from their feet as a witness against you. In such an event suggest to them, "Since you refused to answer my questions, and instead became angry, I will go to your Bishop and ask him to send other missionaries who are willing to be more loving, patient, and knowledgeable." In most instances, they will sit down again and the conversation may continue.

Another way to circumvent their "passing the authority" is to pit the two missionaries against each other. This is especially effective when you are primarily quoting the Bible or their scriptures. For example, you might ask if *The Book of Mormon* teaches Mormon doctrine. When they answer in the affirmative, then you might say, "Well, then, *The Book of Mormon* must certainly teach your doctrine of God—that there are many gods and that our Father was once a man like us." Again, they will generally answer in the affirmative. Now ask one of the missionaries to read, for example, Alma 11:28, 35, from *The Book of Mormon*, which states emphatically that there is only one God. Then ask the second missionary for his opinion. He can't possibly ask the first missionary to take his authority—it was the first missionary who read the passage that contradicted his doctrine! The Christian can then present the Bible's teaching about God, showing that the Bible and *The Book of Mormon* agree on monotheism, while *Doctrine and Covenants* and *The Pearl of Great Price* teach polytheism (see Chapter 3 of this book).

A second method of presentation learned by the missionaries is one that all good salesmen also learn. The missionary is taught to never, under any circumstances, deviate from his prepared presentation. In the Mormon presentation manual, *The Uniform System for Teaching Families*, we find:

> . . .At first memorize the discussions exactly as they appear. As you use them more, you may be more comfortable and effective using your own words. . . . Be careful not to change the spirit or intent of the questions . . . . keep the presentation organized by tactfully deferring irrelevant questions to a more appropriate occasion.
>
> Page A-1

The Christian should have little problem in stopping this form of evasion, by persistently keeping the leadership of the discussion.

A third Mormon method is to never give a dogmatic answer to a touchy question. Instead, the missionary is taught to "answer questions with questions." This way he never has to commit himself and is able to say something in response to every question one asks, even if he doesn't know the answer. This is easily avoided by forcing him to a direct answer. If necessary, one may want to write down the questions the missionary asks in response so that the Mormon will be assured that you will not forget them and that you will answer his questions just as soon as he answers yours. Don't be hostile, but don't give in, either. Be firm.

The final and most popular Mormon method of avoiding unpleasant situations is with a "testimony." This is a purely emotional response and has nothing to do with truth or logic. If the missionary is unable to give you a reasonable answer to a question, he will likely say, "I prayed about it and I can testify that it is the truth." We know that one must be praying to the God of the Bible before he can expect to get an answer that is sound in doctrine (John 9:31). We also know that since God never changes, His answers to prayer must always be in accord with what He has already revealed. We would not dare pray to ask God if we could worship other gods. He has already revealed that we are to worship Him alone (Deuteronomy 5:6, 7). Therefore, since He has already revealed to us not to follow false prophets (Deuteronomy 13:3; 18:22), we cannot follow the Mormon Church and its false prophets, Joseph Smith and Brigham Young.

A quicker answer is to use what is known in logic as an "ad hominem" argument. It is a sectional argument, valid for those who accept the premises, but not for others. In other words, use a premise that the missionary will accept but then draw a logical conclusion from that premise that will refute him. This does not mean that the premise is true, or that you are trying to make the Mormon think it is true. It only means that you are using what *he accepts* to show him that even then his statement is false. This can be done after he "bears his testimony" by saying, "God told me in the Bible that Mormonism is wrong." You have now created a stalemate. You have a testimony, just as he has. The only way to find out who has the true testimony is to test it by what you know God has already revealed. Use the Bible, and show him that your answer to prayer is consistent with what God has *already* revealed, while his answer contradicts God's revelation.

Preach the Gospel

Now that one has a background in Mormon teachings and missionary tactics, what is the best course for him to take in actually witnessing? Although there are several areas that need to be dealt with, it is important that the Christian's attitude toward the Mormon individual and the Mormon Church be clearly defined.

The Christian should keep in mind that his approach to the members of the Mormon Church must always be that of love for the soul and a corresponding aversion to the false doctrines which they preach. Christians should be aware that cultists have feelings and are as much in need of redemption as any other lost souls. We should never attempt to overpower them with clichés or blunt denunciations, for antagonism has no part in witnessing to cultists. Christians would do well to assume the sincerity of those with whom they deal, allowing for the fact that "the god of this age has blinded the minds of unbelievers, so that they cannot see the light of the gospel of the glory of Christ" (2 Corinthians 4:4 NIV). Humiliation of a cultist betrays a definite lack of resources on the part of those who are inept enough to utilize such tactics. Since many cultists do not understand the full implications of their doctrinal positions, it is a good thing to face them with such implications so that they will understand the Christian's concern for their redemption.

In all things, let the Mormon know that his conversion is important, not for the sake of winning an argument, but for the sake of his salvation in the light of Scripture. Tact and patience will pay dividends. The Christian who is faced with this mission field may never live to see the fruit of his efforts, but he can have the satisfaction of knowing that he has been faithful in the task to which God has appointed "all who have longed for his appearing" (2 Timothy 4:8 NIV).

May the Lord grant to us the grace to outwork, outpray, and outevangelize in Christian love those who are under the deceptive yoke of Joseph Smith's "revelation." May they see in those who name the name of Christ in the historic tradition of Christianity a power which can also change their lives, and can grant to them true forgiveness of sins and spiritual baptism in the family of God. This will at length lead, not to man's becoming a god, but instead to man's recognition, adoration, and commitment to the God who became man in Jesus Christ.

The Christian has no right to be hostile to the Mormons. The Scriptures say that "our struggle is not against flesh and blood" (Ephesians 6:12 NIV). The power of God's Spirit alone can take His Word and your prayers and apply them to the souls of these people. The whole time you talk *to* them you must be praying *for* them. The whole time you are working with them you must be remembering that, but for the grace of God, you could be in Mormonism and deceived by it. And never forget that the greatest privilege you and I can enjoy is to share in the joy of their salvation. Let them see Christ in you—the hope of glory, the love, the concern, the compassion that Christ enables you to have for them.

The Authority of the Believer

A second important guideline to follow in witnessing to Mormon missionaries is to be sure that *you* are the one who is leading and directing the discussion. *You* are the teacher; *you* have the Holy Spirit teaching you; *you* have the authority of Jesus Christ. If you lead and direct the discussion, you can keep it on the topics that are the most important to the Mormons' salvation. You can lead them to see that they have been deceived and that they need the real Jesus as their Savior.

Learn to direct the discussion tactfully, however. There is no need to be rude or antagonistic. Just operate on the assumption that you are going to lead the discussion and that the missionary will follow willingly and politely. Remember that the missionary bases much of his belief on experience and emotions. Be careful that you don't hurt his feelings, or else he will not listen to what you have to say because he will "feel" that it is wrong. Gently but with perseverance guide him to see the points that are important. A good way to subtly take command of the situation is to ask if you may open the meeting with a prayer. Then pray, planting the seeds of the gospel and of what you know is important to the discussion. (Never permit them to "take charge" and pray, for they are not praying to the God of the Bible.) Immediately on concluding the prayer, start to ask the missionary questions, and be sure that he answers them directly. You have smoothly and effortlessly taken command and are in a position to present the Christian message.

Be sure to establish the topics of the discussion. Don't wait for the missionary to bring up a topic. It will inevitably be something he has learned by rote and cannot really objectively think about. Instead, get him to agree that certain topics are more important than others. Give him your "canon" or list of topics that mean the most to you. This canon must include *Scripture, God, Christ,* and *salvation.* If one is wrong about any of these three areas, he is wrong enough to miss eternal fellowship with the true God. We must know *what* to accept as Scripture in order to know what God has revealed to us about Himself and our relationship to Him. Once we know what is Scripture, then we are in a position to know who God is and what He requires of us.

Every cult system, whatever its description, will generally be found to be in conflict with these doctrines of Biblical Christianity. Mormonism is no exception. Christians who wish to witness effectively to Mormons should avoid being sidetracked into a discussion of peripheral areas of doctrine (the existence of hell, millennialism, tribulationism, prophecy, baptism, etc.). These areas, while they may be profitable for discussion in a more restricted context, have little bearing on one's salvation. It is far better to confine oneself to the vital doctrines of our faith in order to present the true gospel to the Mormon. You may be able to convince the Mormon that hell is real, but if you are unable to tell him how to escape its torment you have only succeeded in giving him sure knowledge of where he's going, without any way out!

Also be careful not to spend too much time tearing down the structure of Mormonism. There are countless areas where Mormon history, revelation, doctrine, and practice fall far below the standards of thinking Mormons. However, it does no good to antagonize a missionary by destroying every iota of Mormonism and by your antagonizing drive him away before you can present the real Jesus to him. Many times I have heard of cultists who have been literally torn apart by overzealous Christians. The cultist's plea is, "Now that you've destroyed my life, I'm doomed! You didn't give me anything to replace it with! Where do I go from here?" By simply destroying what a Mormon has, you may drive him to another cult, or even agnosticism or atheism, because he has no new standard by which to judge things.

Acknowledging Style and Context

The next step in your discussion with the missionaries should include sound methods of interpreting the Scriptures (hermeneutics). Any discussison of the inspiration of the Bible must include how it is to be interpreted. The Mormon claims of the unreliability of the Bible are almost entirely based on poor hermeneutics. Simply calling the Bible "the Word of God" is insufficient. Unless one knows how to use it, an infallible revelation is of entirely no use. The important thing is to have valid criteria of interpretation and then use those criteria.

Rather than embarking on an extensive tour of the principles of Biblical interpretation, I would like to highlight just a few points and then recommend a small pamphlet that should be owned by every Christian who wants to obey God's command.

> Do your best to present yourself to God as one approved, a workman who does not need to be ashamed and who correctly handles the word of truth.
>
> 2 Timothy 2:15 NIV

The pamphlet is published by InterVarsity Press and is titled "Interpreting the Bible," by J. Stafford Wright. Study what is presented there and utilize every bit of it in your discussions with Mormons.

The most important areas of hermeneutics to be familiar with are *language* (style) and *context*. If one can learn to recognize certain legitimate literary devices in Scripture, one will destroy most of the arguments which Mormonism tries to build from the Bible to support its doctrines. In the same way, if one learns to see a verse in its whole framework, to take a whole passage instead of one verse or a part of a verse, then one will have "defanged" one of the most effective Mormon weapons against the reliability of the Bible.

All of us use figures of speech, metaphors, similes, allegory, and other literary devices every day. Even if we have no schooling in writing or literature, we know to some extent how to express ourselves in a variety of styles. A man might say, for example, in describing his new secretary to a friend, "She's dynamite! A real doll!" Of course he doesn't mean that she is actually a stick of TNT or that he has to wind her up in the morning because she's a plastic and mechanical figurine. We all know that he means his new secretary is extraordinarily beautiful and that he is strongly attracted to her. Unfortunately, if his friend is a Mormon, there is a possibility that he might take him literally, for this is *exactly* what the Mormon missionaries are taught to do with the figurative language of the Bible, wherever it can be "made" to agree with their theology.

Often Christians who have not talked to Mormons are at

a loss to know why the Mormons think that the Bible teaches that God has a body of flesh and bones when the Bible clearly teaches that God is spirit (John 4:24). Then when he asks a Mormon to explain why he believes God has a body, he will find that the Mormon will turn to such verses as those that say that God *spoke,* or God's *hand* was outstretched, to show that the Bible teaches that God has a body and is an exalted man. A quick reference to Psalm 91:4, where God is spoken of as having "wings and feathers," and to such verses as John 6:48 and other metaphorical passages in the New Testament uttered by our Lord, quickly refutes the idea that merely because God is spoken of as possessing human attributes of physical makeup, He therefore is "an exalted man" or the "Adamgod" of historic Mormon mythology. Also, ask the Mormon if he believes as Apostle James Talmage taught, that Jesus was the God of the Old Testament. If he believes this, then remind him that Jesus did not have a body at that time, but was spirit. Their argument fails at this point to prove that God the Father has a body of flesh and bone by using the metaphorical language of the Old Testament.

The second area of hermeneutics that is essential to be familiar with in evangelizing Mormons is that of contextual analysis. Never take a verse for what it says by itself. Even more emphatically, never take a *part* of a verse for what it says by itself. Things have meaning by context, and if it were not for context much of our communication would no longer be communication. What does the word "table" mean? Not much out of its context. One definition is a flat surface raised from the floor, usually by four legs. Another definition is that it is a chart of a certain kind. Still another definition is that it is the level to which rainwater rises in a section of land. Unless one uses the word "table" in a particular context, we cannot hope to know which of the definitions to apply to it. Similarly, a phrase removed from its context is just as meaningless and is often misleading. To quote someone as saying "I quit beating my wife yesterday" means something quite different from quoting the person's entire statement: "The phrase 'I quit beating my wife yesterday' has six words."

The Mormon use of this technique is proficient. One of their more popular Biblical "proofs" for polytheism is obtained by using only the last half of 1 Corinthians 8:5: "As there are gods many and lords many." However, when we take that one portion of a verse and insert it in its proper context, verses 4-6, we see that all Paul is saying is that there is only one who is God by nature (Galatians 4:8), but that people will worship anything to avoid worshipping the true God and true Lord. The whole passage reads:

> As concerning therefore the eating of those things that are offered in sacrifice unto idols, we know that an idol is nothing in the world, and that there is none other God but one. For though there be that are called gods, whether in heaven or in earth, (as there be gods many, and lords many,) But to us there is but one God, the Father, of whom are all things, and we in him; and one Lord Jesus Christ, by whom are all things, and we by him.
>
> 1 Corinthians 8:4-6

As R. A. Torrey used to say, "A text taken out of context is usually a pretext"—and, I might add, usually a pretext for error!

Disproving Discrepancies

The last area that the Mormon Church uses to attack the apostolic authority of the Bible is that of supposed contradictions. Mormons are taught almost from infancy that the Bible is full of contradictions and is therefore not a perfect revelation from God. John Haley, in *Alleged Discrepancies of the Bible*, covers nine hundred of the most popular "contradictions," showing them to be no contradictions at all. In my opinion, *there is not one genuine contradiction in the Bible!* Almost all of what are called contradictions have at least one and usually several valid explanations that remove any hint of "contradiction" from them. One does not have to know all the "contradictions" and their explanations, however, in order to talk to a Mormon missionary. Although they have been taught that the Bible is full of contradictions, they usually can't produce even one example if pressed.

When attempting to establish the reliability of the Bible, the Christian will invariably hear the Mormon say that there have been so many changes and alterations of the Bible that we cannot determine what was originally meant. They will then try to establish the need for "present-day" revelation, in the form of their first three standard works, *The Book of Mormon, Doctrine and Covenants*, and *The Pearl of Great Price*. This is why you need to know that the Bible is reliable.[1] You may also ask the Mormon why "changes" should bother him, since within a relatively short period of time *The Book of Mormon*, which was given "by the gift and power of God" to Joseph Smith in English, has had almost four thousand changes since the original 1830 version was given.[2] The other two Mormon revelations have also had thousands of changes, as well as *The History of the Church.*

If you follow the guidelines discussed below in presenting your "canon" of topic discussion to the missionaries, you will be covering those areas essential to the Mormon's understanding of his responsibility to God.

God's Word

Be sure to establish the authority of the Bible and the

---

[1]For an excellent study on the reliability of the Bible, see Josh McDowell, *Evidence That Demands a Verdict* and *More Evidence That Demands a Verdict.*

[2]See *Joseph Smith Begins His Work*, Vol. 1 (The original 1830 version of *The Book of Mormon*) and Vol. 2 (The original "revelations" of Joseph Smith, known as *The Book of Commandments, Lectures on Faith and Doctrine and Covenants*) (Salt Lake City: Modern Microfilm Company).

lack of authority of the Mormon books (*Book of Mormon, Doctrine and Covenants, Pearl of Great Price*). Point out that the revelations which Joseph Smith alleged were given to him by God are directly contradictory, and that there is more than reasonable doubt as to their being the "restored" Christian gospel for our day. The Mormons lay great emphasis upon these "revelations," claiming them to be an authority equal to the Bible itself. Although the Mormons testify vigorously to their trustworthiness, the Christian can generally discourage this Mormon approach by pointing out the more than 3900 changes in *The Book of Mormon* since its original printing, as well as many internal contradictions among the three main Mormon holy books, including contradictions between science, history, archeology, anthropology, and the Mormon scripture (see Chapter 2 of this book).

In his discussion with Mormon missionaries, the Christian should always seek to confine the area of spiritual authority to that of the Bible, which is older than all the "sacred books" of the Mormon Church and which, the Mormons claim, does not contradict their "revelation." You will already have shown by the principles of Biblical interpretation that the Bible itself is reliable as a revelation from God. The Christian can now logically state that, if the Bible does not contradict the other books, then the Bible is reliable *without* the other books and can be depended upon for final truth. By thus confining the missionaries to the Christian Scriptures, they can be led to listen to the Biblical plan of human redemption (which is far removed from that taught them by their church). In this way the Christian will have an opportunity to present the gospel of Christ, which is more than simply separation from worldliness (which the Mormons identify with repentance) and is in fact the way God deals with personal sin. The missionaries are not very accustomed to this approach, since they consider themselves to be Christians, so it is well to underscore the necessity of the Biblical God, Biblical redemption, and Biblical authority. Always be sure to use the King James Version of the Bible when witnessing to Mormons, since that is the only version they consider authoritative.

God

With the groundwork laid as to the authority that is acceptable, you are now ready to discuss who God is. The missionaries often attack the historic Christian doctrine of God previously discussed in this book, and they do this by subtly pointing out that the God of historic Christianity as taught by the Bible and the creeds, etc., is "incomprehensible."

The missionaries assert that man, as he is created in the image of God, mirrors the true divine image. Hence, God has a body of flesh and bone similar to man's. Joining this circular reasoning to anthropomorphic statements in Scripture that we have already discussed, the Mormons develop their polytheistic concept. Having "established" their basic premise, they then proceed to systematically question the existence of a God of "pure spirit" and end by pointing to the fact that even the Christian Trinity has been clouded by "human superstition" to the point where three separate persons all share the basic essence of deity. The Mormons then declare that the unity in the godhead is one of purpose, desire, will, and collective attributes, not unity of substance in the historic meaning of the term.

The Christian who is not familiar with the doctrine of the Trinity is, of course, quite bewildered at times by the Mormon's usage of such verses as John 17:11, 14:9, and 10:30. When combined, these texts *appear* to teach that the only unity which existed between Jesus and the Father was one of purpose and will. Christians are also promised that type of unity, but *never* future unity with the very essence of Deity. The answer to the dilemma, of course, is found in the fact that the context of John 10 is *not* one of will or purpose but one of unity of substance (i.e., "the state of being God"), as verse 33 indicates: "you, a mere man, claim to be God" (NIV). The *unity* in John 17 (involving the disciples) is indeed clearly one of will or purpose, "so that the world may believe that you have sent me" (verse 21), and so the issue is at once clarified. In the case of John 14:9, the context also reveals that Christ was speaking of the disciples beholding the Father in the attributes, character, and actions of our Lord. Or, as Saint Paul has so eloquently put it, "For in Christ all the fullness of the Deity lives in bodily form" (Colossians 2:9 NIV). Jesus was in effect saying that if we want to know what the Father is like, study Christ, hear Him. He never taught the Mormon doctrine of progression to godhood that was the antithesis of Rabbinical interpretation and the whole religion of Judaism.

The Christian should also become familiar with the material presented in this book on the doctrine of "Adam-God" which so vexes the average missionary if one can present it in the proper manner (see Chapters 3 and 4). In classic Mormon theology God was once a man, he came to earth with Eve (one of his wives) to people it, and later (after his resurrection) had sexual intercourse with Mary to produce Christ. The Scriptures are entirely against any such concept of God, and even say that the origin of that doctrine rests with Satan, both before he was cast out of heaven (Isaiah 14:12-14) and later in the Garden of Eden (Genesis 3:5). Matthew and Luke unequivocally assert that Mary was a virgin when she gave birth to Christ, and that He was conceived by the Holy Spirit (Matthew 1, Luke 1).

The Mormon religion, as we have shown in Chapter 3, is polytheistic. Joseph Smith taught a plurality of gods, as did Brigham Young, two of the standard works of the church, and many Mormon leaders. The Bible, the oldest and most reliable revelation, declares:

> Ye are my witnesses, saith the Lord, and my servant whom I have chosen, that ye may know and believe me, and understand that I am he; before me there was no God formed, neither shall there be after me.
> Isaiah 43:10

This text alone reveals the one supreme, eternal God of

creation to any Mormon who has been deceived into thinking that he will one day become a god and will rule in the heavens with the other "gods" of Mormondom.

Salvation

Finally, give the Mormon missionaries a way to respond to the "unknown God," hopefully their newfound God, the God of the Bible, the Ruler of the universe, and the Judge of their souls (Acts 17:22-34). It is also characteristic of Mormonism that it denies the great doctrine of justification by faith (Romans 4 and 5). The average Mormon therefore knows nothing of salvation wholly by grace. His salvation is a mixture of grace, faith, works, baptism, and repentance. Mormons are perplexed by the assurance which Christians have of salvation as a gift of God, an assurance shared by all those who have experienced the regenerating action of the Holy Spirit (Ephesians 2:8-10). The Apostle Paul points out,

> For since the creation of the world God's invisible qualities—his eternal power and divine nature—have been clearly seen, being understood from what has been made, so that men are without excuse.
>
> Romans 1:20 NIV

All men are therefore conscious of their isolation from God, their estrangement from His love, and the foreboding certainty of His justice. Augustine aptly put it this way: "Thou hast made us, O Lord, and we are thine and our souls are restless until they rest in Thee."

Mormons are no exception to the law of God in their need of personal redemption. Burn away the dross of their legalistic, polytheistic theology and bring them face-to-face with the necessity of personal reception of the saving grace of the Lord Jesus Christ. To be sure, this is all of grace, and prayer and the adept use of the Scriptures are indispensable tools and should be used by the Christian more as a scalpel than as a broadsword.

Mormonism knows nothing of eternal salvation as a present possession. Its adherents are constantly attempting to achieve salvation in their self-propelled ascendancy toward godhood (cf. Romans 10:3). By emphasizing the need of all men for personal redemption and the great Biblical doctrine of salvation by grace, the Christian can strike at the very heart of Mormon theology. Such passages as John 5:24; 6:47; Acts 16:31; 1 John 5:13; John 10:28; and Romans 4, 5, and 8 are most effective; and the Book of Galatians in its entirety is excellent for showing followers of Mormonism the need for the assurance of personal salvation that only Christ can provide, apart from human works of the law.

Time and again I have seen Mormon missionaries halted in their efforts to proselytize by such references, and I have seen them ponder their own spiritual condition in the light of such evidence. It is, therefore, worthwhile to emphasize personal redemption by grace, for it is the very opposite of the Mormon system of salvation by works.

God's Truth Must Prevail

In the light of these and many other factors which we do not have space to adequately cover, it is apparent that Mormon missionaries can be effectively evangelized. They do not have all the answers, and underneath the surface they are uncertain people, many times sincere, but spiritually blinded (2 Corinthians 4:4) and in need of patient understanding, prayer, and kindly but firm rebuke by informed Christians.

To be faithful to our Lord's command, to love our neighbors and to preach the gospel to every creature, Christians everywhere must study once again the great doctrines of the Bible, taking nothing for granted and striving in every way to speak the truth in love to the Mormon missionary, who is almost certain to knock at their doors in the near future.

We must, however, indoctrinate members of the Christian church to the subtleties of the Mormon approach and to the sure answers from the Word of God. We must highlight the dangerous doctrines of Mormonism. But let us not ever forget that the Mormons themselves are souls for whom Christ died. We dare not neglect our responsibility in this respect. The need is far too acute and the time grows short.

May the Lord provoke us to jealousy when we see the zeal and the dedication of the Mormons to a spiritual delusion, and let the Holy Spirit breathe once again on his church, that we may be aroused and revived to meet this new and growing challenge from the cults.

Down through the ages men have sought for certainty and for truth, only to be led into the labyrinths of corrupted human reason, philosophy, and religion. Jesus Christ alone could say "I am the truth," and He remains the same "yesterday, today, and forever." Mormonism, with its secret teachings and temples, its denial of fundamental Christian truth, and its attempt to masquerade as a Christian church, has created a spiritual maze of doctrinal half-truths. When lightly sprayed with Christian terminology, morality, and ethics, this can almost defy detection. But "the Word of God is not bound," and one day unrepentant Mormons will learn the truth of our Lord's statement:

> Not everyone who says to me, "Lord, Lord," will enter the kingdom of heaven, but only he who does the will of my Father who is in heaven.
> Matthew 7:21 NIV

The will of the Father, Jesus said, is to receive Him as Savior (John 6:39, 40), for only then can man "work the work of God" (John 6:28, 29).

Before that day it is our task both to refute the error of Mormonism's teachings and to seek to reconcile its followers to the one true God and to His Son, whose blood alone is able "to cleanse us from all sin" (1 John 1:7, 9).

APPENDIX A

THE REORGANIZED CHURCH OF JESUS CHRIST OF LATTER-DAY SAINTS

The Reorganized Church of Jesus Christ of Latter-Day Saints (smaller than the Utah church, at 220,000 members) has its headquarters and publishing house in Independence, Missouri, and is a type of historical skeleton in the closet of the Utah church.

The reasons for this split in the assertedly united kingdom of the "saints" is best explained by the literature of the Reorganized Church. By this I don't mean to imply that everything the Reorganized Church states relative to the Utah Church is historically or theologically completely accurate. It is not always. There are very real differences between the two groups, as there are between other break-offs from the Mormon Church. To date there are more than 95 splinter groups from the original Church (Strangites, Bickertonites, Fettingites, Church of the Firstborn, Cutlerites, and so forth. (See *Denominations That Base Their Beliefs on the Teachings of Joseph Smith the Mormon Prophet*, by Kate Carter). The efforts of the Utah

Church to maintain a monolithic structure descended from Joseph Smith have clearly been less than successful. In fairness to the Reorganized Church, they have made a good historical case concerning their rights as successors to Joseph Smith, Jr.°

Joseph Smith, Jr., founded the Mormon church on April 6, 1830, and was its official leader until his assassination in Carthage, Illinois, in 1844. Following the death of Smith, the Church was subject to tremendous persecution and internal strife. Brigham Young was elected to succeed the dead prophet and took charge of the Church until it split, at which time he led his own followers to Utah. This became known as the Utah Church.

The Reorganized Church maintains that Joseph Smith, eldest son of the Prophet, was the one designated to succeed his father, and that it was he who "presided over the reorganization from 1860 until 1914." Frederick M. Smith, his son, succeeded him, and his brother, Israel Smith, succeeded him in 1946. It is the claim of the Reorganized Church that "the great majority of the descendants of Joseph Smith, the Seer, cast their fortunes with the Reorganized Church." None of the Smith family is alleged to have been affiliated with the Utah Mormon Church.

What the Reorganized Church does not like to acknowledge is that, although Joseph was assassinated in 1844, the Reorganized Church did not come into existence until 1860. Though many who later joined them revolted against the authority of Brigham Young as early as 1845 and challenged certain doctrines,[1] the final break did not occur until much later. The Bible states, "Can two walk together, except they be agreed?" (Amos 3:3), and it is obvious that

---

°Gratitude is expressed to Elbert A. Smith of the Reorganized Church for permission to quote from and use *Differences That Persist*. Independence, Missouri: Herald House Publishing Co., 1943.

[1]They also challenged such Mormon sacred books as *The Pearl of Great Price*, the revelations of Brigham Young, and other materials.

there was growing disagreement within the structure of the Mormon Church as Young exerted more and more authority.

Significant doctrinal aberrations on such subjects as polygamy and polytheism caused those who founded the Reorganized Church to manufacture a dichotomy between Joseph the Prophet and these doctrines attributed to him. In the words of one Reorganized Church spokesman:

> "We both believe in the authenticity of the *Book of Mormon*—though we differ radically in our understandings of some of its teachings. We both accept and publish many of the revelations given through the Prophet Joseph Smith in our respective versions and editions of the *Doctrine and Covenants*.
>
> Divergence comes here at two points. First, the Utah Mormons include in their book some sections, most notably a purported revelation on celestial marriage (section 132), that we challenge. Secondly, our *Doctrine and Covenants* continues to us as an open canon of Scripture and we have added and continue to add revelations as they come to us from time to time through the prophet of the church; while the Mormons have added nothing to their book of revelations, that has been received by them since they set foot on the soil of Utah (with the possible exception of the 'Manifesto' which was not published as a revelation.[2]

From this it may be seen that they are challenging Section 132 of *Doctrine and Covenants*, which is unimpeachably authentic from a historical viewpoint and which was interpreted by Joseph Smith, Jr., Brigham Young, and the early Mormon followers right up until the split in 1860 as a direct reference to the practice of polygamy. That particular doctrine was superseded by a "Manifesto" from the pen of Wilford Woodruff, President of the Utah Church, as previously noted, but it cannot be denied from a historical perspective that the Mormons practiced polygamy based upon Section 132 and other statements of Joseph Smith,

---

[2]*Differences That Persist.*

Brigham Young, and leaders of the Church. For further evidence, consult such sources as Fawn M. Brodie's *No Man Knows My History*, T. B. Stenhouse's works, and other excellent historical sources both inside and outside Mormonism.

Secondly, the claim that the Church in Utah has not added revelations from their prophets since they set foot on the soil of Utah is absolutely false and without foundation. It is true that they have not added to *Doctrine and Covenants*, but they have revised *The Pearl of Great Price* (as previously discussed) and made more than 3900 "corrections" to *The Book of Mormon*.

In addition, significant revelations have come from the Mormon leadership since the Church's establishment in Utah. We discussed at length in Chapter 3, for example, Brigham Young's authoritative revelations concerning Adam-God and Blood Atonement which were "as good as Scripture."

The Reorganized Church also states:

> On the surface, both churches believe in and affirm the fundamental principles of the gospel, commonly referred to as the "first principles." Both make these the basis of pioneer missionary preaching and the basis of their statements of faith and doctrinal belief.
>
> A difference develops soon when the Mormons set forth the doctrine of "celestial" marriage, including polygamy, as an added revelation of doctrine, a "new and everlasting covenant," through which salvation and exaltation are assured—whereas we hold that the principles of the gospel referred to are themselves quite adequate to assure salvation and any degree of exaltation possible ever to achieve through righteous living in obedience to the will of God.[3]

It should be observed that *The Pearl of Great Price* was accepted without reservations by all Mormons until the split in 1860. It was only when Brigham Young began to

---

[3]*Differences That Persist.*

assert the doctrines of Adam-God and polygamy as a divine obligation that those who became the Reorganized Church revolted.

The Reorganized Church also denies that Joseph Smith, Jr., was a polytheist, and maintains that he believed in the existence of only one God (in harmony with *The Book of Mormon*, as we discussed in Chapter 3). However, one cannot read the King Follet discourse, one of Joseph's last sermons, or a number of his other utterances (catalogued in Chapter 4), without recognizing immediately that he was thoroughly polytheistic, that he contradicted *The Book of Mormon* through his translation of *The Pearl of Great Price*, and that the historical veracity of these statements simply cannot be impugned. Those who left the Mormon Church in 1860 to form the Reorganized Church were not publishing or challenging these statements or the authority and power of Brigham Young or his revelations until more than fifteen years after Joseph Smith's assassination, a fact of no small import. Reorganized spokesmen state:

> When we canvass differences, ordinarily we think first of our disagreement on the marriage question; but that difference grows out of other differences quite as fundamental. One of these is in our understanding of the character of God. The two churches join in the initial statement of the Epitome of Faith drafted by the Prophet Joseph: "We believe in God the Eternal Father." But at the very start when we endeavor to interpret the *character* of God there comes the widest imaginable divergence in views.
>
> We think of God as eternally unchangeable, and commonly assume that there can scarcely be any other view taken. But our Mormon friends do take a very different view.[4]

The Reorganized Church is quite correct here in affirming the eternity of God. This statement has been affirmed by *The Book of Mormon* most emphatically

---

[4]*Differences That Persist.*

(3 Nephi 24:6; Mormon 9:9, 19; Alma 41:8; Moroni 8:18), but they simply will not face the fact that Joseph Smith contradicted himself and declared that God was indeed changeable and, in fact, by his own theology cannot be eternal. This is the fallacy of infinite regression of the gods. They do not know an eternal God any more than they know attaining eternal life in Him through the Lord Jesus Christ, which is why Joseph and Brigham and the Utah Church have taught eternal progression, rather than eternal completion in the true gospel as proclaimed in historic Christianity.

Malachi 3:6 reminds us of the changeless nature of the God of the Bible: "I am the Lord, I change not." Joseph Smith simply did not believe this, but the Reorganized Church ignores his polytheism at this point.

The Reorganized Church denies what Smith, Young, Heber Kimball, and B. H. Roberts (perhaps Mormonism's greatest historian), all affirmed, "a God who is Himself progressive" (*Articles of Faith*, James E. Talmadge, edition 1899, Deseret News Press, Salt Lake City, Utah). The title page of that book states "Written by appointment and published by the church." Obviously this is authoritative, being endorsed by the Church, and yet it is *not* one of the so-called four standard works, proof once again of what we have consistently maintained, namely, that the "standard works" of the Church, insofar as doctrinal authority is concerned, do not stand alone.

One of the great failings of the Reorganized Church is its unwillingness to face the fact that Joseph Smith not only contradicted himself but repeatedly contradicted both the Bible and *The Book of Mormon*, the very book he had allegedly translated and claimed was "the most correct of any book on earth." *The Book of Mormon* forbids polygamy (Jacob 1:15; 2:23, 27; 3:5), but when the Reorganized Church was faced with considerable evidence to the effect that Joseph Smith, Jr., practiced polygamy and gave it as a divine revelation in *Doctrine and Covenants*, Section 132, they maintain, ". . . we cannot accept as coming from the same source the subsequent alleged revelation on polygamy." In effect, what we see in the Reorganized Church is the attempt to have one's cake and eat it too, by retaining Joseph Smith, Jr., as a prophet of God and ignoring the contradictions within his system of theology and his obvious confusion in the early development of the Mormon theological system.

The Reorganized Latter-Day Saints also reject the doctrine of Joseph Smith and Brigham Young that man progresses eternally and that he may indeed become a god. What happens is that wherever the Reorganized Church finds anything which contradicts what they *believe* Joseph Smith, Jr., taught, irrespective of any historical, theological, or logical evidence which can be adduced as proof, they simply affirm that Joseph was a prophet of God and therefore couldn't possibly have said these things. It is admirable that they recognize that a true prophet of God would not teach these things, but it is utter folly to ignore the evidence, for Joseph did indeed proclaim them.

The Reorganized Church claims that at a conference in January, 1853 polygamy was condemned by divine revelation, controverting Brigham Young's declaration (August 29, 1852) ·that ". . . it [polygamy] will be fostered and believed in by the more intelligent portions of the world, as one of the best doctrines ever proclaimed to any people" (*Supplement to Millennial Star*, 15:31). The Utah Church rightly challenges the validity of the claims of the dissident group, who took nine years from the death of their prophet to resist the authority of the Church, vested in Brigham Young. The Reorganized Church, however, does have a good point when it states, "They [the Utah Church] still hold to a belief in the divinity of the doctrine while renouncing its present practice so that the matter still remains a live issue. . . ."

It is the basic contention of the Reorganized Church that the Utah Church received the doctrine of polygamy from Brigham Young, and reject his testimony that it came from Joseph Smith, in favor of the testimony of Emma Smith, Joseph's legal and first wife, who stated that she had no knowledge of any document referred to by Brigham Young, authored by Joseph Smith, and "revealing" polygamy.

In order not to take up a great deal of time, the reader need only consult the documentation provided throughout this book, and it will be clear that Brigham Young faithfully followed what Joseph Smith did indeed introduce as divine revelation, namely, the doctrine of polygamy. The Reorganized Church finds this abhorrent and the very antithesis of the fabricated character of Joseph Smith, Jr., fashioned from selected materials of his own origin and history in order to maintain faith in his validity as "the Prophet."

Further differences between the Utah and the Reorganized Church involve the Utah Church's insistence upon secret temple services (oaths, covenants, sealings, grips, etc.) which the Reorganized Church rejects on the basis of the words of Jesus Christ: "In secret have I said nothing" (John 18:20). Added to this, of course, is the testimony of our Lord as recorded in Matthew 5, where He specifically states: "I say unto you, Swear not at all, neither by heaven, because it is God's throne, nor by earth, because it is His footstool, nor by the hairs of your head, because you do not have power to make them black or white; but let your yes be yes and your no be no, for anything else comes from the wicked one" (verses 34-37 lit. trans.).

The Reorganized Church is right in stating:

> In any event, from all we have read and heard we have good reason to believe that the Mormon temple service is very complex and includes secret rites, ceremonies, oaths, covenants, sealings, passwords, signs, grips, etc. Without doubt this service has a great hold on the imagination of the Mormon people and is dear to their hearts and is held in reverent respect. We would speak of it with the courtesy that is due the religious convictions of all people. But to us it have no appeal and we find for

it no authority in the Bible, *Book of Mormon,* or any of the revelations from God published during the life of the Prophet Joseph . . .

To us the gospel is a thing open and free. Its ordinances and ceremonies are not secret. No one of the sacraments and ordinances: baptism, confirmation, blessing, administration to the sick, marriage and the sacrament of the Lord's supper, is secret. Their nature may be freely revealed to the world. They are not guarded by secret oaths or obligations or secret covenants.

Even the covenant of marriage is set forth in its exact terms in the section on marriage published in the *Book of Covenants* during the life of Joseph Smith (1835 edition). This covenant was approved by the church and published to the world, by approval of the prophet, with the specific commandment that marriage should be solemnized in a "public meeting." By no means was it to be a secret ceremony hidden from the knowledge of men.

We feel that secrecy is not and was not a part of the divine plan.[5]

With this, of course, we are in complete agreement, particularly in the light of our Lord's statement in Matthew 28:20, where He commands the Church to proclaim "all things whatsoever I have commanded you."

There are many other differences which exist between the Utah and the Reorganized Church. The Reorganized Church, for instance, rejected vigorously the Mormon doctrine of "baptism for the dead," as well as Brigham Young's right to the succession of leadership in the Utah Church. Brigham Young maintained, "Who ordained me to be the First President of this church? I answer, it is the choice of this people, and that is sufficient" (*Millennial Star,* 16:442). The Reorganized Church cites in opposition to this that Joseph's eldest son ascended to the Presidency of their church in 1860, succeeding "an acting or provisional president." They maintain that Joseph's son succeeded his father when he became of age and was in the lineage of the Prophet, but they considerably weaken their case by

[5]*Differences That Persist.*

quoting *Doctrine and Covenants* 102:9 (Utah Edition), which declares:

> The president of the church, who is also president of the council (High Council), is appointed by revelation, and acknowledged in his administration by the voice of the church.

The Reorganized Church appeals to a statement from *Doctrine and Covenants* 124:56-58 (Utah Edition) that pertains to a "boarding house" where God allegedly told Joseph Smith that he and his posterity would continue to live, and "have place therein, from generation to generation;[6] for this anointing have I put upon his head, that his blessing shall also be put upon the head of his posterity after him; and as I said unto Abraham, concerning the kindreds of the earth, even so I say unto my servant Joseph, In thee, and in thy seed, shall the kindred of the earth be blessed."

The so-called revelation contains a blessing upon Joseph's family; it does *not* state that any member of the family shall succeed to the office of the Prophet. The Utah Church, therefore, is on far stronger ground at this point.

The Reorganized Church has twice in the civil courts "been sustained as the successor to the original church presided over by the Martyr Joseph Smith." The courts at that time ruled:

> And the Court do further find that the Plaintiff, the Reorganized Church of Jesus Christ of Latter-Day Saints, is the True and Lawful continuation of, and successor to the said original Church of Jesus Christ of Latter-Day Saints, organized in 1830, and is entitled in law to all its rights and property.
>
> *Court of Common Pleas,*
> Lake County, Ohio;
> see journal entry,
> February term, 1880

---

[6]The Mormon god's revelations are not reliable. The house spoken of no longer exists!

Still another decision, by a Judge Philips, in the Circuit Court of the United States for the Western District of Missouri in the so-called Temple Lot Suit in 1894, generally sustained the decision previously quoted.

In that suit James Whitehead, former secretary of Joseph Smith, Jr., swore under oath:

> I recollect a meeting that was held in the winter of 1843, at Nauvoo, Illinois, prior to Joseph Smith's death, at which the appointment was made by him, Joseph Smith, of his successor. His son, Joseph, was selected as his successor. Joseph Smith did the talking. At that meeting Joseph Smith, the present presiding officer of the complainant church, was selected by his father as his successor. He was ordained and anointed at that meeting. Hyrum Smith, the Patriarch, anointed him, and Joseph his father blessed him and ordained him, and Newell K. Whitney poured the oil on his head, and he was set apart to be his father's successor in office, holding all the powers that his father held.
>
> Plaintiff's Abstract,
> *Temple Lot Suit*, page 28

The Reorganized Church has bested the Mormon Church, Utah, at this point and has underscored just how lightly the Utah Church takes the law of the land when it conflicts with its own religious interpretations.

In the famous Reed Smoot Case (1903-4), Joseph Fielding Smith, then President of the Utah Church (1901-18), maintained that he had received *no* revelations whatever as President of the Church (Volume 1, page 484) and in addition admitted under oath that he had not obeyed the Woodruff manifesto outlawing polygamy, for at that time he had five wives and eleven children. To quote President Smith directly, "Mr. Chairman, I have not claimed that in that case I have obeyed the law of the land" (Volume 1, page 197). When further questioned by Senator Overman, President Smith responded as follows:

> Senator Overman: Is there not a revelation that you shall abide by the laws of the State and of the land? Mr. Smith.—Yes, sir. Senator Overman.—If that is a revela-

tion, are you not violating the laws of God? Mr.
Smith.—I have admitted that, Mr. Senator, a great many
times here.

Proceedings in the Smoot Case,
Volume I, pages 334, 335

Prophets of the Mormon Church have received revelations since the death of Brigham Young which are not recorded in the so-called standard works of the Church, yet
they are revelations nonetheless, for they are doctrine to be
believed. President Smith and a number of Mormons along
with him, as the evidence indicates, deliberately violated
such revelations of Joseph Smith himself (*Doctrine and
Covenants* 58:21) as well as the laws of the United States!

This is a blatant contradiction of the thirteenth chapter
of Romans, which instructs all professing Christians to "be
in subjection to the governing authorities, for there is no
authority except from God. Therefore he who resists
authority has opposed the ordinance of God (Romans
13:1, 2a NASB).

From the foregoing documentation and evidence, it is
clear to any unbiased mind that the Reorganized Church of
Jesus Christ does have very definite points of divergence
from the Utah Church, but that this fact does not entitle
them to be classified as a Christian denomination.

Both groups agree that Joseph Smith, Jr., is a true
prophet of God, that *The.Book of Mormon* is of equal
authority with the Bible, and that salvation comes by faith,
repentance, baptism, and good works. Both groups maintain that all churches are in a state of apostasy from the initial revelation of the New Testament and that they alone
are the people of the "restoration." Enough has been written in this volume to refute these teachings, and further
comment is unnecessary. Christians should beware of the
Reorganized Church's attempt to claim Christian status by
opposing the Utah Church, for there is sufficient agreement
between them on erroneous doctrines to exclude both
groups from orthodox consideration.

Theology of the Reorganized Church

1. The Reorganized Church endorses and publishes "The Inspired Version" of the Bible, which is an alleged translation by Joseph Smith, Jr., wherein he alters many Biblical texts and contradicts Biblical revelation in many places. The Scriptures specifically forbid adding to the Word of God (Proverbs 30:6), and the Book of Revelation declares that God will add plagues and subtract names from the Book of Life for people who add to or subtract from the Word of God.

2. Salvation or redemption by grace alone is a fundamental doctrine of New Testament theology which the Reorganized Church does not follow. For them, baptism is necessary for the removal of sin, and good works are necessary in order to either attain salvation or retain it. As we have noted in Ephesians 2, the past tense of the Greek rules this out forever: "For it is by grace you have been saved, through faith—and that not of yourselves, it is the gift of God—not of works, so that no one can boast. For we are God's workmanship, created in Christ Jesus to do good works, which God prepared in advance for us to do" (verses 8-10 lit. trans.). We have dealt with this subject under the Mormon doctrine of salvation, but the Epistle to the Galatians alone is sufficient, along with Romans 4, 5 and 8, to establish the doctrine irrefutably.

3. The Reorganized Church accepts Joseph Smith's first vision and believes that all churches are wrong, that all their creeds are an abomination in the sight of God, and that all their professors are corrupt. They believe that Christendom is in apostasy and that they are the church of the restoration. This is one of the great marks of cultism (consider, for example, Jehovah's Witnesses, the World Wide Church of God, and the Utah Mormon Church).

The record of history shows that there has never been any universal apostasy from Christianity, but rather that the church has had cycles of great spiritual strength and of weakness, and even of corruption, but that God has never left Himself without a witness. Such names as Athanasius, Augustine, Aquinas, John Huss, Martin Luther, John Calvin, Zwingli, Wycliffe, Tyndale, Knox, Wesley, Finney, and Moody, not to mention the great confessions of the church and the historic denominational structures which rose from the Reformation from the tradition of Roman Catholic and Greek Orthodoxy, refute the cultists' arrogant pretensions.

4. The Reorganized Church recognizes *The.Book of Mormon* as the Word of God, despite the fact that there are more than 3900 changes° from the 1830 edition to the present day (and the Missouri version differs from the Utah version). The Bible flatly declares in Jude 3, "When I wrote to you, brothers, concerning the common salvation, it was necessary for me to put up a good fight for the faith *once-for-all* delivered to the saints" (lit. trans.). Notice that the faith was once-for-all delivered; it was not to be changed or contradicted.

That is not to say that God cannot communicate today if He so chooses, but those who claim that He has or is now doing so must submit such claims to the authority of Scripture, for it is Scripture which tests all things, and *not* the experience of man.

5. The Reorganized Church accepts *The Doctrine and Covenants* given by Joseph Smith, with the exception of passages which they maintain are spurious because they conflict with *The.Book of Mormon* and the Bible. As has been pointed out, they assume that Joseph Smith was a true prophet, and that therefore contradictions cannot exist. However, we have shown abundant evidence that Smith made these statements and claimed that they came from God. Therefore, the only evidence that we have that he was a true prophet is his own word. The content of the revelations which he claimed were given to him by God make Smith's claim clearly spurious. The unmasking of his Egyp-

---

°See Chapter 2 for documentation.

tian alphabet, his fraudulent translation of *The Book of Abraham*, his utter racism toward Negroes, and his false prophecies, previously examined, refute Joseph Smith forcefully at this point. It is unnecessary to mention in detail Joseph's now-established conviction as a fortune-teller and "glass-looker," which he denied and which the recently found court bill established beyond reasonable legal doubt (see Chapter 1).

6. The Christian doctrine of the Trinity, which declares that within the nature of the one God are three eternal Persons—the Father, the Son, and the Holy Spirit—is not acknowledged by the Reorganized Church, but is redefined so that there is genuine confusion as to the nature of God, the functions of the members of the Trinity, and the place and application of the Trinity in historic Christian theology.

7. Joseph Smith, Jr., taught that Adam was Michael the Archangel, the Ancient of Days—a totally unbiblical position. In fact, the Bible makes a very clear distinction between Adam and Michael: Adam was the first man created by God (1 Corinthians 15:45); and Michael, first in rank of the angels after Lucifer, by divine command drove Satan from heaven to his present position as prince of the powers of the air.

8. The Reorganized Church accepts Joseph Smith's story of his encounter with the angel Moroni and the existence of a restored priesthood. We have already shown in Chapter 6 the Biblical refutation of this position and the great deception Smith wrought in both the Moroni fiction and the fiasco of the Priesthood.

It would be possible to go on stating other areas relative to the theology of the Reorganized Mormon Church, but the evidence of both history and theology in New Testament revelation rules out the Reorganized Church as a Christian body and rightly classifies them as a non-Christian cultic system.

APPENDIX B

UNANSWERED QUESTIONS ON THE MORMON GOSPEL*

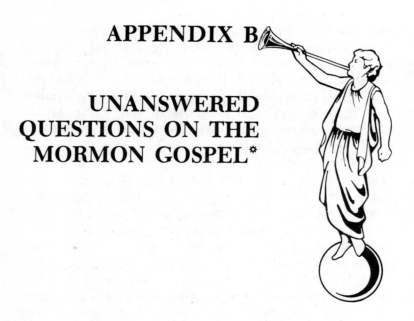

1. We are consistently taught that *The Book of Mormon* is the "most correct book" and that it contains the truth, the Word of God, and the fullness of the gospel (*Doctrine and Covenants* 19:26; 20:9; 27:5; 42:12; 135:3). Exactly where in *The Book of Mormon* are the following doctrines or concepts taught?

- God has a body of flesh and bones.
- God is an exalted man.
- God is a product of eternal progression.
- The plurality of gods.
- God "organized" the world rather than "created" it.
- There is no eternal hell and punishment.
- Men can become gods.
- "Intelligences" are eternal.

---

*We express our thanks to Bob Witte of Christian Communications, Inc., for preparing these questions.

- Pre-existing spirits of men.
- Marriage for eternity.
- Polygamy is *not* an abomination in the sight of God.
- Three degrees of glory.
- A "mother" in heaven.
- A Melchizedek priesthood consisting of the offices of Elder, Seventy, and High Priest.
- An Aaronic priesthood consisting of the offices of Deacon, Teacher, and Priest.
- Negroes are to be denied the priesthood.
- The functions and offices of Evangelists, Bishoprics, Stake Presidencies, Assistants to the Twelve, a First Presidency, and a President of the Church.
- *The Book of Mormon* is the "Stick of Joseph."

2. How could Nephi and just a small handful of men build a temple like Solomon's when it took Solomon 7½ years using more than 180,000 workers to complete the temple in Jerusalem? According to 2 Nephi chapter 5, the Nephites completed their temple in less than 20 years! In addition, were precious ores such as Solomon used available to Nephi or not? Verse 15 says that they were in *great abundance*, but the very next verse (5:16) says that they were *not to be found upon the land!*

3. If *The.Book of Mormon* is true and God is at least consistent (if not unchanging) why don't the disobedient turn black (2 Nephi 5:21-23)? More importantly, why don't Lamanites turn white and delightsome within one year after accepting the gospel, as they did in 3 Nephi 2:11-16?

4. Jacob 4:1 tells us that only a little of the words can be written because of the difficulty of engraving the plates. Why then did God inspire the Nephite prophets to be so wordy? There are numerous examples. Many sentences are 200 to 300 words long. There are 2000 "and it came to pass" phrases. But the best example has to be in 4 Nephi 1:6,

where 57 words are used to merely say that 59 years had passed by.

5. Apostle James Talmadge said that *The Book of Mormon* contained no absurdities and nothing unreasonable (*Articles of Faith*, p. 504). If that is true, what about Jared's barges? Ether chapter 6 tells us that a "furious" wind propelled the barges to the promised land. It took the furious wind 344 days to blow the barges to the new world. Even if the furious wind could only push the barges at 10 miles per hour, the distance traveled would have been 82,560 miles, or enough for more than *three trips around the globe*! Is that reasonable?

6. What is the explanation for the current teaching that there is no eternal hell, when both the Bible and *The Book of Mormon* teach that there is? (See 1 Nephi 14:3; 2 Nephi 9:16; 28:21-23; Mosiah 3:25; Alma 34:35; Helaman 6:28; 13:25-26.)

7. The "law" of eternal progression teaches that Gods are men who have passed through an earth life, obeyed the "laws of the gospel," and received their exaltation. How can the Holy Ghost be a God without a body? How could Christ have been a God, since He too was without a body until 2000 years ago? If God the Father was once a man, why isn't that fact clearly spelled out in *Doctrine and Covenants*? Since it is clear that only God the Father had a body at the creation, why didn't He say "let us make man in *My* image" rather than "our" image?

8. Since *The Book of Mormon* does not teach that God has a body, the LDS usually goes to the Old Testament to prove that God has a body (Moses speaking "face-to-face" etc.). But we are taught that it is Jehovah (Jesus Christ prior to the incarnation) who deals with Man exclusively after the Fall. Therefore, all the verses used in the Old Testament (after Genesis 3) to prove that God has a body of flesh and bone *cannot be used*, because Jesus did not receive His body until after the completion of the Old Testament. What is the answer to this theological paradox?

9. If Jesus Christ wasn't conceived by the Holy Ghost, but is instead the literal "only begotten" of the Father, how could He have been born of a *virgin*, as is required by the Old Testament and is taught in both the Bible and *The Book of Mormon* (Alma 7:10)?

10. If murder is an unpardonable sin (*Doctrine and Covenants* 42:18, 79; 132:27), how could Moses appear. in *glory* on the Mount of Transfiguration (Exodus 2:12; Matthew 17:3)?

11. If the President of the Church receives revelations, why haven't there been any additions to the canon of Scripture since 1847, especially since the Church now has in its possession the original papyri to complete the translation of the Book of Abraham? If the supposed answer to this question is that the "revelations" consist of the teachings of the General Authorities (especially at conferences), why then do the current leaders of the Church repudiate the concepts of Adam-god, individual blood atonement, and rebaptism of the membership, and ignore the many false prophecies given in the last century by the (then) General. Authorities? A final thought on this subject comes from Orson Pratt, who continually taught in many of his speeches and written works that the prima facie evidence of the Christian church's apostasy was the fact that they hadn't added any more books to their canon of Scripture. Well, neither has the LDS Church for almost 130 years, which is 89% of the time that the Church has existed. By analogy, doesn't this tend to bring an indictment of apostasy against the LDS Church?

12. Everyone talks about the "Angel Moroni," but if he was a great prophet and leader of the Nephites and was a righteous and devout man of God, why hasn't he attained godhood along with Abraham, Isaac, and Jacob (*Doctrine and Covenants* 132:17, 37)?

13. Why wasn't there a published revelation for the filling of the First Council of the Seventy? This is especially important since it has lain dormant all these years (an aside

question—Why?) and is not being filled according to the pattern set down by the original revelation. *Doctrine and Covenants* 107:95 clearly states that the seven Presidents of the first quorum are to be the ones to select the other 63 members, not the President of the Church.

14. What is the explanation for the fact that Oliver Cowdery wrote eight letters in the *Messenger and Advocate* beginning in 1834 which contain well over 15,000 words dealing with Joseph's and Oliver's baptism by an angel, yet he didn't once identify the angel as being John the Baptist? Yet in later years, both he and Joseph said that they knew at the time (1829) that it was John the Baptist.

15. Why aren't there any references in the Book of Commandments concerning the First Vision, the identity of Moroni, the restoration of the priesthood, the identity of Peter, James and John, or of John the Baptist?

16. If the First Vision was supposed to be generally known at the time it happened and was the cause of "great persecution" of Joseph (Joseph Smith 2:22), why aren't there *any* references to it prior to 1831? Nothing is mentioned in any known LDS sources (private journals, letters, sermons, revelations, or other church publications) or even in "unfriendly" sources such as non-Mormon newspapers, magazines, etc.

17. Joseph had a "revelation of Jesus Christ" in Section 84 of *Doctrine and Covenants* where Jesus said in verses 21 and 22 that no man can see the face of the Father and live *unless* he has the Priesthood. Joseph didn't receive the Priesthood until 1829, yet he said that he saw both the Father and the Son in 1820. Where is the error—in Section 84 or in Joseph's story of the Vision?

18. Why do *The Times and the Seasons, Millennial Star,* and Lucy Mack Smith's biography on Joseph all agree that the angel who appeared to Joseph Smith in 1823 was named *Nephi*?

19. *Doctrine and Covenants* 104:1 has Jesus saying that the United Order was an everlasting order until "I come," yet

the United Order *failed* and has been disbanded, and the Lord hasn't come yet. Why?

20. *The Book of Mormon* declares that nobody can read "Reformed Egyptian" because it was "altered" (Mormon 9:32-34). Yet Joseph related the story of Martin Harris (Joseph Smith 2:62-64) visiting Professor Anthon, who supposedly said that the translation of the characters was "correct." How would Anthon know if they were correct, if *The Book of Mormon* is true? Also, what is the reconciliation with the fact that Professor Anthon publicly denied the details of the story as related by Harris and went on to say that he told Harris that the whole thing was a hoax?

21. The importance of the Urim and Thummim in effecting the translation of *The Book of Mormon* is greatly stressed today. What is the explanation for the fact that the principals involved with the translation process (Emma Smith, Martin Harris, Oliver Cowdery, and David Whitmer) agreed that most of the translation was accomplished with Joseph having his face buried in his hat with a stone in it, and that the golden plates were usually not even present?

22. The LDS claim that Peter, James, and John were the original First Presidency of the Church, but they were numbered among the Twelve. Why are there now 12 apostles *plus* 3 in the First Presidency? Also, about 10 years ago President McKay expanded the First Presidency until it had a total of *six* members (without benefit of a change in the Scriptures), with the statement that the need was because of the increased workloads and growth of the church. Yet, Joseph Fielding Smith returned the number to the original three, where it remains to this day, even though the numbers in the church today far exceed those of 10 years ago. What is the explanation?

23. What is the Scriptural basis (Latter-day or otherwise) for the office of "Assistant to the Twelve" being a General Authority?

24. How could there be a *total* apostasy when there was at least one apostle, John (and possibly four, if one considers the 3 Nephite "disciples" as holding the office of apostle, as some in the Church do),when the current teaching is that as long as one Elder remains alive *he* has the power to reorganize the Church and all its structured systems?

25. There isn't a single LDS-produced standard work that hasn't undergone hundreds and even thousands of changes, additions, deletions, and corrections, many of which are much more than "typographical" in nature, and all of which were done without indications or acknowledgement of the actions taken. Even granting Joseph the "right" to revise what God had told him before (even though it is difficult to do so when we are talking about cases involving historical facts), why is there the deception associated with these changes? None of the dates are moved up to the time that the revelations were revised, there is not a single heading in the *Doctrine and Covenants, The Pearl of Great Price,* or *Book of Mormon* that indicates a revision, nor is it acknowledged openly by the Church leaders that there were such changes made. Some Church leaders have even lied in public about these situations. Why?

26. If baptism for the dead is a "suppressed" Christian doctrine dating from the apostolic age, why did Paul use the pronoun "they" instead of the personal "we" or "ye" when referring to the practice? In the same light, if the apostatized Christian church is responsible for stopping the practice, and is also guilty of removing "many plain and precious things" from the Bible, *and* Paul's reference refers to a Christian group baptizing for the dead, why then did this reference remain in the Bible, especially in a chapter devoted solely to doctrinal arguments for the resurrection?

27. If nobody can receive the Holy Ghost without the laying on of hands by one "having authority," how can the cases of Cornelius (Acts 10:44-48), Joseph and Oliver (Joseph Smith 2:73), the Nephite 12 disciples (3 Nephi 9:13), and Adam (Moses 5:9-20) be properly explained?

28. If the Bible isn't correctly translated, and even granting that Joseph "didn't complete" the translation (although *Documented History of the Church* 1:324, 368, *The Times and Seasons* 6:802, and the LDS Church Chronology all agree that the New Testament was finished on February 2, 1833, and the Old Testament was finished on July 2, 1833), why haven't any of the other eleven Presidents of the Church finished the job? This is especially important because there are 18 sections of the *Doctrine and Covenants* which contain the Lord's commands and specific instructions relating to the revision of the Bible and its publication to the world. (See *Doctrine and Covenants* 73:4; 93:53; 124:89 as examples.) Haven't *all* the Presidents been sustained as "Prophet, Seer, and Revelator" of the LDS Church?

29. Why didn't Joseph know that Esaias is the Greek name for Isaiah (*Doctrine and Covenants* 76:100)? Why didn't he know that Elias is the Greek name for Elijah (*Doctrine and Covenants* 110:12-13), and therefore couldn't possibly have been the name of a Hebrew prophet at the time of Abraham?

30. *Doctrine and Covenants* 84:4 said that the New Jerusalem and the temple would be built "in *this* generation" by the gathering saints. It has *not* been built yet. More than 143 years have gone by since that prophecy was given. Even granting the extended (and unprecedented) concept of 100 years in a generation (4 Nephi 18, 22), the time for completion is long overdue. The gathering of the saints to Zion has stopped, and Brigham Young, Orson Pratt, and other General Authorities of the time all taught that "this generation" clearly meant the generation alive in 1832. But they have all passed away. The question is, how can one escape the conclusion that Joseph was a false prophet as is required by the test of a true prophet found in Deuteronomy 18:20-22, unless Brigham Young is the one who is the false prophet?

31. How could Joseph carry the golden plates around so

easily, and how could the witness have "hefted" the plates without (a recorded) difficulty when the plates had to weigh at least 230 pounds? (The plates are said to have been 7" X 8" X 6" high, and gold weighs 1204.7 pounds per square foot—figure it out for yourself.)

32. Brigham said that "the only men who become gods, even the sons of God, are those who enter into polygamy" (*Journal of Discourses* 11:269). Now that the Church has yielded to government pressure and suspended the practice of polygamy, how can Mormons hope to become gods?

33. If genealogy is so important, why does the New Testament twice condemn seeking after genealogies, and why is *The Book of Mormon* silent on the subject altogether? (See 1 Timothy 1:4; Titus 3:9).

34. Throughout the New Testament we are taught that the blood of Jesus pays the debt for our sin and cleanses us. *The Book of Mormon* also confirms this doctrine (Mosiah 4:2-3). Why did Brigham Young (and others) teach that there are sins that the blood of Jesus cannot wipe out and that can only be atoned for by the shedding of our *own* blood? (See *Journal of Discourses* 3:247; 4:49, 53, 54 for examples.)

35. Why does the Book of Abraham conflict with the Book of Moses in the terminology "the gods" as opposed to "I, God" when referring to the creation?

36. God rejected the fig-leaf aprons which Adam and Eve had made (Genesis 3:21). Why is the fig-leaf apron used in the temple ceremony to memorialize the Fall?

37. When the Metropolitan Museum of Art gave the LDS Church the original papyri in 1967, why didn't the President of the Church undertake the task of *completing* the translation of the Book of Abraham instead of turning the papyri over to Dr. Nibley for "further research and study?" John Taylor said that Joseph promised to furnish the church with "further extracts from the Book of Abraham" (*Times and Seasons* 4:95), but we know that he didn't accomplish what he promised. So what is stopping the incum-

bent Seer from completing Joseph's work? **Dr.** Nibley hasn't given us the further extracts; in fact, the First Presidency has disavowed any sanction or approval of what Nibley *did* do! (See letter to John L. Smith, August 22, 1975.)

38. Much is made of the name of the Church by its missionaries, who claim that there was *no* church on the face of the earth called "The Church of Jesus Christ" when the "church" was restored in 1830. What is the explanation for the fact that the Church changed its name *twice* in the first *eight* years of its existence? According to *The Book of Mormon* (3 Nephi 27:7-8) it was to be called after Christ's name; and for the first four years, it *was* called "Church of Christ." In 1834 the name was changed to "Church of the Latter-day Saints." Finally, in 1838, it became "The Church of Jesus Christ of Latter-Day Saints." Wouldn't one think that there is a serious problem of contradiction here, because Jesus made a point to instruct the Nephites on what the Church should be named, and one should reasonably assume that Christ would have informed Joseph in 1830 *exactly* what he wanted the Church to be called, yet He didn't speak to the point until 1838—after two different names had been used already?

39. If the LDS Church is a restoration of the New Testament church organization, how can a boy of 12 be a deacon? (See 1 Timothy 3:8-12.) The argument that "times have changed" cannot be used, since Brigham Young very strongly agreed with Paul that a deacon's calling was not the business of young boys (*Journal of Discourses* 2:89).

40. Was Enoch 430 years old when he was translated (*Doctrine and Covenants* 107:49; Moses 8:1), or was he 365 years old (*Teachings of the Prophet Joseph Smith*, page 120; Genesis 5:21-23)?

41. Time and time again we are told that Joseph "sealed his testimony with his blood," went "like a lamb to the slaughter," and "died a martyr's death." Yet the specifics of the dastardly murder of Joseph as related in the

Documented History of the Church 6:xli, 618, 620; 7:102)
clearly reveal that he died in a blazing gunfight—John
Wayne style—and he is reported to have killed a couple of
the Mobocrats in the fracas. *Lambs* do not fight to the
death with six-shooters. How can the LDS Church insist
that Joseph was a martyr, knowing that Joseph fought for
his life, when the universally accepted definition of a martyr is one who dies *willingly* and *without resistance*?

APPENDIX C

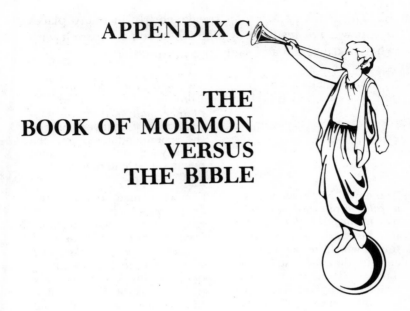

THE
BOOK OF MORMON
VERSUS
THE BIBLE

Listed below are a few of the contradictions between the Bible and *The Book of Mormon*.

1. *The Book of Mormon* tells us that Lehi "dwelt at Jerusalem in all his days," (1 Nephi 1:4) in about 600 B.C. and was a prophet of God from the tribe of Manasseh. Yet we find that his son, Nephi, tells us that his father spoke in a strange language.

> Yea, I make a record in the language of my father, which consists of the learning of the Jews and the language of the Egyptians (1 Nephi 1:2).

The Egyptian language was a very corrupt language from idol worshipping people who had persecuted the children of Israel as Hitler did the Jews in the terrible holocaust during World War II. No prophet of God would have ever used a corrupt language to convey God's message at this period in history. See Nehemiah 13:23-25 for a prophet of God's reaction to use of a mixed and corrupt language.

2. *The Book of Mormon* speaks clearly in many places that it was *not* inspired by God when you compare it with what God has already said about inspiration.

. . . . and I make it according to *my*° knowledge (1 Nephi 1:3).

Ye *shall not add unto the word*° which I command you, *neither shall ye diminish anything from it,* that ye may keep the commandments of the LORD your God which I command you (Deuteronomy 4:2).

And now I, Nephi, *do not make a full account of the things which my father hath written,* for he hath written many things which he saw in visions and in dreams; and he also hath written many things which he prophesied and spake unto his children, of which I shall not make a full account. . . . Behold, I make an *abridgement* of the record of my father. . . . (1 Nephi 1:16, 17).

For what man knoweth the things of a man, except the spirit of man which is in him? *Even so the things of God knoweth no man,* but *the Spirit who is of God;* that we might know the things that are freely given to us of God. Which things also we speak, *not in the words which man's wisdom* teacheth, *but which the Holy Spirit teacheth,* comparing spiritual things with spiritual (1 Corinthians 2:11-13).

Nevertheless, I do not write anything upon plates save it be that I *think they are sacred.* And now, if I do err, even did they err of old; not that I would excuse myself because of other men, but because of the weakness which is in me, according to the flesh, I would excuse myself (1 Nephi 19:6). See also 2 Nephi 11:1; 25:7; 33:1.

Knowing this first, that no prophecy of the scripture is of any *private interpretation. For the scripture came not at any time by the will of man,* but holy men of God spoke as they were *moved by the Holy Spirit* (2 Peter 1:20, 21).

As the reader can see by comparison, Joseph Smith the author and proprietor of *The Book of Mormon* had ab-

---

° Emphasis ours.

solutely no idea of the power of God. Prophets of the Bible never made any excuses for themselves, for they did not speak their own words but God's. When God says something it is accurate, it will come true, and we must not make "abridgements" of His Word.

3. In 1 Nephi 10:11 (which was supposed to have been written about 600 B.C.), the term "Holy Ghost" is used. In reality it is Elizabethan English and was unknown in Old Testament times. However, the translators of the King James Version used it often as they translated the New Testament into English.

4. 1 Nephi 10:17 refers to "faith on the Son of God." (Keep in mind this was allegedly written between 600-592 B.C.) This phrase never was used by an Old Testament prophet. The Messiah, who would be King and Deliverer was expected, but He was not referred to as "the Son of God."

5. 1 Nephi 10:17 says, ". . . he spake by the power of the Holy Ghost; which power he received by faith on the Son of God." This is referring to the gifts of the Holy Spirit and the power given by God which did not occur until the day of Pentecost. If it was available at the time Nephi allegedly was written, Jesus would not have said to His disciples before He ascended to Heaven, "But ye *shall* receive power, after the Holy Ghost is come upon you; . . ." Acts chapter two records the coming of the Holy Spirit in power.

6. 1 Nephi 10:18 states, "For he is the same yesterday, today, and forever." This is a quote from Hebrews 13:8, 600 years before it was written.

7. Over 600 years before the Apostle Paul was born, *The Book of Mormon* quotes his statement from Romans 7:24, "O wretched man that I am" (2 Nephi 4:17).

8. 2 Nephi 1:3 cites America as the "land of promise" for these Israelites. But the Bible informs us that for the children of Israel the land of Canaan was the promised land. (See Genesis 13:14-18.)

9. 2 Nephi 10:7 proclaims, ". . . When the day cometh that they shall *believe in me, that I am Christ then* have I covenanted with their fathers that they shall be restored in the flesh, upon the earth, unto the lands of their inheritance." Verse three of this same chapter tells us this is speaking of the Jews. *This is a false prophecy!!* The Jews *are* back in their own land and they do *not* believe that Jesus is the Christ. Someday they will believe when they see Him, but that was not a condition for their restoration, which is clearly evident since they do occupy the land of their inheritance once again.

10. 2 Nephi 25:19 says, . . . "and according to the words of the prophets, and also the word of the angel of God, his name shall be Jesus Christ, the Son of God." "Christ" was not His last name. It means "The Annointed One" or "The Messiah." The name "Jesus" was not foretold in Old Testament times by an angel to anyone in reference to the "Son of God." (See Isaiah 9:6.) The first time an angel revealed what His name would be was when Gabriel appeared to the Virgin Mary as recorded in Luke 1:31, "and thou shalt call His name JESUS."

11. *The Book of Mormon* is purported to be "a second witness to the Bible"—a witness that condemns and claims the Bible is in error. 1 Nephi 13:24-40 informs us that many "plain and precious things" are taken from the Bible, (verse 28), and 2 Nephi chapter twenty-nine states that anyone who claims the Bible is sufficient and they need no other book is "a fool."

12. 2 Nephi 29:11-13 tells us that every nation would be commanded to write the Word of God and that we should be judged by all these writings. In Old Testament times God spoke to and through Hebrew prophets and dealt only with the nation Israel. In the New Testament, (John 12:47, 48) Jesus tells us we are to be judged in the last days by the things He *has* spoken.

13. The book of Omni, in *The Book of Mormon* speaks of the *gifts of the Holy Ghost* operative in 279 B.C. (See also

Ether 12:14; Helaman 5:45.) Compare this with what our Lord Jesus said in Luke 3:16 and in John 7:37-39. The gifts of the Holy Ghost could not have been given at the time indicated for Jesus was not yet glorified.

14. Mosiah 2:3 gives the instruction, ". . . offer sacrifice and burnt offerings *according to the law of Moses.*" In *The Book of Mormon* the "Nephites" and "Lamanites" were from the tribe of Manasseh (Alma 10:3). No descendent of Manasseh could give attendance at the altar *according to the law of Moses.* Exodus chapters twenty-eight to thirty-one, Numbers 3:7, Nehemiah 7:63, 65 and Hebrews 7:12-14 tell us only the tribe of Levi and particularly the sons of Aaron could give attendance at the altar.

15. Alma 7:10 tells us that Jesus was to be born at Jerusalem. The Bible tells us in Micah 5:2 and in Luke 2:4 that Jesus was born in Bethlehem. Jerusalem is a city. Bethlehem is also a city. The Mormon argument is that "Jerusalem" referred to the general vicinity, but in 1 Nephi 1:4 Jerusalem is called a city. If, as a Jew, you knew where Jerusalem was, you would also know where Bethlehem was for the two cities are not far apart. This is an error perhaps an ignorant farm boy would make, but not the Holy Spirit.

16. Alma is supposed to be a prophet of God and of Jewish ancestry in *The Book of Mormon.* In Hebrew Alma means a betrothed virgin maiden—hardly a fitting name for a man.

17. Alma 46:15 tells us there were people known as "Christians" in 73 B.C. The Bible contradicts that in Acts 11:26, they "were called Christians first in Antioch."

18. The story in Ether 1:34-37 tells us there was a group of people at the tower of Babel who did not want their language confounded and so, they said, God decided not to confound it. This contradicts Genesis 11:9 where it says the language of *all* the earth was confounded.

19. In Ether 1:43 the Jaredites are promised by the God of *The Book of Mormon* that they will be the greatest nation on earth and that there would be no greater nation. However, in the Abrahamic Covenant, (Genesis 15:1-5; 17:1-9;

19; 18:17, 18; Romans 2:2) this promise is made to Abraham and to his descendents. In Deuteronomy 7:6, 7 Moses says, "For thou art an holy people unto the LORD thy God: the LORD thy God hath chosen thee to be a special people unto himself, above *all* the people who are upon the face of the earth. The LORD did not set his love upon you, nor choose you, because ye were more in number than any people; for ye were the fewest of all people." The seed of Abraham is with us to this day and the Messiah came through that lineage. The Jaredites (so the story goes) destroyed each other to a man and within a few generations ceased to exist.

20. Throughout Ether chapter two, we find the God of *The Book of Mormon* needs to be given instructions and corrections and suggestions, for his instructions are foolish and the whole account of the "barges" is one of utter nonsense. However, it is a very amusing farce in an otherwise dull and humorless book. See Job chapters thirty-eight to forty for God's reaction to anyone who might try to instruct Him!!

21. In Ether 3:9-13, 19 the brother of Jared is told by the "Lord" of *The Book of Mormon* that he is "redeemed from the fall" because he saw the finger of the "Lord". Compare Hebrews 9:11-15, 22. Without the shedding of blood there is no remission of sin. See also Abel's offering. It was accepted and Cain's was rejected (Genesis 3-7).

We listed only a few of the contradictions between the Bible and *The Book of Mormon* to demonstrate the impossibility of the book being inspired by the God of the Bible. We did not go into the hundreds of areas where this book defies reason or common sense. Rather than belabor the point, one should ask the question: "How many lies do you have to find in a book before you know it is not from God?"

Plagiarisms From the King James Version

The following quotations from *The Book of Mormon* and the King James Version are presented for the reader's analysis and are particularly interesting because the King

James Version was translated in A.D. 1611, while *The Book of Mormon* purports to date the same material between 600 B.C. and A.D. 421 in perfect Elizabethan English!

King James Version	*Book of Mormon*
the Holy Ghost descended in a bodily shape like a dove upon him (Luke 3:22)	the Holy Ghost come down out of heaven and abide upon him in the form of a dove (1 Nephi 11:27)
bare record that this is the Son of God (John 1:34)	bear record that it is the Son of God (1 Nephi 11:7)
through the power of the Holy Ghost (Romans 15:13)	by the power of the Holy Ghost (1 Nephi 10:17)
the same yesterday, and today, and forever (Hebrews 13:8)	the same yesterday, today, and forever (1 Nephi 10:18)
the earth did quake, and the rocks rent (Matthew 27:51)	the earth and the rocks, that they rent (1 Nephi 12:4)
first shall be last; and the last shall be first (Matthew 19:30)	last shall be first, and the first shall be last (1 Nephi 13:42)
all sick people that were taken with divers diseases . . . and those which were possessed with devils (Matthew 4:24)	who were sick and who were afflicted with all manner of diseases, and with devils (1 Nephi 11:31)
pervert the right ways of the Lord (Acts 13:10)	pervert the right ways of the Lord (1 Nephi 13:27)
endureth to the end shall be saved (Matthew 10:22)	endure unto the end . . . shall be saved (1 Nephi 13:37)
made them white in the blood of the Lamb (Revelation 7:14)	made white in the blood of the Lamb (1 Nephi 12:11)
that old serpent, which is the Devil (Revelation 20:2)	that old serpent, who is the devil (2 Nephi 2:18)
blood, and fire, and vapour of smoke (Acts 2:19)	blood, and fire, and vapor of smoke (1 Nephi 22:18)

death and hell delivered up the dead (Revelation 20:13)

death and hell must deliver up their dead (2 Nephi 9:12)

he which is filthy, let him by filthy still: and he that is righteous, let him be righteous still (Revelation 22:11)

they who are righteous shall be righteous still, and they who are filthy shall be filthy still (2 Nephi 9:16)

shall be saved; yet so as by fire (1 Corinthians 3:15)

shall be saved, even if it so be as by fire (1 Nephi 22:17)

and there shall be one fold, and one shepherd (John 10:16)

and there shall be one fold and one shepherd (1 Nephi 22:25)

by the works of the law shall no flesh be justified (Galatians 2:16)

by the law no flesh is justified (2 Nephi 2:5)

I know whom I have believed (2 Timothy 1:12)

I know in whom I have trusted (2 Nephi 4:19)

endured the cross, despising the shame (Hebrews 12:2)

endured the crosses of the world, and despised the shame (2 Nephi 9:18)

shalt be thrust down to hell (Luke 10:15)

shall be thrust down to hell (2 Nephi 9:34)

He that is not with me is against me (Luke 11:23)

they who are not for me are against me, saith our God (2 Nephi 10:16)

by grace are ye saved (Ephesians 2:8)

through the grace of God that ye are saved (2 Nephi 10:24)

grind him to powder (Matthew 21:44)

grind them to powder (2 Nephi 26:5)

for there is nothing covered that shall not be revealed (Matthew 10:26)

There is nothing which is secret save it shall be revealed (2 Nephi 30:17)

the Lamb of God, which tak-

the Lamb of God, which

eth away the sin of the world (John 1:29)

should take away the sins of the world (2 Nephi 31:4)

darkness rather than light (John 3:19)

darkness rather than light (2 Nephi 26:10)

withered; and men gather them, and cast them into the fire, and they are burned (John 15:6)

wither away, and we will cast them into the fire that they may be burned (Jacob 5:7)

the lake of fire (Revelation 20:14)

a lake of fire (2 Nephi 28:23)

one faith, one baptism (Ephesians 4:5)

one faith and one baptism (Mosiah 18:21)

he which is filthy, let him be filthy still (Revelation 22:11)

he who is filthy shall remain in his filthiness (Alma 7:21)

this Melchisedec . . . to whom also Abraham gave a tenth part of all (Hebrews 7:1, 2)

this same Melchizedek to whom Abraham paid . . . of one-tenth part of all (Alma 13:15)

the elements shall melt with fervent heat, the earth (2 Peter 3:10)

the elements should melt with fervent heat, and the earth (3 Nephi 26:3)

an anchor of the soul, both sure and steadfast (Hebrews 6:19)

an anchor to the souls of men, which would make them sure and steadfast (Ether 12:4)

old things are passed away; behold, all things are become new (2 Corinthians 5:17)

Old things are done away, and all things have become new (3 Nephi 12:47)

partakers of the heavenly calling (Hebrews 3:1)

partakers of the heavenly gift (Ether 12:8)

and heard unspeakable words, which it is not lawful for a man to utter (2 Corinthians 12:4)

and heard unspeakable things, which are not lawful to be written (3 Nephi 26:18)

the name of thy holy child Jesus (Acts 4:30)	the name of his Holy Child, Jesus (Moroni 8:3)
all these worketh that one and the selfsame Spirit, dividing to every man severally as he will (1 Corinthians 12:11)	all these gifts come by the Spirit of Christ; and they come unto every man severally, according as he will (Moroni 10:17)
Charity suffereth long, and is kind; charity envieth not . . . is not puffed up . . . seeketh not her own, is not easily provoked, thinketh no evil; rejoiceth not in iniquity, but rejoiceth in the truth; beareth all things . . . hopeth all things, endureth all things (1 Corinthians 13:4-7)	charity suffereth long, and is kind, and envieth not . . . is not puffed up, seeketh not her own, is not easily provoked, thinketh no evil, and rejoiceth not in iniquity but rejoiceth in the truth, beareth all things, . . . hopeth all things, endureth all things (Moroni 7:45)
the Judge of quick and dead (Acts 10:42)	the Eternal Judge of both quick and dead (Moroni 10:34)

There are many more such blatant plagiarisms from the King James Version, but the reader can see for himself the obvious point and draw his own conclusions about the trustworthiness of Joseph Smith, Jr., the "translator."

APPENDIX D

CHARACTER REFERENCES ON JOSEPH SMITH, JR.*

I am now going to introduce a document of the very greatest importance, which will enable the reader to see Joseph, Emma and the Gold Bible humbug in a kind of family picture, not brilliantly drawn, but full of the color of life. It is a letter from the brothers Hiel and Joseph Lewis, sons of the Rev. Nathaniel Lewis, of old Harmony, Pennsylvania, and all of them near relations of Emma Hale. It is dated Amboy, Lee County, Ill., April 23, 1879. The original belongs to Mr. James T. Cobb, the above-named pathfinder in early Mormon history. The document concerns what the two gentlemen "saw and heard of the sayings and doings of the Prophet Joseph Smith while he was engaged in peeping for money and hidden treasures and translating his Gold Bible in our neighborhood, township of Harmony, Susquehannah County, Pa., our home and residence being within one mile of where he lived and transacted his business." The

---

*From Dr. W. Wyl, *Mormon Portraits* (Salt Lake City: Tribune Printing & Publishing Co., 1886), pages 77-82 and pages 20-21.

most prominent citizens of the little town of Amboy, the mayor, aldermen, attorneys, editors, merchants, bankers, justices of the peace, etc., testify that the witnesses are "truthful, honorable, Christian gentlemen," and that "their statements are entitled to the fullest credence." Here is the document:

> "Some time previous to 1825,* a man by the name of Wm. Hale, distant relative of uncle Isaac Hale, came to Isaac Hale and said that he had been informed by a woman by the name of Odle, who claimed to possess the power of seeing under ground (such persons were then commonly called *peepers*), that there were great treasures concealed in the hill northeast from Isaac Hale's house, and by her directions Wm. Hale commenced digging. But, being too lazy to work and too poor to hire, he obtained a partner by the name of Oliver Harper, of York State, who had the means to hire help. But after a short time operations were suspended, for a time, during which Wm. Hale heard of PEEPER Joseph Smith, jr., and wrote to him and soon visited him, and found Smith's representations were so flattering that Smith was either hired or became a partner with Wm. Hale, Oliver Harper and a man by the name of Stowell,† *who had some property.* They hired men and dug in several places. The account given in the history of Susquehanna County,

---

*This would be, according to Mormon annals, after the time when "the Father and the Son" appeared to the prophet Joseph and held a conference with him.

†Lucy Smith, the mother of the prophet . . . lets a good-sized cat out of her big bag in her biography of Joe. She confesses in it, unwittingly, to all the money-digging part of the prophet, and this was one of the reasons that made Brigham put her gossipy little book on the Mormon Index librorum pro-hibitorum [of prohibited books] . . . . Lucy says (pp. 91-92): "A man by the name of Josiah Stoal came from Chenango County, N. Y., with the view of getting Joseph to assist in digging for a silver mine. He came for Joseph on account of having heard that he possessed *certain keys* by which he could discern things invisible to the natural eye. Joseph endeavored to divert him from his vain pursuit, but he was inflexible in his purpose, and offered high wages to those who would dig for him in search of said mine, and still insisted upon having Joseph to work for

p. 580, of a *pure white dog* to be used as a *sacrifice to restrain the enchantment,* and of *the anger of the Almighty* at the attempt to *palm off on Him a white sheep for a white dog,* is a fair sample of Smith's revelations, and of the God that inspired him. Their digging in several places was in compliance with 'Peeper' Smith's revelations, who would attend *with his peepstone in his hat, and his hat drawn over his face,* and tell them how deep they would have to go; and when they found no trace of the chest of money, he would *peep* again and *weep like a child,* and tell them that the enchantment had removed it on account of some sin, or thoughtless word, and finally the enchantment became so strong that he could not see, and the business was finally abondoned. *Smith could weep and shed tears at any time if he chose to.*°

"But while he was engaged in looking through his peepstone and *old white hat,* directing the digging for money, and boarding at uncle Isaac Hale's, he formed an intimacy with Mr. Hale's daughter, and after the abandonment of the money-digging speculation, he consummated the elopement and marriage to the said Emma Hale, and she became his accomplice in his humbug *Golden Bible* and Mormon religion.

"The statement that the prophet Joseph Smith made in our hearing at the commencement of his translating his book in Harmony, as to the *manner of his finding the plates,* was as follows: He said that by a DREAM he was informed that at such a place in a certain hill, in an *iron* box, were some gold plates with curious engravings, which he must get and translate, and *write a book*; that the plates were to be kept concealed from every human being for a certain time, some two or three years; that he

---

him. Accordingly, Joseph and several others returned with him and commenced digging. After laboring for the old gentleman about a month, without success, Joseph prevailed upon him to cease his operations, and it was from this circumstance of having worked by the month at digging for a silver mine, that the *very prevalent* story arose of Joseph having been a moneydigger." [The italics are mine:]

° Let any half-witted person compare this testimony with those of Ingersoll, Chase and others, . . . and deny that Joseph was the champion humbug of our time!

went to the place and dug till he came to the stone that covered the box, when he was knocked down; that he again attempted to remove the stone, and was again knocked down. This attempt was made the third time, and the third time he was knocked down. Then he exclaimed: 'Why can't I *git* it?' or words to that effect, and then he saw a man standing over the spot, who, to him, appeared *like a Spaniard* [Oh, you great son of Lucy!], having a long beard down over his breast to about here *(Smith putting his hand to the pit of his stomach)*, WITH HIS (the ghost's) THROAT CUT FROM EAR TO EAR, AND THE BLOOD STREAMING DOWN, who told him that he could not get it alone; that another person whom he (Smith) would know at first sight must come with him, and then he would get it; and when he saw Miss Emma Hale he knew that she was the person, and that after they were married she went with him to near the place and stood with her back towards him while he dug after the box, which he rolled up in his frock, and she helped carry it home; that in the same box with the plates were spectacles;° the bows were of gold and the eyes were stone, and by looking through these spectacles all the characters on the plates were translated into English.

"In all this narrative there was not one word about visions of God or of angels or heavenly revelations; all his information was by that DREAM *and that* BLEEDING GHOST. The heavenly visions and messages of angels, etc., contained in Mormon books, were *afterthoughts, revised to order.* While Smith was in Harmony he made the above statements, in our presence, to Rev. N. Lewis. It was here, also, that he *joined the Methodist Episcopal Church.* He presented himself in a very serious and humble manner, and the minister, not suspecting evil, put his name on the class-book in the absence of some of the official members, among whom was the undersigned, Joseph Lewis, who, when he learned what was done, took with him Joshua McKune and had a talk with Smith. We told him plainly that such a character as he was *a dis-*

°The celebrated "Urim and Thummim" of Mormon history. One can "catch on" nicely here: Spaniards having buried treasures, whether of *gold* or *golden* plates, the *ghost* of a Spaniard would naturally have to stand guard over them, whatever the state of his windpipe.

grace to the church; that he could not be a member of it unless he broke off his sins by repentance, made public confession, renounced his fraudulent and hypocritical practices, and gave some evidence that he intended to reform and conduct himself somewhat nearer like a Christian than he had done. We gave him his choice, to go before the class and publicly ask to have his name stricken from the class-book, or stand a disciplinary investigation; he chose the former, and immediately withdrew his name. So his name as a member of the class was on the book *only three days.* It was the *general* opinion that his only object in joining the church was to bolster up his reputation and gain the sympathy and help of Christians; that is, putting on the cloak of religion to serve the Devil in."

When interrogated as to the time of Joe's joining the Methodist Church, Mr. Hiel Lewis wrote back that it was in June, 1828.

This disclosure will prove vastly edifying to the world in general, and to Mormons in particular. Joseph, with the sacred plates in his possession and while he is "translating" them, BECOMES A METHODIST!! And this, too, after the Lord's (both the Father and the Son) telling him that all existing religions are false and corrupt and on no account to join any of them, he being the favored instrument elected by Them in *founding the true one!!* I think the great jury, called public opinion, Mormons included, might give their verdict in the imposter's case without leaving their seats.

Our letter goes on:

"We will add one more sample of his prophetic power and practice. One of the neighbors, whom Smith was owing, had a piece of corn on a rather wet and backward piece of ground, and as Smith was owing him, he wanted Smith to help hoe corn. Smith came on, but to get clear of the work and debt, said: 'If I kneel down and *pray in your corn,* it will grow just as well as if hoed.' So he prayed in the corn and insured its maturity without cultivation, and that the frost would not hurt it. But the corn was a failure in growth and killed by the frost. This sample of prophetic power was related to us by those present, and no one questioned its truth."°

The "revelation on celestial marriage" is a much more candid document than could be supposed. It permits us to "peep" into the peeper's household. We see how he tries to overcome the desperate resistance of the strong wife against—let me use the exactly significant term—religious whoredom. What scenes must there have been enacted in that prophetic household! He begs and flatters, thunders and threatens—all in vain. Finally, he changes tactics. He tells Emma, it is "all spiritual, my dear." "Let us show the people"—he may have said—"that you *do* look at celestial marriage in the right light, by being present at such a cere-mony. It means marriage for the other world, and it is ne-cessary that you should dispel, through a fearless act of yours, the ugly rumors spread everywhere. I may have sinned now and then, dearest, but from now on—you will see—everything will be strictly spiritual."

Emma, perplexed and exhausted, consents. The Par-tridge girls are to be sealed to her husband in her presence. "It is only a formality, deary, and will strengthen my po-sition very much," says the prophet. It was in May or June, 1843, before the revelation was dictated to the "pard." An elder was selected, whose talents and profession promised something extraordinary in the way of impressive solem-

---

°This startling document, which I have copied from the original most carefully, is attested in the following manner:

STATE OF ILLINOIS,)
Lee County.　　)ss.

I, Everett E. Chase, a Justice of the Peace in and for the County of Lee, State aforesaid, do hereby certify that the above named Joseph Lewis and Hiel Lewis, personally known to me to be re-spectable, truthful and honorable men, came before me and in my presence signed the above statement, and each of them before me made affidavit to each and all of the allegations therein set forth according to their best memory.

EVERETT E. CHASE,
J.P.

nity. His name was George J. Adams, and he was a strolling player and great libertine besides. He performed the sealing ceremony and all went well for—two or three hours. Emma found out what the word "spiritual" really meant with that chaste husband of hers. She demanded imperiously the immediate annulment of the ceremony. Joseph hesitated, but the blood of old Isaac Hale was up in the veins of the prophet's wife. She threatened to arouse the city with a terrible display of matrimonial fireworks. The Prophet had to give in. Emma went on suffering what she could not prevent, but her official honor as a wife was safe. She remained the queen of her household instead of stooping to the role of concubine. She did not go to Washington to use her shame as an argument in debate. She did not write pamphlets about it, either.

JOSEPH SMITH AND HIS PLATES

The Prophet's Curious Proposition to His Bosom Friend, Bennett—The Same Fully Confirmed by Mrs. Pratt

The truth about the golden plates, from which Joseph pretended to "translate" the Book of Mormon, has been established since 1834, by E. D. Howe. I give the substance of the very curious affidavits, obtained by him from Smith's neighbors, in the Appendix to Part I. of this book. There were never any plates of any kind. The book, a stupid historical novel, was written by Solomon Spaulding, stolen and "religiously" remodeled by Sidney Rigdon and published through Joseph Smith, whose wide-spread fame as "Peeper" and "Treasure-finder" enabled him admirably to assume the role of discoverer of golden plates. Sidney Rigdon was a man of taste in the matter of choosing the right kind of a rascal to do his dirty jobs. But he failed in one respect; he thought he found a tool and he really found a master in Peeping Joe.

Now it will surely be interesting to the reader, that I can not only convict Joseph Smith out of his own mouth, giving his full confession of the original fraud, but I am also able to show that he contemplated an additional fraud with the "plates," and that, as usual, he thought to make a pile of money out of the second fraud, too. The witness in the case is Joseph's Nauvoo accomplice, Dr. John C. Bennett. Those who would refuse his testimony, will not be able to contradict that of Mrs. Sarah Pratt.

Bennett says: "Shortly after I located in Nauvoo, Joe proposed to me to go to New York and get some plates engraved and bring them to him, so that he could exhibit them as the genuine plates of the Book of Mormon, which he pretended had been taken from him, and 'hid up' by an angel, and which he would profess to have recovered. He calculated to make considerable money by this trick, as there would of course be a great anxiety to see the plates, which he intended to exhibit at twenty-five cents a sight. I mentioned this proposition to Mrs. Sarah M. Pratt, on the day the Prophet made it, and requested her to keep it in memory, as it might be of much importance." When asked by me in the spring of 1885 about this statement of John C. Bennett, *Mrs. Pratt confirmed it fully* and stated also that Bennett had reported to her this conversation with Joseph on *the very day* when it happened.

APPENDIX E

TERMINOLOGY DIFFERENCES*

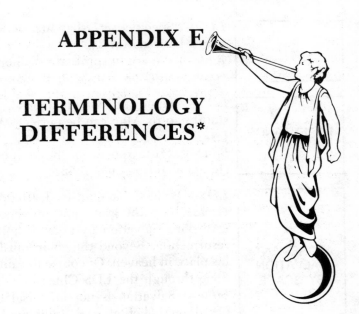

PRE-EXISTENCE	*LDS*— Teach that everyone pre-existed, that we all exist eternally. *Bible*— Only Christ pre-existed—not mankind (John 8:58; Exodus 3:14; Colossians 1:16, 17).
FALL	*LDS*— Teach that the fall brought mortality and physical death, not a sinful nature. Believe Adam was given two conflicting commands and was supposed to fall. *Bible*— God tempts no one (James 1:13, 14). Man is basically a sinner (Romans 8:5-8; 1 Corinthians 2:14).

---

*Reprinted by permission from Jerry and Marian Bodine, *Witnessing to the Mormons* (Anaheim, CA: Christian Research Institute, 1978), pages 28-29.

SIN	*LDS*— Specific acts that are done, not man's basic nature. *Bible*— We are in spiritual rebellion until conversion (Ephesians 2:3; Romans 5:6).
REPENTANCE	*LDS*— Repent of individual acts and not sinful nature. Man can be perfect. Wasn't Jesus? *Bible*— Must repent of basic rebellion (Jeremiah 17:9; Luke 5:32).
ATONEMENT-SALVATION BY GRACE	*LDS*— Believe that Christ's death brought release from the grave and universal resurrection. Salvation by grace is universal resurrection. Beyond this, man must earn his place in heaven. Of course this must be done through the LDS Church. *Bible*— Salvation is not universal but is based on belief of each individual (Romans 1:16; Hebrews 9:28; Ephesians 2:8, 9).
REDEEMED	*LDS*— From mortal death only and not sinful rebellion or spiritual death. *Bible*— Christ redeems from more than mortal death—From *spiritual* death also (Romans 6:23; Ephesians 2:1).
GOSPEL	*LDS*— The Mormon Church system and doctrines. *Bible*— The message of Christ's death, burial, and resurrection as the atonement for our sins (1 Corinthians 15:1-4; Galatians 1:8).
BORN AGAIN	*LDS*— Baptism into the "true Church" (LDS). *Bible*— We are spiritually dead until our spiritual rebirth (1 Peter 1:23; 2 Corinthians 5:17).

TRUE CHURCH	*LDS*— Only the Mormon Church. The church Christ "set up" was lost until Joseph Smith restored it. *Bible*— As born-again individuals we are part of God's church (1 Corinthians 12:12-14; Matthew 18:19, 20; 16:18).
AUTHORITY OR PRIESTHOOD	*LDS*— Teach that only LDS have authority to baptize, ordain, etc. Have two-part system of priesthood—Aaronic and Melchizedek. *Bible*— Christ brought an end to the Aaronic priesthood and is the *only* High Priest after the manner of Melchizedek (Hebrews chapters 5-9; 2 Timothy 2:2).
BAPTISM	*LDS*— Must be performed by LDS priesthood. *Bible*— Emphasis is on the *believer* —*not* on priesthood authority (Mark 16:15, 16).
SONS OF GOD	*LDS*— We are all literal spirit-children of God. *Bible*— We become a child of God at conversion (John 1:12).
ETERNAL LIFE	*LDS*— Exaltation into Celestial Kingdom with ability to bear children in heaven. *Must* have a Temple marriage. *Bible*— Not limited to certain ones in heaven. There is no mention of parenthood or temple marriage, but eternal life is given to *all* Christians (1 John 5:12, 13).
IMMORTALITY	*LDS*— Universal gift and ability to live forever, but not eternal life. *Bible*— Refers to the nature of God and the resurrected body of the redeemed (1 Corinthians 15; 2 Timothy 1:10).

HEAVEN	*LDS*— This is divided into three king-doms: Celestial, Terrestrial, and Telestial. A place for almost everyone. *Bible*— Only mentions two con-ditions—everlasting *punishment* or eternal life (Matthew 25:31-46).

KINGDOM OF GOD	*LDS*— Means Celestial Kingdom only. And those in Celestial Kingdom are in God's presence. Those in other kingdoms are not in the presence of the Father. *Bible*— *All* redeemed will be in God's presence (Revelation 21:1-3). *All* be-lievers are part of God's Kingdom (Mat-thew 13:41-43).

HELL	*LDS*— Hell as an institution is eternal. In-mates come and go as in jail. Do not spend eternity there. A person stays until his debt has been paid to God. *Bible*— No mention of people getting out of hell (Revelation 21:8; Matthew 13:24-43, 47-50; Luke 16:26).

GODHEAD	*LDS*— Father God is a resurrected man with a physical body. Christ is a separate resurrected man with physical body. The Holy Ghost is a separate man with a spir-itual body. There are three totally separ-ate gods. *Bible*— God is not a man (Numbers 23:19; Hosea 11:9; Isaiah 46:5). There is only one God (Isaiah 43:10, 11; 44:6; 45:21, 22). The Father is spirit and is invisible (John 4:24; 1 Timothy 1:17).

HOLY GHOST	*LDS*— Is a separate God from Father and Son. Is different from Holy Spirit. The Holy Ghost is a person. The Holy Spirit is an influence from the Father and is not personal. *Bible*— Same Greek word is used for Holy Ghost and Holy Spirit (1 Corinthians 3:16; 6:19).
VIRGIN BIRTH	*LDS*— Believe God, as a resurrected physical man, is literal father of Jesus. The Father came and had sexual relations with Mary for Jesus to be conceived on earth. They believe Matthew 1:18 is in error. *Bible*— Says Mary was "with child of the Holy Ghost" (Matthew 1:18, 20; Luke 1:35).

The original "Terminology Differences" list was prepared by Sandra Tanner, of Salt Lake City, who, along with her husband, Jerald, have long been in the ministry of disseminating the truth by their publication of many original and long-forgotten documents, diaries, manuscripts, etc.

Remember that it is extremely important when witnessing to make sure that both parties understand what is being said. We must be sure to understand, for example, what a person means when he says "salvation." Remember, in Mormonism, *everyone, except the sons of perdition,* is going to have "salvation" (resurrection). All will be resurrected because Christ died.

APPENDIX F

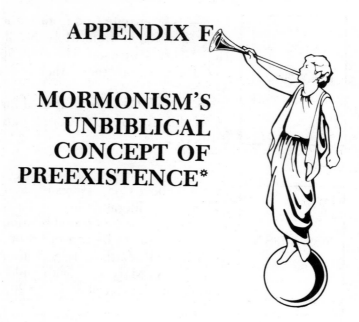

MORMONISM'S UNBIBLICAL CONCEPT OF PREEXISTENCE*

Important in Mormon theology is the doctrine of preexistence. By this concept, the heretical teaching concerning the person of Christ is formed. Mormonism is *man*-centered and NOT *God*-centered, as it elevates man to being a god and demotes God to a mere, exalted man.

The Jesus of Mormonism is "another Jesus," as is shown us in 2 Corinthians 11:3, 4. The Jesus of Mormonism is the literal firstborn (in heaven) spirit child of Father and Mother God, both of whom possess bodies of flesh and bones!

At one time the Father God of Mormonism lived on an earth such as this and had many wives. He proved himself worthy to his Father God by living an obedient and chaste life. Eventually he, his wives, and his children died and

---

*Reprinted by permission from Jerry and Marian Bodine, *Witnessing to the Mormons* (Anaheim, CA: Christian Research Institute, 1978).

were subsequently resurrected. He continued to be exalted to a higher position until he arrived at the station of a god; then, along with his wives, they were given a planet of their own. There, throughout all eternity, they would people it by sexually procreating children in spirit form. Of course their firstborn was Jesus, then Lucifer and possibly Adam and Eve were next. According to Mormonism, all the people who have inhabited earth were born first in spirit form in heaven.

When the Mormon tells you that all of us are, after all, children of our heavenly Father, they mean that literally. When they say Jesus is our "elder brother," they mean it in a very literal sense.

According to Mormonism, Jesus was chosen over Lucifer to be the Savior of the world, thereby assuring the resurrection of all mankind, for the Mormon is taught that salvation means resurrection. As the story goes, Lucifer offered to go to earth and be the Savior! He wanted to force everyone to be saved! But as Jesus desired to give man "free agency," the Father chose Jesus' plan over that of Lucifer's. This of course made Lucifer very angry. He rebelled against the Father's preferential treatment and caused one-third of the existing spirits to take sides and in turn rebel also. This is known in Mormonism as "the war in heaven" and the reason why this group was cast out of heaven to become the Devil and his demons.

Concerning pre-existence, the Mormon Apostle *Bruce R. McConkie* makes this statement in his book *MORMON DOCTRINE,* page 589:

> *Pre-existence* is the term commonly used to describe the *pre-mortal existence* of the spirit children of God the Father. Speaking of this prior existence in a spirit sphere, the First Presidency of the Church (Joseph F. Smith, John R. Winder, and Anthon H. Lund) said: "All men and women are in the similitude of *the universal Father and Mother,* and are literally the sons and daughters of Deity"; as spirits they were the "offspring of *celestial parentage.*"

Continuing on, the Apostle says:

> To understand the doctrine of pre-existence two great
> truths must be accepted: 1. That God is a personal Being
> in whose image man is created, an exalted, perfected,
> and glorified Man of Holiness (Moses 6:57), and not a
> spirit essence that fills the immensity of space; and 2.
> That matter or element is self-existent and eternal in
> nature, creation being merely the organization and re-
> organization of that substance which "was not created or
> made, neither indeed can be." (D. & C. 93:29.)

McConkie further states:

> Unless God the Father was a personal Being, he could
> not have begotten spirits in his image, and if there had
> been no self-existent spirit element, there would have
> been no substance from which those spirit bodies could
> have been organized.

Joseph Smith, the founder of Mormonism, just prior to his
death in June, 1844, said:

> The first principles of man are self-existent with God.
> God himself, finding he was in the midst of spirits and
> glory, because he was more intelligent, saw proper to in-
> stitue laws whereby the rest could have a privilege to ad-
> vance like himself. The relationship we have with God
> places us in a situation to advance in knowledge.
> *Teachings of the Prophet Joseph Smith,* page 354.

In *Mormon Doctrine,* by Apostle McConkie, he has this to
say about the Negro in relation to his pre-existence with
God:

> In the pre-existent eternity various degrees of valiance
> and devotion to the truth were exhibited by different
> groups of our Father's spirit offspring. One-third of the
> spirit hosts of heaven came out in open rebellion and
> were cast out without bodies, becoming the devil and his
> angels (D&C 29:36-41; Rev. 12:3-9). The other two-
> thirds stood affirmatively for Christ; there were no
> neutrals. To stand neutral in the midst of war is a philo-
> sophical impossibility. The Lord said: "He that is not

with me is against me; and he that gathereth not with me scattereth abroad" (Mt. 12:30). Of the two-thirds that followed Christ, however, some were more valiant than others . . . The whole house of Israel was chosen in pre-existence to come to mortality as children of Jacob (Deut. 32:7-8). Those who were less valiant in pre-existence and who thereby had certain spiritual restrictions imposed upon them during mortality are known to us as *negroes*. Such spirits are sent to earth through the lineage of Cain, the mark put upon him for his rebellion against God and his murder of Abel being a black skin (Moses 5:16-41; 7:8, 12, 22). Noah's son Ham married Egyptus, a descendant of Cain, thus preserving the negro lineage through the flood (Abra. 1:20-27).

Negroes in this life are denied the priesthood; under no circumstances can they hold this delegation of authority from the Almighty. . . . The gospel message of salvation is not carried affirmatively to them. . . . Although sometimes negroes search out the truth, join the Church, and become by righteous living heirs of the celestial kingdom of heaven. . . . The present status of the negro purely and simply rests on the foundation of pre-existence. Along with all races and peoples he is receiving here what he merits as a result of the long pre-mortal probation in the presence of the Lord. . . . The negroes are not equal with other races where the receipt of certain spiritual blessings are concerned, particularly the priesthood and the temple blessings that flow therefrom, but this inequality is not of man's origin. It is the Lord's doing, is based on his eternal laws of justice, and grows out of the lack of spiritual valiance of those concerned in their first estate.

Mormon Doctrine, pages 526-28.

Joseph Smith said that God revealed the following through him:

And every plant of the field before it was in the earth, and every herb of the field before it grew. For I, the Lord God, created all things, of which I have spoken, spiritually, before they were naturally upon the face of the earth. For I, the Lord God, had not caused it to rain upon the face of the earth. And I, the Lord God, had created all the children of men; and not yet a man to till the ground; for in heaven created I them; and there was not yet flesh upon the earth, neither in the water, neither in the air; Moses 3:5 (Compare 1 Corinthians 15:46).

1. We now understand what the Mormon means when he says "God." To him, God is a finite creature, as we all are, having a beginning. He was a sinner who was smarter (more intelligent) than those around him, and through his own effort he made it to Godhood, as all Mormons hope for.

2. Man is eternal in the same sense that the spirit matter he was organized from is eternal. Man is self-existent and eternal, as God is.

3. Man is co-equal to Jesus. The *only* difference is that their god, with a resurrected body, had sexual relations with Mary—"Instead of letting any other man do it" (*Journal of Discourses* 4:218). Thus he is called the son of God, not the Son of the Holy Ghost, for he was not begotten by the Holy Ghost.

4. We see a doctrine (man becoming a God) whose author is "*a liar, and the father of it. . . . He was a murderer from the beginning*" (John 8:44), and the one who said, "*I will ascend above the heights of the clouds, I will be like the Most High*" (Isaiah 14:13). He is also the one who originally cast doubt on God's Word (Genesis 3:1-4) and continues to do so in the cults today, that being a COMMON mark.

5. Next we see man's unvarnished bigotry and racial hatred, and saying that God is the author of this. Webster's Dictionary says "valiant" means "brave; heroic; courageous." According to Mormon mythology, the Negro has a black skin because he was less valiant. This apparently happened even after the Negro had sided with Jesus against Lucifer. Wouldn't that have qualified him as being "brave, heroic, and courageous" in that he resisted Lucifer? Mormonism teaches that the spirits were angels, became human, and in some cases return again as angels—a very occultic doctrine, to say the least. If the Mormons want a god who contradicts God's Word, who

changes and progresses, they are welcome to him. But that is not the God of the Bible!

DOES THE BIBLE TEACH PRE-EXISTENCE FOR MANKIND?

John 1:1—The *Logos* was in the beginning with God and *was Himself* God (Micah 5:2; John 8:23, 24; 44-59).

1 Corinthians 15:46—The body is first natural, then will be spiritual—not the opposite.

Hebrews 11:3—The world was created by the spoken word of God.

Romans 4:17—God calls the things that are not (in existence) as though they were.

The following are some proof-texts the Mormon will use. Study them entirely and in context to have an answer—the God-given answer. Genesis 2:4; Jeremiah 1:5; Job 38:1-7; Isaiah 49:1-5; 14:12-20; Proverbs 8:22-31; Deuteronomy 32:7, 8; Luke 10:18; Jude 6; 2 Peter 2:4.

APPENDIX G

UNFULFILLED PROPHECIES*

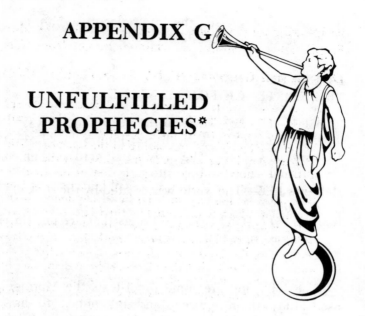

The Biblical test of a true prophet of God is found in Deuteronomy 18:20-22: "The prophet which shall presume to speak a word in my name, which I have not commanded him to speak, or that shall speak in the name of other gods, even that prophet shall die. And if thou say in thine heart, How shall we know the word which the Lord hath not spoken? When a prophet speaketh in the name of the Lord, if the thing follow not, nor come to pass, that is the thing which the Lord hath not spoken, but the prophet hath spoken it presumptuously; thou shalt not be afraid of him." See also Deuteronomy 13:1-5; Jeremiah 14:13-15; 28:9; 23:15-40, especially verses 16, 24, 31, 32.

Because God's Word is unchanging and will endure forever, we should test by God's Word all people who claim to

---

*Jerry and Marian Bodine, *Witnessing to the Mormons* (Anaheim, CA: Christian Research Institute, 1978).

be speaking for God. Now let us examine what the Mormon Prophet, Joseph Smith, Jr., claimed he got from God.

Doctrine and Covenants 84:1-5, 31 (September 1832):

A revelation of Jesus Christ unto his servant Joseph Smith, Jun., and six elders, as they united their hearts and lifted their voices on high. Yea, the word of the Lord concerning his church, established in the last days for the restoration of his people, as he has spoken by the mouth of his prophets, and for the gathering of his saints to stand upon Mount Zion, which shall be the city of New Jerusalem. Which city shall be built, beginning at the temple lot, which is appointed by the finger of the Lord, in the western bounderies of the State of Missouri, and dedicated by the hand of Joseph Smith, Jun., and others with whom the Lord was well pleased. Verily this is the word of the Lord, that the city New Jerusalem shall be built by the gathering of the saints, beginning at this place, even the place of the temple, which temple shall be reared in this generation. For verily this generation shall not all pass away until an house shall be built unto the Lord, and a cloud shall rest upon it, which cloud shall be even the glory of the Lord, which shall fill the house . . . which house shall be built unto the Lord in this generation, upon the consecrated spot as I have appointed. . . .

Doctrine and Covenants 97:19 (August 1833):

And the nations of the earth shall honor her, and shall say: Surely Zion is the city of our God, and surely Zion cannot fall, neither be moved out of her place, for God is there, and the hand of the Lord is there. . . .

Doctrine and Covenants 101:17-21 (December 1833):

Zion shall not be moved out of her place, notwithstanding her children are scattered. They that remain, and are pure in heart, shall return, and come to their inheritances, they and their children, with songs of everlasting joy, to build up the waste places of Zion—And all these things that the prophets might be fulfilled. And, behold, there is none other place appointed than that which I have appointed; neither shall there be any other place appointed than that which I have appointed, for the work of the gathering of my saints—Until the day cometh when there is found no more room for them; and then I have other places which I will appoint unto them, and they shall be called stakes, for the curtains or the strength of Zion.

All of the above prophecies failed! The Latter-day Saints *never* built a temple in Missouri at "the place appointed." Zion *was* "moved out of her place" *two weeks prior* to Smith receiving this "prophecy." On July 20, 1833, the LDS newspaper presses were destroyed and leading LDS officials tarred and feathered, then run out of town. *But Smith was in Kirtland, Ohio, and was unaware of the Missouri problem when he gave the "revelation."*

Today, LDS leaders tell us that Zion was "re-established" in Salt Lake City. Notice in the above-quoted "revelation" (Doctrine and Covenants 101:17-21) that there was to be *"none other place appointed."* So much for Salt Lake City being "the place appointed"!

Let us listen to former LDS leaders and what they understood the prophecy to mean.

Elder George A. Smith, speaking in the Tabernacle in Salt Lake City, March 10, 1861:

Who is there that is prepared for this movement back to the centre stake of Zion, and where the architects amongst us that are qualified to erect this temple and the city that will surround it? . . . And let me remind you that it is predicted that this generation shall not pass away till a temple shall be built, and the glory of the Lord rest upon it, according to the promises (*Journal of Discourses* 9:71).

Elder George Q. Cannon, October 23, 1864, Salt Lake City, in the Tabernacle:

The day is near when a Temple shall be reared in the Center Stake of Zion, and the Lord has said his glory shall rest on that House in this generation, that is in the generation in which the revelation was given, which is upwards of thirty years ago (*Journal of Discourses* 10:344).

Elder Orson Pratt, April 10, 1870, Salt Lake City:

> We have just as much confidence in returning to Jackson county and the building of a great central city that will remain there a thousand years before the earth passes away, as the Jews have in returning to Jerusalem and re-building the waste places of Palestine. In fact we have more faith than they have; for they have been so many generations cast out of their land that their descendants have almost lost their faith in returning. But the Latter-day Saints are fresh, as it were. There are many of the old stock, who passed through all those tribulations I have named, still living, whose faith in returning to Jackson county, and the things that are coming, is as firm and fixed as the throne of the Almighty (*Journal of Discourses* 13:138).

Apostle Pratt, again in Salt Lake City, May 5, 1870:

> . . . God promised in the year 1832 that we should, before the generation then living had passed away, return and build up the City of Zion in Jackson County; that we should return and build up the temple of the Most High where we formerly laid the corner stone. He promised us that He would manifest Himself on that temple, that the glory of God should be upon it; and not only upon the temple, but within it, even a cloud by day and a flaming fire by night.
>
> We believe in these promises as much as we believe in any promise ever uttered by the mouth of Jehovah. The Latter-day Saints just as much expect to receive a fulfilment of that promise during the generation that was in existence in 1832 as they expect that the sun will rise and set tomorrow. Why? Because God cannot lie. He will fulfill—all His promises. He has spoken, it must come to pass. This is our faith (*Journal of Discourses* 13:362).

A generation, according to Webster's Dictionary, is ". . . a step in a pedigree; all persons born about the same time; the average in which children are ready to replace their parents . . . about 30 years."

A generation, according to the Bible, is 35 to 40 years: "After this lived Job an hundred and forty years, and saw his sons, and his sons' sons, even four generations" (Job 42:16).

And we are even told in *The Book of Mormon* that a generation is 110 years. ". . . they were blessed and prospered until an hundred and ten years had passed away; and the first generation from Christ had passed away, and there was no contention in all the land" (4 Nephi 18).

Listen again to Joseph Smith Jr., in February 1835:

> . . . and it was the will of God that those who went to Zion, with a determination to lay down their lives, if necessary, should be ordained to the ministry, and go forth to prune the vineyard for the last time, or the coming of the Lord, which was nigh—even fifty-six years should wind up the scene (*History of the Church* 2:182).

Joseph Smith, Jr., on January 4, 1833, had this to say:

> And now I am prepared to say by the authority of Jesus Christ, that not many years shall pass away before the United States shall present such a scene of *bloodshed* as has not a parallel in the history of our nation; pestilence, hail, famine and earthquake will sweep the wicked of this generation from off the face of the land, to open and prepare the way for the return of the lost tribes of Israel from the north country. . . . therefore, "Fear God, and give glory to Him, for the hour of His judgment is come." . . . there are those now living upon the earth whose eyes shall not be closed in death until they see all these things, which I have spoken, fulfilled (*History of the Church* 1:315-16; *Teachings*, pages 17-18).

Joseph Smith, Jr., again said:

> . . . I prophesy in the name of the Lord God of Israel, unless the United States redress the wrongs committed upon the Saints in the state of Missouri and punish the crimes committed by her officers that in a few years the government will be utterly overthrown and wasted, and there will not be so much as a potshered left . . . (*Teachings*, page 302).

Doctrine and Covenants 124:56-61 (January 19, 1841): Here we have Joseph's "Lord" telling him He wanted a boarding house to be built for Him and ". . . for the boarding of strangers" and that "my [the Lord's] name be named upon it. . . ." But Joseph named the building "Nauvoo House." The financing of this undertaking, according to the Lord, was to be by certain men who were to purchase stock in the building. This "revelation" should be read in its entirety. Further on, in verse 78, Isaac Galland is encouraged to put stock into the house and then is flattered by reminding him that "I, the Lord, love him for the work he hath done, and will forgive all his sins. . . ." Who in the world could resist a promise like that? After all these instructions and promises we are told that the Lord said:

> . . . let my servant Joseph and his seed after him have place in that house, from generation to generation, forever and ever, saith the Lord. And let the name of that house be called Nauvoo House; and let it be a delightful habitation for man, and a resting-place for the weary traveler, that he may contemplate the glory of Zion, and the glory of this, the corner-stone thereof; That he may receive also the counsel from those whom I have set to be as plants of renown, and as watchmen upon her walls (verses 59-61).

The "Nauvoo House" *was never finished*, for Joseph Smith was killed before these "prophecies" could come true. The house is not owned by the Smith family today but by the Reorganized Church of Jesus Christ of Latter-Day Saints.

The revelation in *Doctrine and Covenants* 87 was allegedly given on December 25, 1832, and mentions a rebellion which was to begin in South Carolina and divide the North from the South. However, this information was in newspapers across the land *six months prior* to Smith's "prophecy"! On July 14, 1832, the U.S. Congress passed a tariff act which South Carolina refused to accept, declaring it null and void. President Andrew Jackson alerted the U.S. troops, and the nation expected war. See any good U.S. history book or even the Mormon newspaper, the *Evening and Morning Star*, for more details. This "prophecy" was not printed in the first editions of the *Doctrine and Covenants* or the *Book of Commandments; it did not ap-*

pear until after the Civil War began! A close study of the prophecy itself will reveal much more inaccuracy. (The above comment was taken from *Mormon Claims Answered,* by Marvin Cowan.)

Doctrine and Covenants 97:22-24:

> For behold, and lo, vengeance cometh speedily upon the ungodly as the whirlwind; and who shall escape it? The Lord's scourge shall pass over by night and by day, and the report thereof shall vex all people; yea, it shall not be stayed until the Lord come; For the indignation of the Lord is kindled against their abominations and all their wicked works.

Doctrine and Covenants Commentary, published by the Mormon Church, has notes by Apostle Hyrum M. Smith and Janne M. Sjodahl, which include this interesting comment concerning the above quotation:

> The enemies of the saints had also made a compact, but that did not save the States from the 'scourge,' when the horrors of the Civil War rolled over the country.

These Mormon writers likened the "scourge" to the Civil War, and thus stated that this is what the "revelation" meant. Notice the wording: "It shall not be stayed until the Lord come." The Civil War ended, and the "scourge" was stayed, but the Lord has not yet returned.

Brigham Young in *Journal of Discourses* 13:271 (July 24, 1870):

> Who can tell us of the inhabitants of this little planet that shines of an evening, called the Moon? . . . When you inquire about the inhabitants of that sphere you find that the most learned are as ignorant in regard to them as the most ignorant of their fellows. So it is with regard to the inhabitants of the sun. Do you think it is inhabited? I rather think it is. Do you think there is any life there? No question of it; it was not made in vain. It was made to give light to those who dwell upon it, and to other planets; and so will this earth when it is celestialized.

There are many other Mormon "revelations" and "prophecies" that did not come true, even though they were uttered by people calling themselves "Prophets of God." However, the above quotations should be sufficient to demonstrate that these people are false prophets, and as God says, ". . . if the thing follow not, nor come to pass, that is the thing which the Lord hath not spoken, but the prophet hath spoken it presumptuously; thou shalt not be afraid of him" (Deuteronomy 18:22).

BIBLIOGRAPHY

Anders, Hyrum L. *Documentary Commentary on the Pearl of Great Price.* Salt Lake City: Deseret Book Company, 1967.

Anderson, Edward H. *A Brief History of the Church of Jesus Christ of Latter-Day Saints.* Jackson County, Missouri: Zion's Printing and Publishing Company, 1928.

Anderson, Einar. *Inside Story of Mormonism.* Grand Rapids, Michigan: Kregal Publications, 1973, 1974.

Anderson, Einar. *Mormonism.* Chicago: Moody Press, 1956.

Arbaugh, G.B. *Gods, Sex, and the Saints.* Rock Island, Connecticut: Augusta Press, 1932.

Arbaugh, G. B. *Revelation in Mormonism.* Chicago: University of Chicago Press, 1932.

Bales, James D. *Apostles or Apostates.* Concord, California: Pacific Publishing Company, 1954.

Bales, James D. *The Book of Mormon?* Rosemead, California: Old Paths Book Club, 1958.

Beadle, J. H. *Polygamy, or the Mysteries and Crimes of Mormonism.* Philadelphia: The National Publishing Company, 1882; *Life in Utah,* or *Mysteries and Crimes of Mormonism.* 1870.

Bennett, John C. *Mormonism Exposed.* New York: Leland & Whiting, 1842.

Bennett, Wallace Foster, *Why I Am A Mormon.* New York: T. Nelson, 1958.

Berrett, William Edwin ed. *Readings in L. D. S. Church History From Original Manuscripts*, First edition. Salt Lake City: Deseret Book Company, 1953.

"Bible and Modern Religions." *Interpretation* Magazine, Vol. I, No. 4, 1956.

Bodine, Jerry and Marian. *Witnessing to the Mormons.* Anaheim: Christian Research Institute, 1978.

Book of Commandments. Salt Lake City: W. W. Phelps and Co., 1833.

Bowes, John. *Mormonism Exposed.* London: Manchester, Fletcher & Tubbs, 1840.

Brewer, David L. "Utah Elites and Utah Racial Norms." Ph.D. dissertation, University of Utah, 1966.

Brodie, Fawn M. *No Man Knows My History.* New York: Alfred A. Knopf, 1945, 1971.

Brooks, Juanita. *John D. Lee.* Glendale: The Arthur H. Clark Company, 1973.

Brooks, Juanita ed. *On the Mormon Frontier, The Diary of Hosea Stout*, Vols. I, II, 1844-1861. Salt Lake City: University of Utah Press, 1964.

Brooks, Juanita. *The Mountain Meadows Massacre.* University of Oklahoma Press, 1950, 1962, 1974.

Budvarson, Arthur. *The Book of Mormonism—True or False?* Grand Rapids: Zondervan Publishing House, 1961.

Call, Lamoni. *2000 Changes in the Book of Mormon.* Salt Lake City: Modern Microfilm Company.

Cannon, Frank J. *Brigham Young and His Mormon Empire.* New York: Fleming H. Revell Company, 1913.

Cannon, Frank J., and Harvey J. O'Higgins. *Under the Prophet in Utah.* Boston: E. M. Clark Publishing Company, 1911.

Clark, John A. *Gleanings by the Way.* Philadelphia: W. J. and J. K. Simon, 1842.

Codman, John. *The Mormon Country.* New York: United States Publishing, 1874. Reprint. New York: AMS Press, 1971.

Corrill, John. *A Brief History of the Church of Christ of Latter-day Saints.* Salt Lake City: Modern Microfilm Company, 1839.

Cowan, Marvin. *Mormon Claims Answered.* Salt Lake City: Marvin Cowan, 1975. (Marvin Cowan, publisher, PO Box 21052, Salt Lake City, Utah 84121)

Cowdrey, Wayne, Howard A. Davis, and Donald R. Scales. *Who Really Wrote the Book of Mormon?* Santa Ana, California: Vision House Publishers, 1977.

Deming, A. B. *Naked Truths About Mormonism.* Oakland, California: A.B. Deming, 1888.

Draper, Maurice I. *Christ's Church Restored.* Independence, Missouri: Herald Publishing House, 1948.

Erickson, Ephraim E. *The Psychological and Ethical Aspects of Mormon Group Life.* Chicago: University of Chicago Press, 1922.

Etzenhouser, R., and A. B. Phillips. *Three Bibles Compared.* Independence, Missouri: Herald Publishing House, 1954.

Evans, R. H. *One Hundred Years of Mormonism.* Salt Lake City: Deseret News, 1905.

Folk, Edgar E. *The Mormon Monster.* New York: Fleming H. Revell Company, 1901.

Foster, Ralph Leonard. *The Book of Mormon on Trial.* Klamath Falls, Oregon: R. L. Foster, 1963.

Fraser, Gordon H. *Is Mormonism Christian?* Chicago: Moody Colportage Library, 1957.

Froiseth, Jennie Anderson ed. *The Women of Mormondom, As Told By Themselves.* Detroit: C. G. G. Paine, 1882.

Gibbs, Josiah. *Lights and Shadows of Mormonism.* Salt Lake City: Salt Lake Tribune Publishing Company, 1909.

Gibbs, Josiah F. *The Mountain Meadows Massacre.* Salt Lake City: The Tribune Publishing Co., 1910.

Hanson, Klaus. *Quest for Empire.* East Lansing, Michigan: Michigan State University Press, 1967.

Hickman, Bill. *Brigham's Destroying Angel.* Salt Lake City: Shepard Publishing Company, 1904.

Hield, Charles R., and Russell F. Ralston. *Baptism for the Dead*. Independence, Missouri: Herald Publishing House, 1953.

Hougey, Hal. *A Parallel: The Basis of the Book of Mormon*. Concord, California: Pacific Publishing Company, 1963.

Hougey, Hal. *Archeology and the Book of Mormon*. Salt Lake City: Modern Microfilm Company.

Hougey, Hal. *Latter Day Saints, Where Do You Get Your Authority?* Concord, California: Pacific Publishing Company, 1971.

Hougey, Hal. *Truth About the 'Lehi Tree-of-Life' Stone*. Salt Lake City: Modern Microfilm Company, 1963.

Howe, E.D. *History of Mormonism*. Plainsville, Ohio: E.D. Howe, 1834, 1840.

Hunter, Milton R., Ph. D. *The Gospel Through the Ages*. Salt Lake City: Stevens & Wallis, Inc., 1945.

Hunter, Milton R. *The Gospel Through the Ages, Melchizedek Priesthood Course of Study*. Salt Lake City: Church of Jesus Christ of Latter-day Saints, 1945-46.

Improvement Era, Vols. 43-65. Salt Lake City: Church of Jesus Christ of Latter Day Saints, 1940-1962.

Ivins, Stanley S. *The Moses Thatcher Case*. Salt Lake City: Modern Microfilm Company.

Jenson, Andrew. *Church Chronology*. Salt Lake City: Deseret News, 1899.

Jenson, Andrew. *Plural Marriage*. Salt Lake City: Modern Microfilm Company.

Jonas, Larry. *Mormon Claims Examined.* Salt Lake City: Modern Microfilm Company.

Joseph Fielding Smith Geneological Society, Church of Jesus Christ of Latter-day Saints. *The Way to Perfection.* Salt Lake City: Deseret News, 1958.

Journal of Discourses, (26 vols.). Liverpool, England; F. D. Richards, Latter-day Saints' Book Depot, 1855.

Journal of Wilford Woodruff. Church Archives. Salt Lake City: Church of Jesus Christ of Latter-day Saints.

Koch, Kurt. *Between Christ and Satan.* Grand Rapids, Michigan: Kregel Publications, 1962.

Kraut, Ogden. *Michael/Adam.* Dugway, Utah: Ogden Kraut.

Lamb, M. T. *The Golden Bible.* Salt Lake City: Modern Microfilm Company.

Lee, John D. *Confessions of John D. Lee* (1880). Salt Lake City: Modern Microfilm Company.

Lee, John Doyle. *A Mormon Chronicle.* San Marino, California: Huntington Library, 1955.

Lewis, William. *The Church of Jesus Christ: How Shall I Know It?* Independence, Missouri: Herald Publishing House.

Linn, William Alexander. *The Story of the Mormons.* New York: Macmillan Company, 1902.

Lyford, C. *The Mormon Problem.* New York: Hunt and Eaton, 1866.

Marquardt, H. M. *The Book of Abraham Papyrus Found.* Salt Lake City: Modern Microfilm Company, 1975.

Martin, Stuart. *The Mystery of Mormonism.* New York: E. P. Dutton & Company, 1920.

Martin vs. Johnson, Corp. of the President, California Anaheim Mission, Santa Ana Institute of Religion, Fountain Valley First Ward, Costa Mesa First Ward, Costa Mesa Institute of Religion, Irvine Institute of Religion, Case No. 229099, The Superior Court of the State of California, for the County of Orange, January 22, 1976.

Martin, Walter R. *The Kingdom of the Cults.* 2nd rev. ed. Minneapolis: Bethany Fellowship, 1977.

Martin, Walter R. *The Rise of the Cults.* 3rd rev. ed. Santa Ana, California: Vision House Publishers, 1980.

Martin, Walter R. *Walter Martin's Cults Reference Bible.* Santa Ana, California: Vision House Publishers,1981.

McConkie, Bruce R. *Mormon Doctrine.* Salt Lake City: Bookcraft, 1958, 1966.

Melchizedek Priesthood Handbook. Salt Lake City: First Presidency of the Church of Jesus Christ of Latter-day Saints, 1970.

Messenger and Advocate. Salt Lake City: Modern Microfilm Company, 1834-1837.

Millennial Star, Vols. 1-51. Salt Lake City: Church of Jesus Christ, Latter-day Saints, 1840-1870.

Mulder, Wm. *Among The Mormons.* New York: Knopf, 1958.

Nelson, Dee Jay. *The Joseph Smith Papyri—A Translation and Preliminary Survey.* Salt Lake City: Modern Microfilm Company, 1968.

Nelson, Dee Jay. *A Translation and Study of Facsimile #3 in the Book of Abraham.* Salt Lake City: Modern Microfilm Company, 1969.

New American Standard Bible. La Habra, California: The Lockman Foundation, 1971.

Nibley, Dr. Hugh. *The Message of the Joseph Smith Papyri: An Egyptian Endowment.* Salt Lake City: Deseret Book Company, 1975.

Nibley, Dr. Hugh. *The Myth Makers.* Salt Lake City: Bookcraft, 1961.

Nutting, J. D. *The Little Encyclopedia of Mormonism.* Cleveland: Utah Gospel Mission, 1927.

O'Dea, Thomas F. *The Mormons.* Chicago: University of Chicago Press, 1957.

Orson Pratt's Works. Salt Lake City: Deseret News Press, 1945.

Orson Spencer's Letters. Salt Lake City: Modern Microfilm Company.

Paddock, Mrs. A. G. *The Fate of Madame La Tour.* New York: Fords, Howard, & Hulbert, 1881.

Pamphlets by Orson Pratt. Salt Lake City: Modern Microfilm Company.

Passantino, Robert and Gretchen. *Answers to the Cultist at Your Door*. Eugene, Oregon: Harvest House Publishers, 1981.

Pearl of Great Price, 1851 edition. Liverpool, England: F. D. Richards, 1851.

Pearl of Great Price. Salt Lake City: Latter-day Saints' Printing and Publishing Establishment, 1878.

Pearl of Great Price. Salt Lake City: The Church of Jesus Christ of Latter-day Saints, 1967.

Peck, Reed. *Reed Peck Manuscript*. Salt Lake City: Modern Microfilm Company. (Originally written in 1839.)

Penrose, Charles, *Mormon Doctrine*. Salt Lake City: The Juvenile Instructor Office, 1888.

Petersen, La Mar. *Problems in Mormon Text*. Salt Lake City: Modern Microfilm Company, 1957.

Petersen, Mark E. *Race Problems, As They Affect the Church*. Address at the Convention of Teachers of Religion on the College Level. Provo, Utah: Brigham Young University, 1954.

Pratt, Orson. *The Seer*. Salt Lake City: Eugene Wagner, Publisher, 1853-1854.

Pratt, Parley P. *Key to the Science of Theology*. Liverpool, England: F. D. Richard, 1955.

Reiser, A. H., and Marian G. Merkley. *What It Means to Be A Latter-day Saint. Course of Study for the First Intermediates Dept.* Salt Lake City: Church of Jesus Christ, Latter-day Saints, 1946.

Reorganized Latter Day Saints Church History. Independence, Missouri: Herald House Publishing Company.

Revealing Statements by the Three Witnesses to the Book of Mormon. Salt Lake City: Modern Microfilm Company.

Reynolds, George. *A Complete Concordance of the Book of Mormon.* Salt Lake City: Deseret Book Company, 1972.

Richards, LeGrand. *A Marvelous Work and A Wonder.* Salt Lake City: Deseret Book Company, 1950.

Ropp, Harry L. *The Mormon Papers.* Downers Grove, Illinois: InterVarsity Press, 1977.

Rosten, Leo. *Religions in America.* New York: Simon and Schuster, 1963.

Rushton, John W. *The Apostasy and the Restoration.* Independence, Missouri: Herald House Publishing Company.

Schindler, Harold. *Orrin Porter Rockwell: Man of God, Son of Thunder.* Salt Lake City: University of Utah Press, 1966.

Senate Document 189. (February 15, 1841). Salt Lake City: Modern Microfilm Company.

Shook, Charles A. *The True Origin of the Book of Mormon.* Cincinnati: The Standard Publishing Co., 1914.

Smith, Elbert A. *Differences That Persist Between the Reorganized Church of Jesus Christ of Latter Day Saints and the Utah Mormon Church.* Independence, Missouri: Herald House Publishing Company, 1943.

Smith, Elbert A. *The Latter Day Glory; Question Time: Answers to 457 Often-Asked Questions.* Independence, Missouri: Herald House Publishing Company, 1955.

Smith, Ethan. *View of the Hebrews.* Salt Lake City: Modern Microfilm Company.

Smith, John L. *I Visited the Temple.* Little Rock, Arkansas: The Challenge Press, 1972.

Smith, Joseph. *A Book of Commandments, for the Government of the Church of Christ, Organized According to Law, on the 6th of April, 1830.* Zion: W. W. Phelps & Co., 1833.

Smith, Joseph, Jr. *A Book of Commandments, for the Government of the Church of Christ.* Salt Lake City: W. W. Phelps and Co., 1833.

Smith, Joseph, Jr. *The Book of Mormon.* Palmyra, New York: E. B. Grandin, 1830.

Smith, Joseph, Jr. *The Book of Mormon.* Salt Lake City: The Church of Jesus Christ of Latter-day Saints, 1952; *Doctrine and Covenants*; *The Pearl of Great Price.* 1953.

Smith, Joseph, Jr. tras. *The Book of Mormon.* Salt Lake City: The Church of Jesus Christ of Latter-day Saints, 1974.

Smith, Joseph. *The Doctrine and Covenants of the Church of Jesus Christ of Latter-day Saints.* Salt Lake City: The Church of Jesus Christ of Latter-day Saints, 1968.

Smith, Joseph, ed. *The Elder's Journal.* Salt Lake City: Modern Microfilm Company, 1837-1838.

Smith, Joseph, Jr. *History of the Church of Jesus Christ of Latter-day Saints*, Vols. 1-7. Salt Lake City: Deseret Book Company, 1976.

Smith, Joseph, Jr. *Holy Scriptures, Inspired Version, Containing the Old And New Testaments: An Inspired Revision of the Authorized Version. Reorganized Church of Jesus Christ of Latter Day Saints.* Independence, Missouri: Herald House Publishing Company, 1974.

Smith, Joseph, Jr., Oliver Cowdery, Sidney Rigdon, and Frederick G. Williams, compilers. *Doctrine and Covenants of the Church of the Latter-Day Saints.* Kirtland, Ohio: F.G. Williams & Co., 1835.

Smith, Joseph Fielding. *Doctrines of Salvation*, compiled by Bruce McConkie, vols. I, II, III. Salt Lake City: Bookcraft, 1955.

Smith, Joseph Fielding. *Essentials in Church History. 11th ed.* Salt Lake City: Deseret News Press, 1946.

Smith, Joseph Fielding. *Gospel Doctrine.* Salt Lake City: Deseret Book Company, 1977.

Smith, Joseph Fielding, and Assistants in the Historian's Office compilers. *Teachings of the Prophet Joseph Smith.* Salt Lake City: Deseret Book Company, 1972.

Smith, Lucy. *Biographical Sketches of Joseph Smith the Prophet and His Progenitors for Many Generations.* Liverpool, England: S. W. Richards, 1853.

Snowden, James H. *The Truth About Mormonism.* New York: George H. Durant Company, 1926.

Spalding, F. S. *Why Egyptologists Reject the Book of Abraham.* Salt Lake City: Modern Microfilm Company.

Spalding, Rev. Solomon. *The Manuscript Story.* Lamoni, Iowa: Reorganized Church of Jesus Christ of Latter-day Saints, 1885.

Starks, Arthur E. *A Complete Concordance to the Book of Mormon.* Independence, Missouri: Herald House Publishing Company, 1950.

Stenhouse, T. B. *The Rocky Mountain Saints.* New York: B. Appleton Company, 1873.

Stenhouse, Mrs. T. B. H. *Tell It All.* Hartford: A. D. Worthington & Company, 1875.

Sterwart, J., and William Berrett. *Mormonism and the Negro, Part II.* Salt Lake City: Bookmark, 1960.

Stewart, George. *Priesthood and Church Welfare.* Salt Lake City: Deseret Book Company, 1939.

Strong, A. H. *Systematic Theology.* Westwood, New Jersey: Fleming H. Revell, 1907.

Swartzell, William. *Mormonism Exposed.* Pekin, Ohio: William Swartzell, 1840.

Talmage, James E. *The Articles of Faith.* Salt Lake City: The Church of Jesus Christ of Latter-day Saints, 1952, 1974.

Talmage, James E. *Jesus the Christ.* Salt Lake City: Deseret News Press, 1915, 1916.

Tanner, Jerald and Sandra. *The Case Against Mormonism*, vols. I, II, III. Salt Lake City: Modern Microfilm Company. 1967, 1968, 1971.

Tanner, Jerald and Sandra. *Changes in Joseph Smith's History*. Salt Lake City: Modern Microfilm Company, 1961.

Tanner, Jerald and Sandra. *Changes in the Key to Theology*. Salt Lake City: Modern Microfilm Company.

Tanner, Jerald and Sandra. *Changes in the Pearl of Great Price*. Salt Lake City: Modern Microfilm Company.

Tanner, Jerald and Sandra. *Falsification of Joseph Smith's History*. Salt Lake City: Modern Microfilm Company.

Tanner, Jerald and Sandra. *Joseph Smith and Polygamy*. Salt Lake City: Modern Microfilm Company.

Tanner, Jerald and Sandra. *Joseph Smith's Curse Upon the Negro*. Salt Lake City: Modern Microfilm Company.

Tanner, Jerald and Sandra. *Joseph Smith's Strange Account of the First Vision*; also, *A Critical Study of the First Vision*. Salt Lake City: Modern Microfilm Company.

Tanner, Jerald and Sandra. *The Mormon Kingdom*. Salt Lake City: Modern Microfilm Company.

Tanner, Jerald and Sandra. *The Mormon Papyri Question*. Salt Lake City: Modern Microfilm Company, 1967.

Tanner, Jerald and Sandra. *Mormonism—Shadow or Reality?* Salt Lake City: Modern Microfilm Company, 1964, 1974.

Tanner, Jerald and Sandra. *Mormons and Negroes.* Salt Lake City: Modern Microfilm Company, 1972.

Tanner, Jerald and Sandra. *The Negro in Mormon Theology.* Salt Lake City: Moderm Microfilm Company.

Tanner, Jerald and Sandra. *3913 Changes in the Book of Mormon.* Salt Lake City: Modern Microfilm Company.

Taylor, John. *The Mediation and Atonement.* Salt Lake City: The Church of Jesus Christ of Latter-day Saints.

Temple Mormonism. New York: A. J. Montgomery Co., 1931.

Times and Seasons, Vols. 1-6. Salt Lake City; Commerce, Illinois; Nauvoo, Illinois (Early Mormon Newspapers), 1839-1846.

Topical Guide to the Scriptures of the Church of Jesus Christ of Latter-day Saints. Salt Lake City: Deseret Book Company, 1977.

Tucker, Pomeroy. *The Origin, Rise and Progress of Mormonism.* New York: D. Appleton and Company, 1867.

Tullidge, Edward W. *The Women of Mormondom.* New York, 1877; Fourth reprint, Salt Lake City, 1975.

Turner, Rodney. *The Position of Adam in Latter-day Saint Scripture and Theology* (Thesis). Provo, Utah: Brigham Young University, 1953.

Turner, Wallace. *The Mormon Establishment.* Boston: Houghton Mifflin Co., 1966.

The Uniform System for Teaching Families. Salt Lake City: Corporation of the President, Church of Jesus Christ of Latter-day Saints, 1961.

Vine, W. E. *Vine's Expository Dictionary of New Testament Words.* Old Tappan, New Jersey: Fleming H. Revell Company, 1966.

Walters, Wesley P. "Joseph Smith Among the Egyptians." Quoted from *The Journal of the Evangelical Theological Society* 16:1. Winter, 1973.

Walters, Wesley P. *Joseph Smith's Bainbridge, N. Y., Court Trials.* Salt Lake City. (Reprinted by permission from the *Westminster Theological Journal,* Vol. 36, No.2, Winter 1974).

Walters, Wesley P. *New Light On Mormon Origins from the Palmyra (N. Y.) Revival.* Salt Lake City: Modern Microfilm Company, 1967.

Wardle, James D. *Selected Changes in the Book of Mormon.* Salt Lake City: Modern Microfilm Company.

Weldon, Roy. *Other Sheep: Book of Mormon Evidences.* Independence, Missouri: Herald House Publishing Company, 1956.

Westminster Review, vol. 59, (January and April), New York: Leonard Scott & Company, 1853.

Whitmer, David. *An Address to All Believers in Christ.* Richmond, Missouri: David Whitmer, 1887.

Whitmer, John. *John Whitmer's History.* Salt Lake City: Modern Microfilm Company.

Widtsoe, John. *Discourses of Brigham Young*. Salt Lake City: Deseret Book Company, 1973.

Widtsoe, John A. *Evidences and Reconciliations*. Salt Lake City: Bookcraft, 1960.

Widtsoe, John A. *Joseph Smith's Egyptian Alphabet and Grammar*. Salt Lake City, Modern Microfilm Company.

Widtsoe, John A. *Joseph Smith: Seeker After Truth*. Salt Lake City: Deseret Books, 1951.

Widtsoe, John A. *Priesthood and Church Government*. Salt Lake City: Deseret Book Company, 1939.

Wood, Wilford C. *Joseph Smith Begins His Work*, vol. 1. Salt Lake City: Deseret News Press, 1958.

Wood, Wilford C. *Joseph Smith Begins His Work*, vol. 2. Salt Lake City: Deseret News Press, 1962.

Wyl, Dr. W. *Mormon Portraits*. Salt Lake City: Tribune Printing and Publishing Company, 1886.

Young, Brigham. *Journal History*. Salt Lake City: Church Archives, Church of Jesus Christ of Latter-day Saints, 1846.

OTHER WRITINGS BY WALTER MARTIN . . .

BOOKS

Jehovah of the Watchtower
The Rise of the Cults
Essential Christianity
The Kingdom of the Cults
Screwtape Writes Again
The New Cults
Walter Martin's Cults Reference Bible

BOOKLETS

Jehovah's Witnesses
Christian Science
Mormonism
Herbert W. Armstrong and the
    Worldwide Church of God
The Riddle of Reincarnation
Abortion — Is It Always Murder?
Exorcism, Fact or Fable?